BOWLING

★ ★ ★ ★ ★ ★

ACROSS

★ ★ ★ ★ ★ ★

AMERICA

★ ★ ★ ★ ★ ★

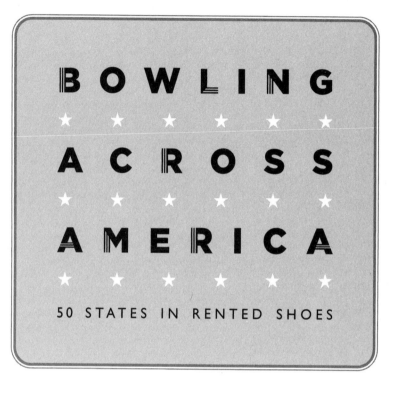

BOWLING

ACROSS

AMERICA

50 STATES IN RENTED SHOES

★ MIKE WALSH ★

ST. MARTIN'S PRESS ≋ NEW YORK

www.stmartins.com

Design by Greg Collins

Library of Congress Cataloging-in-Publication Data

Walsh, Mike.
    Bowling across America : 50 states in rented shoes / Mike Walsh.
      p. cm.
    ISBN-13: 978-0-312-36619-3
    ISBN-10: 0-312-36619-1
    1. Bowling—United States.   2. Bowling alleys—United States.   I. Title.
  GV908.U6W34   2008
  794.60973—dc22   2008024763

First Edition: November 2008

10 9 8 7 6 5 4 3 2 1

For Mom

s of some

changed.

For Mom

CONTENTS ★

ACKNOWLEDGMENTS ★

THIS book is in this binding thanks to John Murphy, who made it happen after the bowling was done and the car was parked. Talented, thoughtful editing by Tom Mercer and Marc Resnick improved the writing immensely.

Many people opened their homes to me during this adventure despite knowing there was a decent chance I would never leave. Some are mentioned in these pages and some are not; I am grateful to you all. My guest room, my couch, my hide-a-bed, my futon, my air mattress, my bare wood floor with a foam pad and a few blankets are yours at a moment's notice. For those who underwrote the trip in other ways—sponsorship, meals, introductions, letting me bowl with you—my thanks abounds.

To Amy, for a place to stay in D.C., and for all that that one gesture will lead to for us.

To Ann, Pat, Peter, Molly, and Regan: what a reassuring safety net and loud cheering section five siblings can be. Like looking over and seeing Leo and Jan on the sidelines.

To Dad, for setting goals both large and whimsical, and for setting such an example.

To Mom. For strength, for humor, for integrity, for letting us all go, and for keeping us all together. And least of all (though it seemed important at the time), for the wheels.

PREFACE ★

EIGHTER from Decatur," he always said when his score was eight and it was his turn to serve. I usually cringed when I heard it, in part because a grown man shouldn't be employing such a silly rhyme, and in part because it meant I would soon be losing nine to zero. I was never a very good handball player, and certainly no match for someone who'd played twice a week for the last forty years. Against me he said it to lighten the mood and soften the crushing blow of defeat a twenty-year-old feels at losing in athletic competition to a sixty-year-old. Against a better-matched player he would say it to unsettle his opponent with the appearance of nonchalance, or at least annoy him with the rhyme's puerility. Years later I would realize that this nonsensical phrase was among my father's last words, but on the wintry Saturday morning when my brother Peter phoned me with the news of his death, heavier thoughts took hold.

Our father was sixty-six. He'd just finished a handball game, stepped off the court for some water, and suddenly collapsed into a taupe-colored chair. It is the type of chair common to athletic clubs, the sort that's upholstered with faux leather so the sweat can be easily wiped away with a gym towel. The kind of chair that's only comfortable if you're exhausted, that you'd never put in your own home. Not the sort of chair you'd choose to die in, but there's not always time to plan.

His friend and opponent, Dick Carr, tried to help him, brought my father's limp, leaden body to the industrial-strength carpet and performed CPR, did everything he could to revive him, but he was gone before the ambulance even arrived. Astonishing. Unbelievable. Completely unexpected.

Perhaps it shouldn't have been. After all, my father had often stated his desire to die on the handball court, "with his gloves on," to paraphrase the soldier's refrain about boots. Had we believed him, we might have been a bit more thoughtful when saying our good-byes to him on his way to play every Saturday morning. But as it stood, his vision of the event was a tad too glorified to take seriously.

It would be game point, his serve. His T-shirt would be saturated with sweat, darkened several shades from its original heather gray. His dingy leather handball gloves, worn to protect the hard rubber ball from sweat more than to protect the hands from pain when hitting it, would also be drenched and nearing the limit of their effectiveness. A couple of weaselly racquetball players would be impatiently waiting for their scheduled turn on the court. They would probably be acting whiny and effeminate, wearing collared shirts tucked into matching shorts with matching headbands. They would be fretting about making their manicure appointments in time following their game. Dad would be in no hurry to yield the court to them, having always regarded the need for a racquet as a sign of weakness. Checking Dick's position, bouncing the ball a couple of times, and saying a brief warrior's prayer under his breath ("protect me, Father, in this great and final battle . . ."), he would raise his right hand high behind him and swat the ball as it bounced from the ground, delivering the serve of his life. Dick would return it, miraculously, and an intense volley would ensue. Vulgarities would be grunted as the two men lumbered about the court, slamming into the walls, pushing each other out of the way, and each using every possible angle to put the next shot out of his opponent's reach. At last, Dick would manage to hit an unreachable ball, a ball so far away and bouncing at such an angle that the laws of physics would prohibit Dad's hulking body and remanufactured knees from possibly, humanly, reaching it before it bounced a second time. But he'd get there, leaping and making his entire six-three frame parallel to the ground (this part, I believe he envisioned, would occur in slow motion with a pause in midair) as he smacked a kill shot into the front left corner. The ball would roll smoothly out from the front wall, making it impossible to return. The last thing he would see would be the blue orb rolling past his prostrate body. The last sound he would hear as he grinned his dying grin would be Dick's frustrated voice, ripped with agony, echoing in the humid court. "Damn you, Leoooooo!"

When I first spoke with my oldest brother, Pat, knowing only that Dad had been playing handball when he died, I asked rhetorically, "I wonder if he won?"

Pat, always equipped with profound perspective, replied through tears, "He won all his life."

By that night all six of his children returned home, the first time we'd all been at 2152 Middlesex Road together in years. We'd come to comfort our mother, one another. We'd come to celebrate our father's life.

Planning a funeral is a lot like planning a wedding, only at a much faster pace and without all the cake tastings. You order flowers, invite everyone you know, reserve the church, select readings and music, print programs, order a limo to pick you up after the service, and bicker with loved ones over the details. The differences between the two events tend to be subtle: invitations go out by phone instead of calligraphy-scrawled stationery; people stop by with hams and casseroles instead of china and toasters. And instead of an engagement announcement for the paper, you write an obituary.

Writing an obituary by committee is no easy task. My mother would ultimately steal away in her bedroom to draft the version that would appear in the paper, but not before we explored some potential leads and inclusions as a family. This was the first time any of us laughed since our father, a very funny man, had made us all cry that morning.

"Maybe we should make it a singles ad," my mother suggested, channeling her terror at suddenly being alone into humor. "Newly widowed redhead seeks wealthy boy toy . . ."

Though I believed he was being truthful, I saw the obit as a chance to debunk Dick Carr's contention that he'd won the last game he and Dad played. "Leo Walsh, 66, suddenly, after beating Dick Carr in handball," was my suggestion for the lead. That way we could explain to Dick that with no other living witnesses to confirm his story, we'd have to believe the newspaper's account.

Regan, my twenty-three-year-old sister, insisted that we list her residence as "New York" despite the fact that she lived across the Hudson River in Hoboken. "I don't want my old high school classmates to think I live in *Jersey*." (This piece of spin actually made the final draft. Karmic retribution for the Garden State would come years later when the headline for Regan's wedding announcement—appearing in a section that far more of her peers read than the death notices—proclaimed: "To Reside in New Jersey" beneath a beautiful picture of her and her husband, John. If spirits can manipulate this world from beyond, this was Dad's mischievous hand.)

We continued to cry aplenty, but the fine emotional line between that release and laughter enabled us to find humor in the grimmest of situations. Shopping for caskets led to faux debates over the aesthetics and benefits of a box we'd see only once and whose primary user wouldn't know the difference.

"This one looks fast," Peter said. "Maybe we should get it—Dad liked fast cars."

"Ooh, feel how soft this one is! I bet it's comfortable."

"Do you have this in ecru?"

"Is the rust-proofing package optional?"

At the cemetery, the woman helping us select a resting place for

Dad (and de facto for Mom, since she would one day be buried along-side him) bore the real brunt of a sarcastic family's grief.

"Now, this plot is nice because it faces south, so it gets a little more sunlight," she said of one site, a selling point that hadn't occurred to us for a 5-by-10 patch of land we might see once a year.

"It's nice," someone replied, "but could you move the Calvano grave away from it? I don't want my parents to be buried next to any Italians."

"Yeah, where are all the Irish graves?"

"Okay, there's another site over here that is available and has some nice shrubbery at the head of the plot," she said, trying to move on.

"Where might we find some existing graves where the wife's dead, but the husband's still alive? We're looking for a rich widower for our mother."

At some point our saleswoman began showing us sites of five graves together, suggesting that some of us might want to make a down payment on our own graves so that we might be buried with our parents. That or she was wishing more of us dead.

"I think we're okay with just buying two holes in the ground today, but thanks."

"Can we get Astroturf?"

Morbid, yes, but this is how some people cope. By the time Regan and I were finished lying down as stand-ins for our parents' corpses so Mom could visualize where the plot and headstone would be ("I think you guys looked more peaceful in that last plot"), our saleswoman lost her will and went to wait in the car until we'd made our decision.

Dad's wake was epic. I felt pity for the other families with deceased relatives at the funeral home that night, because Dad's friends and family were so numerous that we were crowding everyone else out. The receiving line to pay respects to my mother was over an hour long. Imagine waiting an hour not to get on a roller coaster but to have a brief, awkward, emotional encounter with a woman so distraught she probably won't even remember your being there. (This is why funeral homes have guest books.)

An ex-girlfriend's father whom I'd always assumed (probably with merit) hated me came with a kind word.

Pat Blume, who'd taught several of us first and second grade, said what a great man Dad was.

Emil Colissimo, the friend and barber who'd cut his hair the morning he died, disapproved of the job the mortician had done on Dad's hair and pulled out a comb and corrected it right there in the viewing room.

Several of my father's business associates talked about how he'd trusted them and given them credit to buy inventory when they were starting their businesses.

A boy he'd mentored in a Big Brother program decades ago and since lost touch with came to pay respects.

Family and friends from a dozen states and Puerto Rico came to remember Leo Walsh and lift his family with their presence.

The mass was beautiful. Pat gave a touching eulogy, as did Mike Petrie, a close friend of Dad's, and my godfather. For the recessional hymn, instead of some slow, depressing dirge we insisted the organist fire up "Battle Hymn of the Republic." The "Glory! Glory! Hallelujahs!" spilled out into the parking lot around the casket like it was in a parade, not a recession.

It was the perfect day for a burial, in the sense that one would like to think the deceased is going to a better place. The temperature was 12 degrees, the sky gray, and the wind whipped light, prickly flurries about the air as we left the church.

The line of cars en route to the cemetery stretched for more than a mile of headlights behind us, and the lone sheriff's deputy who pulled motorcycle escort duty for the procession executed Knievel-esque traffic management feats along the way. At one point, he was riding 50 miles per hour, holding back freeway traffic with one hand and motioning the hearse to accelerate with the other, all while riding on a gravelly berm and steering by balance. "Dad would have thought this was really cool," someone said. As we neared the cemetery, the deputy sped ahead of the procession fast enough to park, dismount his bike, stand at attention, and salute the hearse with Dad's flag-draped coffin inside it as it passed through the gates.

Thanks to a heavy investment Pat made in alcohol the day before, we all got soaking drunk after the burial, our family home filled with friends I never knew my father had.

We told stories and laughed with deep affection and unabashed escapism.

We cried, mostly the kind of tears that come with an appreciative smile.

We set off fireworks in the backyard, a tribute to so many summer evening displays Dad had put on when we were growing up.

We held the silence that followed the final boom. As the last rocket's glare dimmed from our faces we stood briefly in tableau, the last moment before our lives would resume again.

No matter how someone dies—long battle with cancer, kidney failure in a nursing home, shot in bed by mistress's jealous husband—we have a tendency to rationalize it as appropriate, if only for the sake of giving comfort. "He would have wanted to go that way" and "At least he's not suffering anymore" are silver linings of sorts, and more comforting than they are true in most cases. As I returned to Chicago and tried to reinsert myself into my life as though nothing had changed, I convinced myself that my father had all but planned it this way. With hindsight's help, this was easy enough to do.

He had planned to retire at the end of February and made the legal and financial arrangements for Peter to assume control of the family business beginning March 1. Dad's passing on January 20 just accelerated that time line by a few weeks.

He'd just finished a term as president and then chairman of the board for an industry organization he'd been deeply involved in for more than two decades, steering it in a new direction at the beginning of a new century.

The previous summer, for the first time in years, he had gathered us all for a family reunion. We spent a hot, humid Labor Day weekend at a state park in Illinois, not too far from where his grandfather first settled after coming from Ireland. At that event Dad shared with us the results of research he'd been doing on the Walsh family's ancestry, which he had made into laminated printouts for each of us. The description of his grandfather's journey to the United States reads: "One of the photos herewith shows the house from which Grandpa walked, when he left home for the port of Cork . . . probably a 40 or 50 mile walk or ride, if able to hitch one. His farewell 'party' would have been like an Irish wake . . . lots of crying, story telling, speculation of what would be or could have been, and lots of booze." A road map we'd subconsciously followed for Dad's immigration to the afterlife.

His last note to me was a thank-you card for the gift I'd given him for Christmas. Recounting the culmination of their holiday season, he wrote that after forty-four years of marriage he and my mother "finally got New Year's Eve right" with a quiet evening of gin rummy at home.

During a couples' weekend they attended four years earlier, he and my mother had been assigned the task of writing each other a letter about their fears. His read, in part: "I fear a prolonged death and you and the kids having to take care of me. I want to die playing handball."

In every aspect of his life, it seemed, he'd set things right. Nothing was left undone, unsaid, or undecided. If not for the suddenness of his death, one could be forgiven for thinking he'd known it was coming and prepared expressly for it. This was comforting to believe.

Of course it was also completely untrue. He'd left countless things undone, like spending another twenty years with his wife and growing old with her. Like walking his two unmarried daughters down the aisle at their weddings. Like meeting his grandchildren who were not yet born but were no doubt forthcoming. These things only God could bring about now, and only spiritually.

And then there was that one other earthly task Dad had left undone.

It had glared at me from his office on East Fifth Avenue, hanging crooked on the wall behind his desk, two nights after his death when Peter, Pat, and I went there to try to absorb Dad's presence. Of course, all going there did was depress us more, being surrounded by his life's work while his life's last breath was being recirculated throughout an athletic club's HVAC system. But the thing that haunted me most, that captured my gaze and locked my stare upon it, was the map on the wall.

It was a rudimentary map of the United States, measuring 20" × 30" and colored in blue, green, and varying shades of purple and pink, each state a single color and the shades carefully chosen so no state bordered another of the same color. The states' names were written in all caps, and major cities and midsized towns were noted alongside black dots. Alaska and Hawaii were tucked in the lower right-hand corner, doing no justice to Alaska's size or Hawaii's distance from the mainland. According to a copyright notice beneath the legend, the map had been made by a company in Texas. It was mounted on cheap white foam board; taped to its upper edge were a photo of Dad with my sister Molly, and my sister Regan's college business card from when she was president of her sorority.

Only after looking at it for the third or fourth time would one notice the small circular stickers, about a quarter inch in diameter, in either green or yellow, each with a number on it. The numbers were pre-printed, and their placement appeared arbitrary. There was no discernible pattern, no apparent reason that Boise, Idaho, had a green "135" while Huntington, West Virginia, had a yellow "5." Cryptographers would go mad trying to figure out why twenty-eight states had stickers and others had none. But the answer was simple to anyone who knew Leo B. Walsh. And it was obvious that someone had to finish what he'd started.

Though it would take over a year to materialize, there was a journey of epic, if somewhat absurd, proportions in my future.

BOWLING

★ ★ ★ ★ ★ ★

ACROSS

★ ★ ★ ★ ★ ★

AMERICA

★ ★ ★ ★ ★ ★

Reserving the Lanes ★

SCRAWLED in the margins of a yellow legal pad on which I am ostensibly taking notes is a list of states, and next to each the name of someone who lives there and might have a guest room or couch where I could spend the night. "VT—Owen. CA—Josh, Val, Erica. MN—Orths." And so on. Some states have blank spaces next to them; others I just can't remember. I'm having an embarrassingly hard time naming all fifty; I never learned that song children are taught as a mnemonic device to remember them.

Around me people are debating which word, "whiter" or "brighter," would be most effective at getting consumers to pay 30 cents more for their laundry soap, or a similar topic of such monumental importance. I have long since tuned out. I've been doing that a lot lately.

I am one of those advertising executives they portray in the movies gathered around a conference table saying important-sounding things about sketches mounted on black presentation boards. "I think the logo should be bigger" and whatnot. Movie portrayals notwithstanding, what once seemed an exciting world of expense accounts, photo shoots, and high-powered meetings has become a bleak reality of rushed airport dining, prima donna egotists, and windowless conference rooms on beautiful spring days. My interest is waning, has waned, and I've become desperate for something more fulfilling.

Now, I'm self-aware enough to realize I'm being somewhat immature and impatient in this. Who does love their job? There's nothing special about my situation. In fact, I should be happy to have a job that pays me well and involves little more than writing e-mails and talking to people all day. Kids sewing gym shoes in Asia would kill for work like this if they didn't die from the shock of learning that people are paid tens of thousands of dollars to do it. And here I am griping that it isn't fulfilling enough.

I take some comfort that these feelings are, if not universal, perhaps genetic. My dad loved his job, running the business he founded, but he'd once had a yellow legal pad of his own.

He was thirty-seven—a decade older than I am. He had a wife, four children, and a lucrative, secure job as a salesman for Honeywell. In those days, employment at a company such as Honeywell was a lifetime engagement if one so desired. But despite that security and decent pay, he was frustrated, bored, and feeling more ambitious than that corporate culture would allow. He spent his weekends and evenings scribbling his legal pad ragged, showing it to his friend Mike Petrie, talking it over with my mother, and finally getting up the courage to enact its contents: the business plan for Columbus Temperature Control, the company he would leave in Peter's hands upon his death. In 1972 he quit Honeywell, rented a warehouse, and became a wholesale distributor of heating and air-conditioning parts. Aside from a meager amount of inventory, all he had was a lot of confidence and an inventive sales pitch: "Buy something. Anything."

Leaving Honeywell was a tremendous risk. Aside from abandoning the security of working for a major corporation, he had to create his business from scratch. This involved driving from potential customer to potential customer with a trunk full of air conditioner parts, introducing himself, and hoping he could sell enough to feed his family that month and create enough relationships to feed them for years. In the end it worked out, enabling him to send six children to college and look well after his wife, who would later join him as the company's vice president and an invaluable peer in running the business.

His passing, now sixteen months ago, triggered thoughts of making my own break. In trying to recapture what advice he might have given me as I considered the status quo versus taking more dramatic action, I was reminded of a metaphor he often repeated on the subject of risk.

"You can make safe choices and sleep well," he would say, "or you can take risks and eat well. Eating well is a hell of a lot more interesting, but it does keep you up at night."

This from a man whose snoring was a known quantity in the neighborhood. On a summer's night with the windows open, the rhythmic rumble emanating from his sinuses would broadcast from his bedroom and echo off neighboring houses. Sam, an Irish setter belonging to the Dawsons, would be found whimpering under their backyard deck, stricken with fear at what beast had been on the prowl in the subdivision overnight. Over time my mother had learned to live with it, often by leaving their bedroom to sleep in another. This is my memory from the better years, when past risks taken and past sleep lost meant both sleeping and eating well for the Walsh family.

There were lean years, though, when the business was struggling to get off the ground, when an embezzling employee nearly bankrupted the company. In those years there was little snoring to be heard. Dad never fully explained that, when pursuing an "eating well" life course, one's ability to "sleep well" is often interrupted by the inability to eat at all, never mind "well." As novel as it may have seemed to occasionally have "breakfast for dinner," what this meant was that eggs and pancake batter was about as well as we could do.

Though he let his children draw our own conclusions about whether we wanted to pursue a life of eating or sleeping well, it was clear which he favored. Which brings me back to my own legal pad and the growing list of states in its margins, another product of my father's mind.

Dad's more well-known goal with regard to handball (I don't know how widely he shared the whole "wanting to die on the court" thing with others) was to play at least one game in every state and on every continent. This was his personal quest, undertaken like some men decide to climb Everest or run a marathon. This was the task he left unfinished.

Though it was certainly one of his many passions, he never made this round-the-world goal a full-time pursuit. Running the business, raising the six of us, and going on bike rides with his wife took precedence over geographic domination of an obscure indoor sport. Plus, he started late: he didn't begin collecting states until he'd settled in, developed commitments and obligations, mortgages and tuitions. So he would arrange to play when in Minnesota to visit family, in California for a convention, in New York on a trip with his sons. He once wrote to a well-known retired basketball coach who he'd read was a handball player and arranged a game with him in Idaho during a business trip. Dad did it because he loved the game, because the romance of doing something unique in each state inspired him, and because of the profound joy he took from social interaction with the old and new friends he met on the court. This, of course, was the reason for the map and the stickers on his office wall. The colors and numbers on the stickers were a consequence of his grabbing the first thing he'd found in the supply cabinet he could use to mark his newly mounted map. The twenty-eight states with stickers were those in which he'd played a game before playing his last on his home court in Ohio.

More than any specific interests I had in common with him, I shared the sensibility required to fall in love with such a quest. Anyone can merely visit every state. Anyone can see a game at every Major League Baseball park, or ride every wooden roller coaster. And these are noble and worthy goals in and of themselves. But how many people can say they have not only been to but also played a little-known sport within every state? Handball's outsider status in the sporting and social pecking order added a degree of obscurity and quirkiness, a touch of uniqueness, that made it his. I always liked that about it, even if I wasn't a handball player.

During college I announced my intent to bowl in all fifty states as a kind of emulative gesture—a nod to the old man's quest with a bent to make it mine. Granted, I was no more a bowler than I was a handball player, but then it wasn't really about the sport so much as it was about the adventure. Besides, handball hurts your hands.

I figured if I worked at checking off states, perhaps I could catch up to him. Perhaps we could begin to work the missing states together, hitting a handball court and a bowling alley in each. We could make Hawaii the fiftieth for both of us, and celebrate with much fanfare and ceremony. And a steak dinner.

He never asked, because I think he understood, why I would choose bowling of all activities. "Why not badminton or checkers?" others would wonder, exposing the arbitrary nature of my selection of bowling. The answer was that I'd always found bowling alleys to be wildly romantic—in the nostalgic-reminiscence sense of the term, not the cuddle-up-and-listen-to-Barry-White-by-the-fire sense. What other place in American society could you find such a cross section of people? What recreational activity offers more opportunity for both competition and socialization? Bowling's egalitarian accessibility—for around five dollars anyone can borrow all the equipment and roll a game—makes it a great equalizer. Everyone—rich, poor, black, white, male, female, transgendered, handicapped—can get to the foul line and have a shot at the pins. Few do it enough to be good, much less own their own equipment, which puts people of all backgrounds in rented shoes rolling a ball that was made for someone else. It matters not whether it's a group of suburban rich kids, a senior citizens' league, or a family of four spending their only entertainment dollars for the month: everyone looks equally ridiculous in ill-fitting blue and red shoes trying to balance their weight against that of a heavy three-holed ball. Everyone feels equally silly when they roll a gutterball, and equally proud when they roll a strike. The advent of gutter guards for kids and devices to assist the handicapped in getting the ball down the lane means that truly anyone can bowl.

This accessibility makes the bowling alley a rich environment for people watching. Any given bowling alley on any given day becomes a microcosm of the community in which it sits. The bowling alley is a gathering place, and much more transpires within its confines than merely a series of sporting contests divided into ten frames. People don't just bowl in bowling alleys. They eat and drink. They karaoke.

They fall in love. They have sex, as foul as that sounds. They spend the one Saturday afternoon a month they have custody of their son there. They forget about work, home, tragic news headlines. And they smoke. Man, do they smoke.

The romantic feelings I held for bowling were matched in swooning fervor only by those I felt for land travel, specifically that which involved a car, lots of roadside diners, and a general lack of a pressing schedule. This is the other part of the shared sensibility with my father that encouraged such appreciation for a trivial quest. As a family of eight, we were lucky to take a summer vacation, let alone fly anywhere, so our destinations were always reached by highway. I did a lot of my growing up in the backseat of an enormous wood-paneled Ford Country Squire LTD station wagon, watching the landscapes go by and wondering what was going on in that farmhouse, or what people did in that small town beyond the exit ramp. (Incidentally, the Country Squire of my memory is slightly bigger and less fuel-efficient than a Hummer. With all six of us inside along with whatever luggage didn't fit in the cartop carrier, there was still room to build a fort, assemble an elaborate meal from the cooler Mom had packed, fight over who was touching whom, and behave for up to three minutes after Dad threatened to pull over and make someone walk.) But it was more than the cost of airfare that kept us from flying anywhere. My father loved a good car trip, and even after the kids had all moved out and he and my mother could afford to fly on their travels, my dad would lobby hard, if unsuccessfully, to drive instead. Whether through nature or nurture, his love for America's interstate freeway system remains a constant in my psyche. The road beckons.

It does so, as often as any time, during the workday. As the whiter-versus-brighter debate swirls around me, I find myself conspiring and strategizing. In the five years since graduating from college I've managed to add few states to my quest, despite ample opportunity to have done so. While this is a relatively minor failure in the grand scheme of things, the events of the past year and the prospects for the months to come have shone a light on it, compelling me to do something about it. It's now the first warm, sunny day in May. Schools are winding down classes, summer camps are registering campers, and somewhere a father is mapping out a road trip and getting the minivan's oil changed. Spring's transition to summer always evokes memories of loading into the Country Squire's cavernous backseats, Mom sitting shotgun and Dad behind the wheel pointing us toward the horizon. Days like this should be filled with anticipation and outlook.

But today I am in a windowless conference room in Cincinnati and my father is in the ground ninety miles to the north. Tomorrow promises more of the same, as does the next year, the next decade. *This won't do.* I turn to my meeting notes, mostly incoherent scribble that will lead to tedious to-do lists I have no desire to complete.

I continue writing in the margins, crafting my plan throughout the meeting and on the plane ride home to Chicago. By the time the wheels touch down at O'Hare my to-do list, while fraught with risk and uncertainty, is a bit more inspiring. It reads:

1. Quit job.
2. Put belongings in storage.
3. Set course for bowling alleys in all 50 states.

Lacing Up
★ **the Rental Shoes**

PRIOR to quitting my job I spend some time developing convoluted financial survival schemes—written outlines of daydreams, really—that involved my being sponsored by a hotel chain, automobile manufacturer, bowling ball maker, foot odor powder distributor, or wealthy heiress in order to fund the trip, or at least offset my expenses. After all, the few thousand dollars I have in the bank will only get me so far, and the prospect of credit card debt is only so appealing, despite how easy the commercials make it sound. It is one thing to throw away a promising career to drive aimlessly around the country but another thing to add mountains of personal debt on top of one's self. Priority One is signing up a name sponsor to underwrite the trip.

Not that I'll be selling out—my demands of any sponsor will be that they have a light hand, almost no influence whatsoever on the trip, and ultimately be barely noticeable. The last thing I need is to look like a NASCAR driver struggling to move under the weight of logos and patches. No, any sponsor giving me money to pursue a life goal would have to play by my rules: be a product brand I like and seek little to no recognition for its contribution. When you have nothing to lose, such arrogance comes easily for a while. Never mind the fact that I don't even have a car.

I attempt to overcome this first by writing letters to marketing directors of newly launched cars, hoping to convince them to give me just one of their vehicles. My pitch, that I would return their investment many times over in favorable news stories about a twenty-seven-year-old man who chose their car in which to drive aimlessly about the country, alone, garners no response.

I then recall that a friend of a friend runs marketing activities for a line of Chrysler minivans. He had once proposed a very well-thought-out plan when working for Oscar Mayer to circumnavigate the globe in the company's famed Wienermobile. He'd gone to the extent of consulting a world record–holding adventure driver about the permits and paperwork required, calculated expenses, and planned to bring along spare parts and a mechanic to install them just in case. It was sure to become a global news story centered on a vehicle that was built for the very purpose of getting on the news. And still it was rejected. Somewhere on page 7 of the PowerPoint presentation I'm drafting to persuade him, I realize that my plan lacks the kind of executional detail ("the key thing is that I have no set itinerary . . .") important to a major corporation when making funding decisions and/or giving away cars. Never mind that, unlike the Wienermobile, a single man going bowling in a minivan isn't exactly a global news story. I opt not to trouble him.

With less than two weeks left of a steady paycheck, I remain a man about to embark on a long car trip without a car. Luckily, my mother shares my enthusiasm for the project.

Actually, to say she is "enthusiastic" at this point is a tad inaccurate. "Terrified" might be too dramatic. "Cautiously skeptical" seems about right.

"That's nice," she responds the first time I tell her of my plan to quit work to bowl in all fifty states. Her tone is one of feigned interest, patronizing me as she might have when I was a child going on in great detail about my plans to be a fireman while she just wanted to watch the evening news in peace. Only this time she hears what I'm saying and hopes her tone will illustrate the folly of my plan and dissuade me from making such a potentially disastrous life choice.

"Mom, this isn't like the time I brought my friend's pregnant wife home and introduced her as my new girlfriend. This is real."

"You don't even have a car."

"I was thinking of taking the Scorpio or the truck."

The Scorpio is a black 1987 Merkur with leather seats and a big speedometer, a car my father loved too much to get rid of when he bought his next car in 1998. Not that he could have gotten rid of it: Merkur was a Ford product built in Germany that was touted as a European sports sedan with tight handling and a powerful engine. Unfortunately, it was so fraught with maintenance and repair problems that Ford only sold it in the United States for one model year before discontinuing it. The truck is a dark green 1968 GMC pickup with lap seat belts, no radio, and doors that don't lock (hence the missing radio).

Both vehicles are parked on Columbus Temperature Control's back lot. Both smell faintly of gasoline on the inside whenever their tank is filled to capacity. Neither has great prospects for making it to all fifty states without a major breakdown and/or fatal, explosive accident. At least, I tell myself, hardship and tragedy would be character building and present opportunities otherwise unknown. I begin having romantic visions of hitching to a phone booth on a windy Montana highway, the GMC half a mile behind me on the shoulder and a buxom young cowgirl in short shorts and a shirt tied up past her belly button stopping to give me a lift into town. Maybe she'd be lonely and invite me to stay with her while the truck was in the shop and we'd have a brief but memorable affair before I had to break her heart and continue down that lonesome highway en route to bowling alleys unknown. The alternate vision of what might happen was less romantic, and involves being forced into slave labor to work off the two thousand dollars I owe a husky Neanderthal mechanic for two hundred dollars' worth of used parts and a half hour of labor. *Character building,* I reassure myself, halfheartedly.

"Why don't you take the Honda?"

My mother is offering me her car, a nine-year-old Accord that has low mileage, new tires, and no discernable gasoline odor inside the passenger cabin.

I immediately accept her offer.

Janice B. Walsh has now signed on as the Official Automotive Sponsor of my Great American Bowling Road Trip, and Mom's Honda will be the Official Vehicle of same. The sponsorship rights in the beverage, sporting goods, foot odor powder, snack chip, beer, and hotel categories remain available, but the all-important vehicle slot is filled.

Some people's business cards list their title as "Manager," "Associate," or "Director." My first business card told people I was a "Hotdogger."

In 1936, a German immigrant named Carl Mayer offered to help his uncle Oscar, a butcher, promote his sausages. Carl's idea: build a car shaped like a frankfurter, put a driver and a dwarf in it, and cruise around Chicago.

"Little Oscar, the World's Smallest Chef," would sit in an exposed rear cockpit at the tip of the frank, wearing a chef's hat and waving as he passed by, to the delight of kids of all ages. The first Oscar Mayer Wienermobile was made of metal and donated to the World War II effort, possibly making its way to Oscar and Carl's relatives in Germany in one form or another. After the war, several new mobiles were built, several new Little Oscars recruited, and the Wienermobile continued its journey into America's iconographic history. In the decades to come, various iterations of the vehicle and promotional programs came and went. A number of Little Oscars who did tours of hot-dog duty also appeared as Munchkins in the film *The Wizard of Oz*. During the late 1970s and early 1980s the program all but disappeared due to a shift in marketing-dollar prioritization. Then in 1988 a new fleet of Wienermobiles came off the assembly line along with new promotional programs. Little Oscar was replaced by recent college graduates who were given the title "Hotdogger" and assigned to drive around the country generating goodwill. Primarily public relations majors, the new Hotdoggers would spend a year behind the wheel spreading Oscar Mayer's message in public appearances, on TV morning shows, at radio remotes, and driving food critics and automotive writers around for an afternoon in hopes of getting a good article written about the tube steak on wheels.

The latest models of the Wienermobile are twenty-seven-foot-long behemoths weighing in at over five tons. The orange-red hot dog sits atop a yellow bun and is completely hollow inside, with fishbowl windows at the front and a back-lit Oscar Mayer logo across the middle. A single gull-wing door at the center of the passenger side is the only entry and exit, giving the mobile a certain half-DeLorean futuristic feel. Inside are six relish green captain's chairs, a TV, GPS, eight-speaker sound system, hot dog–shaped dashboard, and enough storage for thousands of plastic Wiener Whistles, which the Hotdoggers hand out during scheduled appearances.

Jay Leno once joked in a monologue that it was actually easier to get the job of president than it was to become a driver of the Oscar Mayer Wienermobile. From a pure numbers standpoint, it's true: if ten people run for president in an election year, that's still well over a thousand shy of the number of applicants the Wienermobile program receives annually. I'm not sure exactly how I managed to get the job, but I quickly learned how to answer that question when asked:

"I cut the mustard."

And that's not even the worst of the puns. Over two grueling (*grilling*) weeks of Hot Dog High in Madison, Wisconsin, each class of new Hotdoggers is extensively trained on how, as a Hotdogger, to be gracious ("*franks* a lot!"), to say good-bye ("*ketchup* with you again soon!"), to be appreciative ("I really *relish* my job"), and so forth. It sounds like all fun and games, but at times, as any Hotdogger will tell you, it can be a real meat grinder.

After pun training, which only comprises about the first twenty minutes, and when the newbies aren't practicing their parallel parking (being careful not to scratch the buns, of course), they're getting some of the best public relations training in corporate America.

Anti-meat protesters and other unsavory sorts target Wienermobile events because it's easy to latch onto the attention the vehicle generates on its own. Somehow they've gotten the notion that a clown car and a pair of twenty-two-year-olds handing out toys to children represents all the ills of corporate America and meat-eating humankind. Controversy, even if it's contrived for the exact purpose of getting on the news, draws news crews. The reporters are typically rolling their eyes as they repeat the protesters' killjoy accusations and get an obligatory sound bite from one of the Hotdoggers. But occasionally the reporters get aggressive, perhaps seeing this story as their shot at *60 Minutes* if they can uncover the evil truth about this insidious vehicle. And so each Hotdogger receives extensive training on how to respond to questions like, "You pump pigs full of hormones and raise them in dark, unventilated cages, don't you?" The best response to which, I found, was, "Sounds like someone needs a Wiener Whistle!"

More important, Hotdoggers get extensive training in how to draw the media to events in the first place. Since the program exists to spread goodwill on the roads and over the airwaves, every Hotdogger knows how to write a compelling press release and persuade skeptical reporters into covering a soft-news event. (It helps if it's a slow news day.) As I had successfully placed the Wienermobile on dozens of front pages and news shows, my plan is to use the same formula to gain attention for my bowling trip, and to use that buzz to gain the funding I will need so desperately, so soon. Granted, a twenty-seven-year-old having an early midlife crisis and driving around to bowling alleys in his mom's car may prove less compelling than an iconic vehicle with seventy years of history, but that's no reason not to try.

To help with this I've set up a Web site. Now, this in itself is nothing special. Most fourth graders have Web sites by now, and bowling-roadtrip.com is about as likely to win corporate sponsorship as mypicturesofhorseys.com by Brianna is. While I've primarily set it up as a means of explaining the endeavor to friends and family, it will also serve as a reference for the media and potential sponsors to convince them I'm not making this up, or at least I'm a committed liar. I've designed it as little more than a structured blog, so I can add narratives of each state's adventures and update key statistics like "Highest Score," "Pairs of Rented Shoes Worn," and "Number of Gallons of Nacho Cheese Consumed".

On my last day of work I send the URL in an e-mail to about one hundred friends, family, and co-workers.

To my surprise this yields a wealth of responses, and the first hint that the trip has potential to capture interest, i.e., sponsorship-generating buzz. The people I sent it to sent it to their friends, and their friends in turn sent it on further. If I were in a windowless conference room in Cincinnati I'd be touting this as a case study in successful *viral marketing* and soliciting ideas on how to *leverage* it. Having eschewed that world, however, I'm thinking this is fantastic dumb luck. By the end of the day I begin hearing from complete strangers who are in love with the idea.

From a former client, likely fresh from a windowless conference room:

> Mike,
>
> I wish I were going with you as I read your reasons . . . they did strike a chord with me. Many a time, I'm sure no surprise to you, I look around this place and ask . . . Is there more to learn about life here . . . or in a bowling alley? . . . I think you know the answer.
>
> I also relate to the memory of the "two week load up the car" trips of my youth. I'm an only child, so it used to be me and Mom and Dad headed west . . . Sometimes I can still remember the excitement of going to bed the night before we were leaving, not being able to sleep dreaming of the adventure that was awaiting. Maybe that's some of the innocence we've lost in America.
>
> —Matt

From a stranger in Dallas:

> Mike,
>
> I strongly recommend you visit the Jupiter
> Bowl in East Dallas. It's everything you expect a
> bowling alley to be and more. For my money,
> it's also the best place in Texas to view a large
> gathering of extremely unhealthy people.
> Jupiter Bowl patrons are an unpretentious sort
> who eagerly throw caution into the wind by
> consuming large quantities of fried food, high
> nicotine cigarettes and American beer. I once
> overheard a couple of customers chastising the
> Jupiter Bowl snack bar attendant by saying,
> "She's mean. She didn't give me no gravy."
> Saturday night at the Jupiter includes a strange
> ritual in which one of the employees walks
> around with a cordless microphone announcing
> scores at various lanes (or maybe it's some
> league game I don't quite understand).
> Regardless, I love these people.
>
> —John

From my friend Cam's father, whom I've never met:

> Mike,
>
> All of us my age wish we had done something
> like this but Vietnam, early marriages and life
> prevented it. Have a blast and if you like a
> place, stick around for a while . . . you never
> know what you will find behind the scenes.
>
> —Craig

From another stranger, this one in Indiana:

> Hey bowling guy
>
> I live in Indiana, and I am a tattoo artist in Kokomo, and I hear you like meeting people who are interesting. Well, if you are interested I would like to give you a free bowling themed tattoo. How's that for an experience? So if you're interested you can e-mail me back or get ahold of me at the shop. Its' called Mad City Tattoo in Kokomo, IN.
>
> Sincerely,
> Chad WormBoy Reeves
>
> P.S. Ask for Worm.

And so on. Bowling alley recommendations, stories of sexual exploits in bowling alley bathrooms, and offers of lodging are pouring in. In one e-mail a woman identifying herself as "Bowling Spice" even calls me her hero and makes some innuendo toward me involving bowling equipment, a frightening yet intriguing prospect in itself. And while no corporate sponsors are knocking on my door just yet, a handful of people did send money in response to a semi-facetious offer I have on the site: $150 in exchange for a postcard from every state. And I haven't even begun the trip yet.

Ohio ★

OUR bowling adventure begins, as fate would have it, in a gynecologist's office.

Located a half mile from Lane Avenue Mall and across four lanes of traffic from Taco Bell and Tommy's Pizza, Kingsdale Gynecologic Associates offers a full range of women's reproductive health services. Mammograms, ultrasounds, Pap tests, fertility treatments, and sexually transmitted disease evaluations are administered here with great professionalism and the utmost in medical standards, so I'm told, daily to the women of Upper Arlington, Ohio. This is where I learned to bowl.

Prior to becoming a gynecologists' office, this stretch of Lane Avenue housed Fiesta Lanes, a 1950s-era bowling alley complete with a smoke-filled vinyl-boothed lounge and a snack bar that put out heart-stopping, grease-dripping cheeseburgers and chocolate malts so gritty you'd think you were sipping sand if it didn't taste so good.

A wide, low-profiled building with a set of double doors in the center and a sign reading: "No Outside Food or Drink Allowed," the address's most significant feature was the neon Fiesta Lanes sign that sat high atop a pole near the street. A bona fide landmark, the red, pink, yellow, blue, and green sign with its crooked letters was a beacon marking the edge of Upper Arlington at its border with the Ohio State University campus across Kenny Road. Surrounded by undeveloped land used by OSU's agricultural program, the bowling alley was the first building incoming traffic would pass as it entered Upper Arlington and the last it would see on the way out.

Those neon letters were the unofficial "Welcome to Upper Arlington" sign.

Entering through the front doors, patrons were greeted at a rounded countertop, behind which cubbyholes stuffed with blue and red shoes lined a half wall. A public-address microphone sat on the countertop, enabling the manager on duty to run the operation by simply leaning down, pressing the button, and speaking without leaving their stool. A sweet woman who must have weighed ninety-five pounds often occupied this role, barking out orders with surprising authority.

"Reset on lane fifteen."

"DiPaolo, your lane is ready."

"Hey, kid—no bowling before the guard goes back up. Hey! I mean it, lane thirty-eight. I'm watching you!"

Behind the desk was the lounge, accessible via a cutout window in the wall above the bar. Behind the lounge was the snack bar, a low countertop with stools facing the milk-shake mixers. All of this occupied the building's long, narrow center, which was flanked on either side by forty bowling lanes, lined with racks full of black bowling balls of every weight and finger hole size combination imaginable. While many modern bowling centers have color-coded house balls (green=heavy, pink=light, et cetera) Fiesta's rental balls were almost exclusively previously owned equipment, as evidenced by names like Hank and Betty etched into their shells just above the finger holes. To a first-time visitor the balls may all have looked the same, but regulars could easily spot a favorite by a certain chip by the thumbhole or a familiar blemish or printed marking. My ball of choice was a twelve-pounder with the initials "BBH" stamped into it just above a white triangular AMF logo. I could spot it on any rack in the building all the way from the front door. If I found it was already in use by another bowler when I arrived I would select another, always keeping an eye out for them to finish.

A stone's throw from Upper Arlington High School, Fiesta was an easy loitering spot after school or after Friday night football games. The expansive parking lot and surrounding fields made for easily hidden underage drinking for those seventeen-year-olds not bold enough to just order pitchers of beer from the lounge, which had a reputation for serving even the most baby-faced of patrons. More innocuously, and more common, was for a group of six or eight sophomores to rent a couple of lanes, don rental shoes, and hurl balls down the lanes, the activity for which the place had been built. Within that context, first kisses would be shared, momentarily crushing breakups would occur, cigarettes would be tried, boys would bond, girls would gossip, and parents would pick everyone up at the night's end. The world lacking many places for teenagers to gather with impunity, Fiesta Lanes was a safe place to take the social training wheels off and explore being grown-up for a couple of hours . . . so long as we kept generating income for the proprietors by eating burgers, renting shoes, and buying games.

In autumn of 1999, opening mail in my first apartment in Chicago, a dark, low-ceilinged garden unit on Sheridan Road, I learned of Fiesta's demise. Accompanying a note from my mother was a clipping from the *Upper Arlington News*—a weekly suburban paper with high school football scores and wedding announcements—reporting the closure and sale of the town's only bowling alley. The owners, citing a decline in league participation and overall business and having no heirs interested in continuing the day-to-day operations of the facility, had decided to sell the building and the land around it. Decades of hospitality, community, and friendly competition would be auctioned off to the highest bidder. Whether they sought a buyer who would keep the bowling alley open was unclear, but as events unfolded the development company that purchased the site demolished the building.

The new building, built in 2001, sits back from Lane Avenue with a broad parking lot stretching the width of the building and wrapping around the sides to the back for overflow. The gynecologists' offices share their brick-faced building with a tanning salon, a chiropractor, and a Starbucks. It is a nondescript building, not offensive in its architecture to the newcomer but wildly so to those with some affection for the structure that previously occupied the spot. Atop the pole where the neon sign once welcomed all there is now an interior-lit box sign listing the new occupants' names. Fiesta Lanes has become half a strip mall. A sad-looking drive-up ATM stands in a lonely corner of the parking lot. Overall, the new installation has brought a very transitory feel to what was once a destination for spending a few slow hours with friends.

All is not lost, however.

The developers kept the famous neon sign, only they relocated it. The multi-colored crooked letters now adorn the entranceway to Kingsdale Gynecologic Associates, greeting patients on their way to a potentially dreaded exam with the warm, familiar glow of a neon bowling alley sign.

Herein lies the paradox of bowling in the United States today: as a society we don't bowl with the frequency to keep businesses like Fiesta open, yet we hold sufficient affection for its place in our civic lives to think it wholly appropriate that the old neon sign remain, even if in such an unusual location.

Robert Putnam, who is the Peter and Isabel Malkin Professor of Public Policy at Harvard University, published a book in 2000 called *Bowling Alone.* Putnam's central premise is that over the past quarter century Americans have become less communally inclined and that the decline of group social activity has led to an overall decline in satisfaction with life, as well as increased crime, teen pregnancy, child suicide, and low birth weight, to name a few consequences. (Beyond that it's an optimistic book, though.) As the title suggests, bowling is a key bellwether Putnam cites for these trends. While over 50 million people still bowl annually in the United States, he observes that league participation has declined from its mid-1960s peak when nearly 8 percent of men and 5 percent of women were in a regular bowling league to somewhere around 2 percent for both groups by the mid-1990s. If Americans are not literally bowling "alone," we're at least not bowling in regularly scheduled leagues.

A bowling league is a commitment. Most leagues occur weekly for six months. Each weekly match lasts between two and three hours. Who has three hours to spend away from their family on a Tuesday night? And not just a Tuesday night here and there—*every* Tuesday. There's work to stay late for, soccer to take the kids to, prep work to do for tomorrow's meetings, spouses to see, dinners to make, laundry to pick up, appointment TV to watch. I recently tried to organize a night out with four friends and, after exploring five possible dates, finally settled on one that just three of us could make. Scheduling thirty-six Tuesdays in a row with them would require a cosmic event of some sort. A bowling league, even for a handful of twenty-somethings without children, is a difficult thing to commit to in this age.

Most bowling centers were built around the league model, which presumes the ability to line up a full house of bowlers every night and ideally twice per night—an early league at 6:00 and late league at 9:00. Bowling revenues would pay to keep the lights on and the lanes oiled, and concessions sales would provide the profit. A captive audience who spend three hours playing at least three games per visit, league bowlers consume exponentially more beer and food than a couple stopping in for a game after dinner. The declining league trend signals a need for a dramatic shift in the business model for bowling centers, one that many have failed to successfully implement because they lack either the sophistication or the resources to do so. When AMF, the world's largest owner-operator of bowling centers, recently sought a new CEO it hired the former CEO of a successful restaurant chain—a revealing glimpse at which part of the company's operations would be most important to its survival and growth. Improve the food offering and get back the dining business, if not the leagues. The Fiesta Lanes of the world, it seems, will have to similarly adapt if they are to regain their position as a community destination in a time when community participation is in decline.

The last time I really embarrassed my mother was during a high school talent show attended by some five hundred people, many of whom were friends of hers. During an onstage interview the emcee asked me what had been my most embarrassing moment. I replied that it happened just seconds after I was born when, upon assessing the situation, I realized that I was completely naked in a room full of fully clothed doctors and nurses. "That must have been quite traumatic for you," the emcee played along.

"That's not even the worst part," I continued. "The doctor turned me around and I saw that my mom was there with her pants off!" My mother, sitting front-and-center among her peers, buried her head.

Today I get the sense she's bracing herself for another talent show moment. I've already gathered the crowd: everyone she knows has seen the Web site, and it's put her in a position to have to explain with awkward, perhaps forced, confidence, the nobility of my quest. I can tell she doesn't quite understand it, and the words to better explain it to her escape me. One of her friends has already expressed, rather patronizingly, that it's "nice that Michael is going off to find himself." Words to cringe by, especially for my mother, who expended so much time and energy during her children's formative years making them solid, focused individuals who wouldn't flake out and drive aimlessly around the country. And now I'm taking her car over to Sawmill Lanes for what I've assured her will be the launch of a successful media campaign that will span the entire trip, win me sponsorship, probably lead to a movie deal, and validate the whole endeavor. Her supportive words are underpinned by doubt she's trying not to show—I detect it anyway—and by a fear that I've come home to unintentionally but still undeniably shame her. On her birthday, no less.

I am alone at Sawmill Lanes, explaining to the manager that any minute now a news crew will arrive to interview me live on the local NBC4 morning show.

"It's going to be live, on Emmy Award–Winning Reporter Gail Hogan's show."

He regards me with a mixture of disbelief and disinterest and goes back to what he was doing. I might have told him that when I grow up I'm going to be an astronaut.

I sit at the table in front of lane fifteen. I get up from the table and check the parking lot for the news truck. The producer I spoke with had suggested that a traffic story or a child trapped in a well could pre-empt the bowling guy story, but if not, they'd have someone there, absolutely. Probably. In fact, I would be on live, talking to Emmy Award–Winning Reporter Gail Hogan in the studio via satellite. I would have an earpiece in my ear and a microphone on my lapel and would engage in witty banter. If only the crew showed up with earpieces, microphones, and banter suggestions. The manager looks over with a smirk and shakes his head to himself.

I'm bowling at least, the first official rolls of the trip, with my head turned toward the door watching for a knight with shining camera to rescue me. I roll an 8 and miss the spare. The show I'm supposed to be on has already begun. I roll a 6 and miss the spare again. It's nearly ten minutes into the show now; my mother is no doubt watching at her office and pretending she still thinks I'll be interviewed. "I'll support my son no matter how he humiliates me," she's telling herself, gritting her teeth.

I roll a strike. The light changes: sunlight floods in through an east-facing door that's just swung open. A silhouetted figure walks through it. The sunlight frames him like a soldier, his weapon a camera hanging at the end of his left arm, his ammunition a thick cable draped over one shoulder, across his chest, and under the opposite arm. I nonchalantly rush over to him, stumbling in my rented shoes and over my words. He rigs me with a an earpiece, a lapel mic, and points to me when I'm on in three, two, one—

"What better describes average America than its bowling alleys?" asks Emmy Award–Winning Reporter Gail Hogan, rhetorically. "That is the thought of Upper Arlington native Mike Walsh, who begins a journey today that will take him to all fifty states. Mike joins us today from Sawmill Lanes. Mike, I understand there's a reason you chose Sawmill—it's your home bowling alley, isn't it?"

Everything I learned at Hot Dog High leaves me at this very moment. I stammer through an answer about a 200 game I once rolled at Sawmill and how Fiesta was really my "home court," but it's gone now, so yes, I suppose this is my home bowling alley. *Did I really just correct Emmy Award–Winning Reporter Gail Hogan?*

Emmy Award–Winning Reporter Gail Hogan is unfazed by my stammering and carries me through the next couple of questions until I find my footing. Two minutes into the interview I've managed to somewhat satisfactorily explain what it is I'm doing and why and I'm starting to relax on camera.

EAWRGH asks to see me roll a ball. I do, announcing as I make the approach, "This one's for you, Gail!" It leaves three pins and she kindly mocks me.

"Mike, I've got to ask: you're not married, are you?"

"Well, Gail, I'm hoping to find that right special lady in a bowling alley somewhere."

This elicits an actual laugh from EAWRGH, surprised that I managed a legitimate quip instead of sputtering something awkward.

"Mike, do me a favor and come back and see us when you're all finished."

"Will do, Gail. This one's for you." I roll a ball as the segment ends and leave two pins standing. As the audio fades from my earpiece I hear EAWRGH saying something like, "He really shouldn't dedicate those to me—it doesn't seem to be helping."

A reporter from the *Upper Arlington News* arrives to interview me next, and then the local CBS and ABC affiliates come and shoot video for their evening broadcasts. During breaks in my media junket I take some time to absorb the daytime activity at Sawmill Lanes.

On lanes one and two is a group of middle school children—a special education class—and their three teachers. One child is in a wheelchair, another wears plastic leg braces from just above the knee down, and a third shows a severe case of Down syndrome. None of them bowls particularly well; bumpers keep their slow, wobbly rolls from entering the gutters and the pins barely fall when hit, so slight is the ball's momentum. One child keeps bowling out of turn and being reprimanded by his teacher. The girl in the wheelchair bowls by pushing the ball down a special ramp made of curved metal pipes.

"Way to go, Rachel," calls one of the instructors. "Now how many is that?" She does the math, verifying it on the overhead electronic score display.

Erin, in the plastic braces, is unstable as she picks up her ball. Dutifully another of the kids, a boy named Seth whose disability is less apparent, helps her complete her roll. They high-five as the ball knocks into the pins sixty feet away.

Several lanes over, birthday girl Eleanor Gentile is celebrating her eighty-fifth with the women's league she's been bowling in for forty-six years, most of them at Fiesta until its closure. Eleanor can't weigh much more than her age; it's nerve-racking to see her pick up a ball and go through the motions of bowling, but her brittle-looking bones move fluidly, if slowly, through the approach, and the ball glides smoothly into its target. Textbook form.

"You've been bowling for forty-six years, Eleanor? What's your best score?"

"Oh, I can't remember," she says modestly, then allows a brief moment of pride no one would begrudge her after eight and a half decades. "I have had some very good games."

Between turns she continues to tell me about the league.

"Everybody's friendly. Everybody talks about everybody."

"Eleanor!" I tease, feigning shock. "Are you talking about gossip?"

"Of course—it's women! It wouldn't be any fun without it!"

"It made me sick when Fiesta closed," she says. "I had a lot of memories there." Beyond the venue, however, not much else is different, she explains.

"I don't really think my bowling experience has changed that much over the years. These ladies, even the young ones, are just like we were."

★ ★ ★

I've been inside Sawmill Lanes now, bowling and chatting, for the better part of five hours. It's better than a windowless conference room, I gloat to myself, though my right arm is so sore that I can barely bowl. My brother Peter brings my nephew Jacob, who is five, and my niece Lily, who is three, for the last hour. The kids present me with a parting gift: a road atlas with a ten-dollar bill stapled to each state, accompanied by a rule not to spend one until I reach the state to which it is attached. Who needs corporate sponsors?

By the time my mother arrives home, her answering machine is packed with messages from neighbors and friends who saw me on TV. Now they understand. Now she understands. "Michael, you were so good! When do you think David Letterman will have you on?"

The joviality that masked our sadness when we were picking out my father's grave site is absent as I visit it for the first time since his funeral. Mostly gone, anyway. I do have to smirk at the Italian name on the headstone next to his, recalling our faux protest when we were selecting the plot nearly two years ago.

I never thought I'd be a grave visitor. I suppose once every two years doesn't make me one, at least not a frequent one. It just seems silly to talk to a headstone, and I find I feel self-conscious about it despite being the only (embodied) soul anywhere nearby. I give a black piece of granite and seventy-two inches of earth an awkward update on the family: "Mom's doing okay, Peter and Pat each had another kid, Molly got her master's degree . . . ," and move on to more immediate matters. "Oh, and do you remember that fifty-state idea? I'm going to have a go at it for you, Dad." And suddenly self-consciousness turns to tears.

I return to the car, steer it to the far left lane on westbound I-70, and do what he would have done: speed like a demon. Now, I'm not one to put a lot of faith in the notion of being "watched over," but it's a minor miracle that I manage to get to the last exit before the Indiana border without getting stopped by the notoriously aggressive Ohio State High-way Patrol. Perhaps Dad was able to have a word about my project with, as he would put it, the Great Handball Player in the Sky.

At the Exit 10 truck stop I remove ten-dollars from the Ohio page of my new atlas, purchase and send ten postcards, then cross state one off my list.

You don't know me, but I'm willing to be your little woman with shoe powder and ball cleaner awaiting your return home.

THESE words are among the responses from strangers in response to the "viral" distribution of my departure e-mail. The sender signed her name as Bowling Spice.

I can tell from her e-mail address that she works at a Chicago ad agency, but not one at which I know anyone, so I can't verify her as crazy, beautiful, funny, or otherwise. Her offer of services, clearly tongue-in-cheek, contrasts with some of her other comments: "I needed a new hero. I've been itching to leave my job, itching for a road trip, and I'm a huge bowler." "Your idea brought tears to my eyes." And my personal favorite: "I am numb with awe."

Naturally, I arrange a bowling date with her.

My reply to her e-mail includes probing questions to form a better understanding of what I might be getting myself into.

"Who do you bowl with?" (Do you have a boyfriend?)

"Who are your other heroes?" (Who's my competition?)

"You write: 'I'm a huge bowler'—how often do you bowl?" (What do you weigh?)

Bowling Spice's response to my queries comes with even more innuendo, if read into properly, and I am all for reading into it properly. To a question about what made her favorite bowling alley so great, she replies: "Orgasmic lanes." She also clarifies that when she wrote "I'm a huge bowler" in her first e-mail, she meant she was "passionate" about the sport—not physically large. She describes the opportunity to bowl 10 frames with me as something that would be "a pleasure." *Orgasmic. Passionate. Pleasure. Not physically large.* This looks promising, actually.

As I drive to her apartment to pick her up, I begin to question that conclusion. How sound is my judgment if I'm acting so easily on a stranger's Internet-born advances? Isn't more caution called for here? Is this going to end with people gathered around my casket, shaking their heads at how I could have been dumb enough to go somewhere alone with a complete stranger who approached me through the Internet? What if she's some John Wayne Gacy copycat, a middle-aged man who dresses like a clown and chloroforms young men before molesting and killing them, burying them beneath the house? Or worse (in some ways), what if she's a fourteen-year-old girl and this was all some sting operation and the guy from *Dateline NBC* will be there with a camera crew and the Chicago Police Department Sex Crimes Unit? Not exactly the kind of media attention that will attract a sponsor.

As it turns out, no clowns or camera crews are waiting to pounce on me. Instead, a young woman (at least twenty-three—completely legal) slinks down the concrete steps in front of the row house where Bowling Spice said she'd be. Long auburn hair bounces off her shoulders, faded blue denim clings for dear life to her model-length legs, and a tight, low-cut black T-shirt snuggles against a pair of astonishingly perky breasts.

What's more, and perhaps I'm pre-disposed to this given her physical description and previously e-mailed innuendos, I find myself taken with her personality. *Even if she wasn't hot, I'd like her,* I tell myself. In what could be a very awkward situation for her (if I was worried about meeting a stranger through the Internet, what goes through an attractive young woman's mind?), she is relaxed and charming, witty and engaging. We're firing on all cylinders; first dates don't go this well! But this isn't a first date—that's the beauty of it. This is just a friendly outing with no pressure, just a couple of people with common interests who met by a quirky impetus. I've even brought along a tape recorder to record parts of our interaction to help me document the trip, thinking it provides a layer of academia to the evening. (As it turns out, asking to tape-record everything a girl you've just met says strikes the subject as exceptionally creepy, so I shut it off and toss it in the backseat.) Lacing up my rental shoes at Circle Lanes in Forest Park, I can't help but be disarmed by her pleasant, unassuming smile.

And then Bowling Spice puts on her game face.

With all the steely-eyed friendliness of a linebacker staring down an opponent across the line of scrimmage, this flower of a woman won't break eye contact as she methodically removes each of a half-dozen silver rings from her fingers one by one, tossing them into her bowling ball bag. Lacing her shoes appears to be not so much an act of getting dressed as one of donning armor just before battle. I'm fairly certain I hear her mutter something like, "I'm going to kick your pasty ass, road-trip boy," but when I ask what she said she puts on an innocent face and insists, "What? I didn't say anything. Now let's roll some balls."

Gulp.

Like any good intimidator, Bowling Spice mostly keeps quiet as we bowl, except for the odd taunting when I roll poorly and mentioning that she stole the green ball she's rolling with from a bowling alley in Oregon. Funny, she hadn't seemed like a criminal when she sent me an unsolicited e-mail signed with an alias. That she refuses to let me take her photo without somehow obscuring her face makes me think maybe she *is* a John Wayne Gacy and doesn't want to be recognized via my Web site. Come to think of it, Gacy did his killing not far from here. . . .

We bowl three games, and I rid myself of the paranoia taking comfort that no self-respecting serial killer would wear for a belt buckle a saucer-sized hunk of metal with a blue bowling ball crashing into ten pins above the word "bowling." Bowling Spice beats me in the first two games, and I win the third. When the bowling is done, the playful, borderline flirtatious conversation returns. We drive back to her apartment, shake hands, and I make sure to invite her to my going-away party in hopes of progressing to something more intimate.

Buoyed by my success in Columbus, I thought Chicago, though a much larger market, would at least yield *some* media interest, given that there are more papers, local networks, and radio stations with space and air to fill. But my press releases to the local media go unnoticed, and my follow-up phone calls are met with the same level of commitment a radio DJ expresses when you call in to request a song he has no intention of playing: "We'll see if we can get to it." *Click.*

Just before packing up our apartment so I can road-trip and he can move into a one-bedroom, my roommate, Eric Boyd, and I throw one last going-away party. My ex-girlfriend Kalli shows up and asks with less-than-innocent curiosity, "So, what's the deal with Bowling Spice?"

"Oh, nothing," I reply, clearly still pining for Kalli. "Bowling Spice is just something funny to put on the Web site. She's meaningless." At this moment, I notice Bowling Spice over Kalli's right shoulder. That bridge likely burned now and my breakup with Kalli still fresh enough to seem reversible, I spend the rest of the evening focusing attention none too subtly on Kalli. Our breakup, after all, had been the result of poor communication. We always had fun together, had everything in common, liked the same restaurants, bars, and people. We just never communicated well. Why not start talking on my last night in town?

Deluded by drink into thinking this eleventh-hour strategy will spark a rekindling, I walk her home, try to kiss her, and invite myself in. The floating optimism of a man with nothing to lose. She responds wisely, if contrary to my immediate preferences.

"Good night, Mike. I know your trip will be amazing. Be careful, and good luck."

Leaving Illinois on my way to Wisconsin the next afternoon, I'm a bit jaded over not getting any sponsor-attracting press attention. As I was a Chicago resident, the hometown angle added a more compelling element to my story than I'll have in the remaining forty-eight states; the public relations value of my story will be that much weaker as I move on into even less familiar territory. Reviewing my checking account balance at a gas station ATM near my erstwhile apartment, I'm already becoming more desperate for a sponsor; not having a strong publicity portfolio to present leaves me with a pretty feeble case to bring to Odor Eaters or anyone else for that matter.

Fuck it anyway. I'm going on the road trip to end all road trips. Who cares if I get a sponsor? The experience will pay for itself in . . . experience. That ought to keep me fed.

Pedal down on the Tri-State Tollway somewhere just south of the Wisconsin border, my cell phone rings.

"Mike? This is Mark Brown from the *Chicago Sun-Times*. I've got your press release sitting here. I'm thinking of doing a page-two column on you for tomorrow's paper—do you have a few minutes to talk about your story?"

I suppose. . . .

Wisconsin ★

I can barely sleep, and it's not because the couch in Dan Farrar's corporate apartment lacks comfort. (Dan, a college friend, happened to be in Milwaukee for a week of sales training. Responding to the call of my e-mail, he graciously offered a few nights of free lodging.) Make no mistake, the couch is entirely uncomfortable, but the reason I'm not sleeping is that I am scared silly about how the *Sun-Times* column will turn out. *Was I funny? Will my words, so insightful and witty when I spoke them during the phone interview, appear stupid in print? And what does this Mark Brown guy typically write? Is he going to shred me, make me look self-righteous or like I'm just another lost soul out to "find" himself? Or worse yet, what if he was so underimpressed after speaking with me that he didn't even end up writing it?*

At 3:00 A.M. the *Sun-Times* Web site still has not posted a new Mark Brown column; most papers update their Web sites with the next day's content by midnight. Perhaps the editors decided to cut the bowling guy piece for its complete lack of newsworthiness. Bleary and discouraged, at 3:30 I find a sort-of comfortable position on the couch and stare at the ceiling until I drift to sleep. My cell phone's ring awakens me at 7:00.

"Mike, hi, it's Tiffany." I check the time and figure I must be dreaming. I used to work with Tiffany. She doesn't get up this early.

"They're talking about you on *Eric and Kathy!*"

Eric & Kathy is a highly rated and well-promoted morning show on Chicago's biggest pop radio station.

The *Eric & Kathy Show* is ubiquitous in the city: everyone, even those who find it grating, knows what it is and, like it or not, gets sucked into listening at some point or another. "Eric & Kathy" make appearances at major events around the city. "Eric & Kathy" interview pop stars of international renown. "Eric & Kathy" are Chicago royalty. "Eric & Kathy" are not talking about me. I can't figure out why I'm dreaming that Tiffany is awake, calling my cell phone, and lying to me.

As Tiffany continues to swear it's true (that she's awake *and* that I'm the topic on *Eric & Kathy*) I log onto my e-mail account. There are a dozen new messages, several from strangers. One is from someone named Marlene, with the subject line "bowler of my . . . dreams???" Marlene describes a dream she'd had about my adventure, which seemed strange until she figured out that the radio alarm clock that just woke her up had infiltrated her subconscious. I begin to believe that both Tiffany and I are awake and that "Eric & Kathy" are talking about me. I find Mark Brown's column on the *Sun-Times* Web site—a favorable write-up that captured the spirit of my quest. This is what spawned the radio coverage. I hang up with Tiffany and call Eric. Or Kathy. I'll take either one. I get Eric. Apparently I'm not the first whacko who's called him in his on-air career.

"How do I know you're really Mike Walsh?" he asks.

"Um, I don't know. How can I prove it? I'm driving my mom's car around the country bowling in all fifty states."

"It says that in the *Sun-Times*. Anyone could say that. Give me something better. Prove you're him."

I'm searching my Hotdogger training for how to deal with this. They taught me how to pitch a story. How to deliver sound bites. How to spin negative news. How to do all of this simultaneously and smiling while some hippie animal rights activist is screaming into the reporter's microphone the accusation that I, personally, killed Babe the pig. But never, in all of that training, did anyone bother to teach me how to prove to radio personalities that I am, indeed, me. I am at a loss. It's way too early in the morning for this kind of stumper, but I manage to convince Eric. After coming to the conclusion that he would be unable to verify anything about me that wasn't published in the article anyway, as that was the extent of his knowledge on the matter, my winning argument is all too self-implicating: "Who would claim *this* just to get on the radio?"

I kill on the *Eric & Kathy Show*. I'm hilarious. I'm quick-witted, self-deprecating, coherent, and even manage to plug the Web site. Gail Hogan and her Emmy would have been proud. As apparently happens when there's a slow news day and Mark Brown's column has a quirky story in it, other radio stations want to talk with me. By the day's end I've conducted interviews with a handful of them, from shock jocks to sports commentators. Eric and Kathy's competitor Melissa Forman of WLIT requests that my mother and I both phone in for an interview the next morning.

Mom and I kill together on WLIT. We're hilarious. She's quicker-witted and more me-deprecating than I had been on *Eric & Kathy*. It sounds so pure, this sixty-seven-year-old woman in her first-ever radio interview trying to sound proud of her son; then she throws in a cutting jab: "We've always thought Michael was . . . *special*." She even plugs the Web site before I have the chance. Off-air Melissa and her cohost rave about our performance. We are the Next Big Thing.

I spend the rest of the morning planning what I'll wear on Letterman, how I'll act nonchalant when Dave asks me to have dinner with him after the show. I've conquered Chicago—a huge media market. I never had this much success in a single day in five years of marketing and public relations. This is too easy.

This is too disappointing. *You're telling me that in Milwaukee, home of the American Bowling Congress, freakin' Bowling Town USA, no*

media organization wants to come out and cover the greatest thing to happen to bowling since the advent of graphite balls? You people are idiots. I was on Eric & Kathy! *Did you see page two of yesterday's* Sun-Times?!

Milwaukee's Bowlero Lanes, I'm finding, can be a lonely place for someone as suddenly spotlight craving as I am.

I sent out press releases, made calls, sent e-mail reminders, and still no one has shown up with a video camera to reaffirm me and raise my self-esteem to atmospheric levels. Despite yesterday's success, today's lack of interest hits me surprisingly hard. To paraphrase something Sylvester Stallone once said describing the conundrum of fame: On one hand, it's terribly inconvenient to be unable to venture into public unnoticed. On the other hand, you become so accustomed to the attention that merely the thought of walking through a hotel lobby and not being recognized is terrifying.

Realizing that in my internal monologue I'm equating a newspaper article and a couple of radio phone-ins with fame and, worse, that I'm searching for perspective from Rambo, I decide to get over it and get to know some of the people sharing Bowlero's air with me today.

It's 3:00 P.M. on a Wednesday. A seniors' league is bowling on the left side of the center. An elderly woman named Marion sips her second vodka and soda, putting the leftover ice from the first into the fresh one as the liquid level in the glass lowers. Across the table, her husband, Robert, grudgingly gulps a nonalcoholic beer, the prohibition of alcohol an inconvenient consequence of a newly begun struggle with bone marrow cancer—a struggle that doesn't seem to have curbed his smoking any; he sucks down a Marlboro in ten puffs or less.

Robert shakes his head in disappointment after rolling a six, sits down, and gazes across the lanes, focused on nothing in particular, on something beyond this bowling alley.

"He had to switch to a lighter ball than he's used to," Marion explains, adjusting her ice. "He's just not strong enough anymore to use his regular one."

A quick glance around the group shows varying degrees of infirmity and malady, some outward, like a cane or an oxygen tank, some inward like Robert's.

"We all like coming here every week. We really look forward to it," Marion continues. "I know it sounds stupid, but for lots of us, spending an hour in the lounge having popcorn and talking after we bowl is the highlight of our whole week."

"I'll do anything I can to get out of that big empty house for a few hours," agrees Martha, whose husband died two years ago.

A man named Henry chimes in. "Of course we used to bowl a lot better and drink a lot more!" he laughs.

In his next frame Robert finally rolls a strike and tries not to look too happy as he says to himself, "Now that's more like it," fighting a sheepish smile.

From the aging and optimistic at Bowlero Lanes to the young and jaded at Oriental Landmark Lanes, Dan accompanies me for a night out among our peers. Sort of.

The look and feel of Landmark is decidedly more "authentic" than Bowlero's sterile (for a bowling alley) environs. Where Bowlero had regularly emptied ashtrays and newish carpet, Landmark's ashtrays appeared to have been regularly emptied onto its carpet—though the crowd of twentysomething hipsters was doing its best to refill them. As with my aging friends from the afternoon, the clientele here at Landmark gravitates toward the lounge, its U-shaped red vinyl booths lining every wall making the ideal place to loaf complacently while waiting for a pool table or a bowling lane. An attractive twenty-three-year-old blonde attaches herself to us as we shoot pool and await our lane for bowling.

Where Marion and Robert spoke of companionship and fighting their bodies' deterioration, Heather speaks of recreational drug use and piercings in unusual places.

"My boyfriend got his penis pierced last week," she says matter-of-factly.

"Please don't say any more," Dan says, the first time I've ever seen him not ask an insightful follow-up question in conversation.

"It actually isn't that noticeable," she continues, ignoring his plea and proceeding in far too graphic detail to describe various sexual events in which she has taken part.

Finally, our lane is available. The three of us bowl, and the conversation is largely piercing- and sexual escapade–free. It is late now, and behind our lane a graying man wearing a green and red plaid shirt sits in an orange plastic chair, arms crossed and head bobbing as he does battle with the sandman.

The number of bowlers dwindles until only our threesome remains; the din of pins crashing has quieted from a full roar to the intermittent activity on our lane alone. The man in the chair finally succumbs to sleep, and stirs not a bit as we walk past him to return our rental shoes and settle our tab. After offering to help Heather hail a cab to her newly pierced boyfriend, I find a similarly deep slumber on Dan's couch for my last night in Milwaukee.

Having all but forgotten that my quest to land a sponsor via proven media exposure hit a brick wall in Milwaukee, I'm leaving town having had my fill of cheese and beer, content and propelled by the prospect of meeting more Roberts and Marions and Heathers. I'll worry about running out of money after I've run out of money, I tell myself cheerfully. Again, my cell phone's ring interrupts my drive.

"Mike, this is Rory Gillespie from *American Bowler* magazine. When are you coming to Milwaukee? I'd like to do a story on you and see if we can't get someone from the Milwaukee *Journal Sentinel* to write one as well."

"Funny you should mention it. . . ." My burgeoning penchant for being a media whore kicks in again. I spend the night in the Madison home of Russ Whitacre, my former boss at Oscar Mayer, and return to Milwaukee the next day for an afternoon at the American Bowling Congress Research and Testing Facility.

In addition to publishing *American Bowler* magazine, the ABC serves as bowling's governing body: it establishes rules and equipment standards, and it sanctions tournaments and league play. When someone rolls a perfect 300 game, it's the ABC that verifies it and sends them a commemorative ring. No bowling house worth its shoe-sanitizing spray goes without an official ABC certification sticker on its door. It is to bowling equipment what the FDA is to prescription drugs, and its testing procedures are equally rigorous, as I will soon learn. (Since my visit, the ABC has merged with a number of other bowling organizations to become the United States Bowling Congress.)

Rory has invited me to bowl against the ABC's executive director, former World Bowling Cup champion Roger Dalkin. "Real bowlers are legitimate athletes," Rory explains to me by phone, taking issue with portions of my Web site in which I espouse the traditionally accepted stereotypes associated with the sport: out-of-shape beer guzzlers in rented footwear and such. "That's not real bowling. We'll show you real bowling." His tone is one of a friendly executioner: you'll lose this one, but it's inevitable, so enjoy it.

Rory greets me at the ABC's headquarters, a nondescript office building on Milwaukee's southwest side. With him is Jim Stingl, a columnist from the Milwaukee *Journal-Sentinel*. Rory takes us down a hallway to a door that looks as if it might lead to a windowless conference room, only it doesn't. It leads to a windowless bowling testing facility: eight working lanes, charts and graphs on the walls, machines for testing balls, lane surfaces, lubricants, pins and pinsetters. Every sanctioned piece of equipment, brand of lane oil, type of lane surface, and bowling pin is tested here before being approved. Aside from arranging my humiliation at the hands of a world champion bowler, Rory has brought me here to open my eyes to the science behind the sport. To assist with this, Neil Stremmel, the ABC's director of research, joins us and gives me the dime tour.

"Each of these lanes is made with a different material," he explains, describing the different kinds of real and synthetic wood that are ABC certified. "These represent ninety-five percent of the bowling surfaces in use in the U.S."

Using the charts on the wall, Neil explains the complex physics behind throwing a strike, where each variable—the ball's weight, velocity, rotation, angle of impact—affects the outcome of a roll.

By this time a handful of people, serious bowlers all, have joined us to observe Roger Dalkin beating me soundly in a game. I decide to impress the audience with my wit.

"And here I thought the only skill involved in bowling was pouring the beer from the pitcher without making too much foam," I remark smugly. This elicits a collective cringe from the group.

"Rolling strikes consistently is like having a good golf swing," someone explains. "It's extremely demanding—mentally and physically."

There is a large contraption at the head of one of the lanes, and Rory beckons me to it. It looks like a torture device from a sixties-era Bond movie: a nine-foot-tall glass enclosure with a machine inside it, gears and mechanical arms, hydraulic fittings, hoses and wires all around. "Hey, I was just kidding about the beer thing. . . ."

"This machine is designed to roll a perfect strike," Neil explains. "We input the lane conditions—how the lane is dressed, what material it's made from, and so forth, and it adjusts accordingly." He puts a sixteen-pound ball in the machine's cradle, makes some adjustments on a keypad to reflect the lane's conditions today, and everyone steps back. The machine spins the ball to put the precise rotation on it before releasing it onto the lane at a trajectory to create the exact angle of impact between the headpin and the three-pin. Here, in the temperature- and humidity-controlled conditions of bowling's governing body's testing facility, the strike-throwing machine leaves one pin standing.

Roger Dalkin arrives, and so has the time for my ass-whooping. Rory hands me a new pair of bowling shoes—mine to keep—and a loaner ball that's newer and nicer than any ball I've ever held before. Having not fully learned my lesson about mocking bowling stereotypes, I attempt to talk trash and psych out a man who had won his first world championship before I was born and had devoted his life to the sport. "You know, these conditions aren't quite pristine, if you ask me. There's no secondhand smoke."

Roger's response to my snide remarks and trash talking is, like any good athlete, to put up more points. I proceed to roll one of the better games of my life, which would be exciting if not for the fact that, from the outset, he is on track to beat me by over one hundred pins. The gathered crowd of career bowlers and ABC officials is clearly on Roger's side, but in the spirit of people who purely love the game and want others to enjoy it as well, they also encourage me, offering tips and cheering my better rolls.

Following the game, Neil completes our tour, taking us to a room behind the lanes where floor-to-ceiling shelves are filled with hundreds of bowling pins and balls. Some balls are cut in half to show their core and the different materials and how they're arranged within to provoke a certain type of rotation or spin when rolled a certain way. Most of the pins are beaten and chipped. A pinsetting machine is in the process of testing a new type of pin for certification, setting them up and knocking them down continuously to simulate the wear and tear they'll get from real-world use.

Having sufficiently convinced me that bowling is indeed a serious sport requiring mental and physical stamina and a golflike understanding of physics, Rory is ready to expose me to a more relaxed version of the bowling experience. Along with his colleague Bill Vint and the newspaper's Jim Stingl, we enter a bowling facility that belongs in parallel universe to the ABC's environs. As the crookedly painted letters on the red wall above the staircase announce, "This is Holler House."

Holler House is a bowling alley where dreams come true and nightmares are born, often in the same evening. An absolute dive bar on Milwaukee's near south side, it's run by seventy-six-year-old Marcy Skowronski (just like it sounds). Holler House has been in her family since her in-laws built it in 1908; she's been running it for the past fifty years. As the name suggests, the building is indeed a house—Marcy's family lives upstairs. It sits on a corner, and the main entrance of the lower level opens to a 20' × 40' room with a bar covering the length of the facing wall and three low, circular tables covered with printed plastic tablecloths filling the remaining space. A weathered piano sits in the room's far left corner looking out of tune and neglected—various items of clothing, tools, and boxes are being stored on it. To the right of the bar is a staircase leading down to two bowling lanes—open since 1908 and the oldest lanes to still hold the ABC's certification. A trophy shelf sits above the staircase landing, filled with dozens of awards from long-forgotten bowling games. Each is adorned with a thick, even coating of dust, suggesting contests waged so long ago that many of their winners may have since returned to dust themselves. I'm glad we're drinking straight from bottles, not Holler House glasses.

Glancing around the bar at cracked vinyl seats, sports paraphernalia, photos of regulars, dents in the wall, I notice at least one hundred bras and pairs of underwear dangling randomly from the ceiling around the bar. *If these walls could talk*, I think. Only so long as Marcy's around, they wouldn't get a word in.

"A group of men came in one night," she says. "Usually when they come in groups it's a stag party, so I asked them, 'Who's getting married?' And they just started laughing." The men were seminarians from a nearby Catholic college. "They proceeded to get bombed," she continues, "and they started taking their pants off and that's one of their underwear up there. I told him when he gets ordained I'll wrap them up and send them to him."

Eagles guitarist Joe Walsh once played the piano during a surprise visit, and bowling greats like the late Earl Anthony, who won forty-one Professional Bowlers Association titles during his career, have signed some of the pairs of underwear on the ceiling.

"I lived in Arizona," Marcy starts again, "and you know you'd get so bored! I tried to do some volunteer work—there are so many old people there—so I went to the hospital. The volunteer coordinator was pushing someone in wheelchair. He asked me what I wanted to do and I said, 'I want to read porno to the blind.' Well, he took that wheelchair and started running. . . ."

Marcy lights the room with her personality, a good thing, since Holler House is dark enough on this sunny day to grow mushrooms.

"We had a publisher come in here once wanting to write a book about this place. Well, about twenty people were going to have to leave town! One of the guys who was always coming in with his mistresses said, 'You're not going to use real names, are you?' "

Bill, Rory, Jim, a *Journal-Sentinel* photographer, and I never stop laughing—hearty, high-pitched cackling—at Marcy's commentary during our forty-five-minute visit. The Polish beer she keeps serving us has little to do with it, but it doesn't hurt.

Downstairs, the bowling lanes themselves appear to be somewhat of an afterthought, and a bit of a letdown from the energy upstairs at Marcy's bar. Two side-by-side regulation lanes with manually set pins, they are framed by cinder block walls, one of which has radiator pipes sticking out of it to heat the room. There is no bathroom, no bar, no nothing in the basement but these two lanes. I must bowl here to round out what has been a rather diverse Wisconsin bowling experience.

"You must be Polish," she yells at me from the top of the stairway. She says this because I've just put two unmatching bowling shoes on. Rather than being stored behind a counter in cubbyholes, the rental shoes at Holler House are piled up in a jumble of laces and cheap suede at the head of the bowling area. A couple of wobbly folding chairs, a hammer, and several other hand tools are mixed in with the shoes, and finding a matching pair could take an hour. Search-and-rescue dogs would have trouble finding a body in this mess, though it wouldn't be a complete surprise if they did.

Marcy appears to have no interest in changing this because it gives her the opportunity to affectionately and regularly slander her Polish heritage from the top of the stairwell. She summons her grandson, a junior in high school, from the living area upstairs. He appears, shirtless as though he'd been just about to jump in the shower, and grudgingly climbs behind the manual pinsetters to set the pins and return my ball as I roll my final ten frames in Wisconsin.

Michigan ★

IN 1945 Grand Rapids led an oral hygiene revolution by being the world's first municipality to add fluoride to its water supply. (Imagine the tourism boom.) Since then it seems to have rested on that accomplishment, leading a fairly quiet existence in the Midwest as Michigan's second-largest city, winning high rankings on such survey measures as "best places to earn and save money"—a distinction that suggests a healthy business climate without much to do. To the in-the-know, however, the place is a hopping metropolis. And I'm in the know: I've been here once before.

I had flown into town on a Thursday night for an early meeting Friday, accompanied by a co-worker named Kevin, a brilliant, soft-spoken copywriter who tended to keep to himself. At a bar near our hotel he surprised me by ordering a Manhattan—a pretty stiff libation for a guy with a 7:00 A.M. meeting, not to mention that it's an old man's drink and, like me, Kevin was only twenty-six. To keep pace, I ordered something similarly strong. One drink led to another and barely more than an hour later, swimming in bourbon and Jägermeister, we began asking locals where we might find a more lively bar than the one across the parking lot from the Crowne Plaza. We ultimately took the suggestion of a woman with big hair and big arms who was drinking beer straight from a pitcher. The logic was apparent to us: Want a restaurant reco? Ask a fat guy. Want a bar suggestion? Ask a woman drinking straight from a pitcher.

With a swig and a slightly contemptuous look the woman slurred, "You want to find some college sluts?"

Any feigned offense at being pegged as shallow, one-night-stand-seeking chauvinists quickly disappeared as we clamored for a pen and a napkin to capture the name of the place she was about to recommend.

"You should go to the Buckin' Beaver," she said.

Wow, I thought. *The Buckin' Beaver.* This must be a reference to indigenous Michigan wildlife—not an innuendo-laden invitation to untamable vaginas, right? After all, our friend with the pitcher assured us she was sending us to a bar where all the "young kids" go these days, not some strip club. But why the suggestive name? It violated my theory that only strip clubs and gay bars are named with heavy innuendo. Beyond being a sensational way of drumming up business, it creates a helpful distinction for potential patrons wondering what kind of bar that is on the corner. Few people looking for a relaxed sports bar where they can innocently flirt with young coeds step into places with names like The Man Hole, Cellblock, or The Bush Company. As we arrived, it became apparent that, if not a strip club, the Buckin' Beaver has at least borrowed the strip club's marketing strategy, setting expectations by using the interchangeable letters on its marquee to announce "WILDEST BEAVER IN TOWN!"

Apparently every girl in Grand Rapids with a halter top and pierced navel heeded its call on this night, along with every guy with greased hair and a souped-up Honda Civic. I leaned toward Kevin to smugly muse out of the corner of my mouth, "I can't tell—is this Sodom or Gomorrah?" only to find that he had disappeared to a spot on the dance floor beneath a machine spewing foam, college sluts on all sides.

In one corner of the bar was a six-foot-tall raised platform-cage in which some of the aforementioned girls were dancing, and next to that was a mechanical bull surrounded by fairly hard-looking pads. While the Buckin' Beaver staff wouldn't let us dance in the cage—despite our repeated reassurance that we wouldn't bother the girls—they were more than willing to punish us on the bull for two dollars per ride (three for five dollars). In fact, it became a contest between two of the beefier bouncers to see who could knock the smug, condescending Chicagoans off the bull in the least amount of time. I soon learned that up close the pads were even harder than they looked, though perhaps the fact that the spinning bull was hurling me toward them like a stone from a slingshot had something to do with it. By the night's end we were exhausted, sore, bruised, soaked, and not a little frightened by the whole scene at the BB. And we hadn't even entered the adjoining bowling alley.

"He's one of those cats who enjoy the simple things in life. Once you see his crib, you'll see what I'm talking about."

This is how Trevor, an acquaintance with whom I once drank enough German beer to earn a Viking helmet at Chicago's now-defunct Great Beer Palace, describes his brother. Tim is a complete stranger to me, but one who is willing to put me up in Grand Rapids for a night during this, my second visit, which makes him my kind of stranger. While I have other offers for lodging in Grand Rapids, I opt to stay with Tim because he just last year had walked from Grand Rapids to St. Louis—nearly five hundred miles—relying on the kindness of people he met along the way. He would be sympathetic to the drifting traveler, and would likely have some good road survival tips to share.

When I finally arrive after the three-hour drive from Chicago, it's late afternoon and a typical midwestern autumn day: clouds dominate the sun, not quite brisk enough to be interesting or warm enough to be pleasant. I lock the car and try to give the two teenaged thugs loitering on a pile of nearby cinder blocks the impression there is nothing in it worth stealing—certainly not my laptop, guitar, iPod, or digital camera. Tim's place is a warehouse among warehouses. The area doesn't have the charm, or even the prospect of future charm, of those revitalized industrial neighborhoods found in cities across the country where brewpubs, loft spaces, and stationery boutiques have sprung up inside of former storage depots. These are not the 1920s-era quaint-looking buildings of New York's Meatpacking District or Chicago's River West, where urban industry has given way to Cuban-Cambodian fusion restaurants and hordes of fabulous people. These are stark, plain buildings made from the kind of cinder blocks that are better for loitering upon than for shopping or living within.

I walk through a blue door and up a dark flight of cement stairs. To the right of the top of the stairs is the high buzz of a table saw in the heat of cutting. A tall, skinny man in his midtwenties wearing a worn white T-shirt and sawdust on his blue jeans stops the saw and introduces himself. This is Tim.

Behind him I begin to see what Trevor meant about Tim enjoying the "simple things." The space, floor of wood painted gray, walls painted white, and windows painted shut—except for one window that's just plain missing—is sparsely decorated. A brown pleather couch sits against the wall facing an ancient TV on a spade-shaped coffee table; a white pleather chair sits in the middle of the room, accompanied by a mismatched floral-patterned footstool. Large paintings—splotches of light greens, sky blues, and soft browns—rest against one wall; a classical guitar is propped, one of its nylon strings missing, against the couch.

Tim is immediately friendly, intriguing, and engaging. We talk briefly about what he's making (a window to replace the one that's missing: he thinks the temperature is going to really dip tonight and he'd feel badly having a guest sleep in the cold), what I'm doing, and his own travels. I'm holding back my direct questions ("So where's the rest of the place?" "Is your bedroom in another part of the building?" "Was that a rat?") in favor of comments like "cool place" and "that's some rug," somehow thinking it would lead to a tour of the newly remodeled shower, the guest room, the kitchen.

"If you need a bathroom, it's down the hall to the left."

"I'll just let you finish that window while I freshen up then."

Except that it doesn't require a key chained to a tire iron to open the door, the bathroom could be attached to any roadside gas station: dim, worn-out mirror; dirty, stained sink; half-wadded paper towels spilling out of a rusting metal trash can. The bare 40-watt bulb swinging from the center of the ceiling gives the room a distinct murder-scene quality. I detect no shower or tub, and have a feeling there isn't one; Tim indirectly confirms this by informing me that the landlord "doesn't know I live here." I don't want to ask, as I somehow feel that "So you don't have a shower?" would be insulting to my host.

Oh, you wanted adventure, Walsh. You wanted to quit your job and live the nomad life, free from responsibility and society's constraints. Well, here you go. Does a conference call seem like such an inconvenience now? Does the thought of being "tied down" to an apartment, with its onerous shower and separate sleeping quarters, still seem so burdensome?

A closer look at Tim's habitat reveals an eclectic, ambitious mind. Against one wall in the wood-floored $50' \times 50'$ space is an antique upright piano that was made in Ann Arbor and first tuned in 1915, according to tuning dates scribbled in pencil on the back. An obscure Dylan album plays in mono from a stand-alone turntable and speaker cabinet to which Tim has temporarily hooked up a CD player. "I'm trying to figure out how to fix the turntable," Tim explains. Dozens of vinyl albums sit next to it, waiting for the day he does so to spin again: Burt Bacharach, more Dylan, the Housemartins, Willie Nelson, Johnny Cash. Underneath the TV is a twenty-year-old Atari system, Pac-Man and Home Run game cartridges alongside it. The guitar and piano aren't just showpieces; Tim is teaching himself to play both. To pay the rent and keep the fluorescent lights on he works in the shipping department of a small local company. "I've had offers for graphic design jobs, but I'd rather put my creative energy into my paintings," he says.

Following the tour of his place, Tim hands me a Miller High Life from the fridge in the kitchen/living room/studio/bedroom/guest room and shows me the phone line so I can check e-mail. "I got the phone service because I met a girl and felt weird not being able to give her a number," he explains. "It didn't work out with her, though; I'll probably get rid of the phone."

I've got several new messages from people who read Jim Stingl's piece in the Milwaukee *Journal-Sentinel,* one of which stands out not

only for its potential as a road trip sponsor but also because of the
pure coincidence of the aluminum can Tim just handed me.

> Hey Mike—
>
> I work for Miller Brewing Company's public
> relations firm and recently read about your
> quest to bowl across the country in the
> Milwaukee Journal-Sentinel. What you're doing
> really fits in well with what Miller High Life is all
> about: taking the road less traveled and
> appreciating the little things in life.
>
> Wanted to talk to you about possibly
> developing a relationship with Miller High Life
> for the remainder of your journey. We think this
> is a great opportunity to help you not just
> complete the road trip, but to do it while living
> the High Life. Please give me a call when you
> have a chance.
>
> —Russin Royal

It's hard to keep the devilish cackling to myself, and I quickly explain to Tim that I'm not some psycho he's allowed into his home but
merely a man who until three minutes ago had zero prospects for income for the foreseeable future but was now being solicited by one of
the biggest companies in the world. And it's a beer company, no less!
A product I've always wanted to endorse but never thought I could,
being neither a swimsuit model nor an animated reptile. Granted, this
is by no means an offer to fund the trip just yet. But it's a least a promising sign. Perhaps the choice to lead the nomad life will pay off after
all.

I reply to Russin's e-mail, suggesting we have a conference call—an
act that strikes me as greatly ironic given my recent escape from such
corporate structures. If you loathe something, set it free. If it returns
to you, it's probably a conference call you just have to dial into.

About the time it wasn't becoming known for the fluoride it just added to its water, Grand Rapids was becoming known for something else: bowling. The 1940s and '50s brought a surge in bowling's popularity across the United States, and Grand Rapids boasted the largest per capita population of league bowlers. It was also home to Marion Ladewig, a young woman who fifty years later is still regarded as the greatest woman bowler of all time.

In the midst of a streak in which the Bowling Writers Association of America named her Woman Bowler of the Year five consecutive times, Ladewig won a tournament at the Chicago Coliseum in 1951 with an unprecedented 247.5 average. A Grand Rapids entrepreneur named Chuck Orlikowski witnessed the game and made an offer to the tournament organizers to buy the sixteen lanes on which Ladewig claimed her victory. They accepted, and in 1953 Orlikowski opened Clique Lanes on Stocking Avenue, eight lanes on the ground floor and eight upstairs. Now known simply as The Clique, tonight I visit there with Tim. Chuck Orlikowski, Jr., shows us around the business his father handed down to him and his brother, Tom.

"This is my dad with Marion Ladewig," Chuck says, pointing to a photo within a collage on the wall near the horseshoe-shaped bar. Ladewig is in a long skirt, shaking hands with Chuck Orlikowski, Sr., and holding a trophy.

"This is similar to how it looked back then," Chuck tells us as we survey the red vinyl booths and chairs, the lighting just low enough so that even bowlers look attractive. "It's changed over the years—in the seventies its decor was a lot more disco, like everything was back then. But we like this look a lot better."

"We're in the process of selling the place," he says. Upstairs, the new ownership can be heard doing some renovation on the lanes; electric sanders and hammers whir and pound above us as we talk. The Orlikowskis sold to the former owners of another legendary Grand Rapids bowling center, the Fanatorium, a bowling house where, in

1950, Marion Ladewig won a team tournament. The Orlikowski family may be leaving bowling, but at least the new management has a good pedigree for carrying on the tradition.

The Clique's neon sign is infinitely better than the Fiesta Lanes sign that now hangs in the gynecologic clinic in my hometown, which may be the key to its ability to stay open in the face of the *Bowling Alone* effect that closed Fiesta. The sign is a bowling pin in the midst of falling down with the words "The Clique" beneath it and the words "Beer, Liquor, Bowling" above it. It has a classic, 1950s style that sets the tone for the history that fills the building's interior. On a wall in the lounge is a time capsule of sorts: a photo collage that spans the history of the Clique, of Grand Rapids. Marion Ladewig's photo is surrounded by other black-and-whites—winners of the '55 Peterson Classic and so forth—but also a progression of color photos that show the evolution of American life since then. There is a palpable sense of a changing of the guard from those who ruled bowling's heyday to those who will bring it into the future, whatever it may hold. Marion's long skirt and Chuck Senior's close-cropped hair give way to miniskirts and shaggy, unkempt cuts. As the renovation work continues on the second floor, Tim and I roll a game, straddling the Clique's past and future, and depart for another two-story bowling house.

Wenger's is hosting two leagues tonight: men's downstairs and women's up. Walking into the men's league, we're hit hard by the smell of smoke and bowling equipment, a wall of harsh glares and scornful stares. At the bar some rough-looking men, faces pockmarked beneath patchy mustaches and NASCAR hats, are playing poker between frames using a deck of remarkably graphic X-rated playing cards. I'm carrying a fancy new digital camera and the gayest-looking notepad ever produced. The notepad was a gag gift from my friend Florencio, who thought it would be amusing if strangers in small towns saw me making notes in a book with shirtless, oiled-up Mexican wrestlers on its cover. Hilarious. Tim and I opt to explore the women's league upstairs.

Sitting at the bar on the second floor, surrounded by light-colored wood paneling and Formica, Tim talks about his painting, and about creativity in general.

"More and more I feel like a hack with each new thing I paint," he says. He struggles, as do so many artists, with wanting to create something "original" but feeling like either it's all been done before or it's just different for the sake of being different, which in itself is hacky.

"In high school I painted sports stars as gifts for people, Michael Jordan and that sort of thing," he continues. "I got a lot of praise for them, and that's what I painted for—praise. But I've had enough of that to last a lifetime." Now Tim only paints for himself, which he says comes as a surprise to his former classmates, all of whom expected him to become an enormously successful commercial artist. He speaks of this not with contempt, pride, or wistfulness for times past but with acknowledgment and distance, and some careful observation in case there's something back there to inspire his new tack.

Tim also tells me about bowling on Thursday nights. "We'd all watch *The Cosby Show* together; then Dad would leave for his Thursday night league. When school was out on Friday for parent-teacher meetings, we'd all get to go with him to the alley and stay out all night, which was like eleven thirty."

An older woman, dressed in a pale yellow bowling shirt with "Rita" sewn above the left breast pocket in black, comes to the bar and walks the bartender through making her a White Russian.

"My daughter taught me this drink when I visited her in Tulsa last weekend," she explains. As the bartender searches for cream ("Will milk do?"), Tim asks Rita, "How're you bowling?"

Rita gives the amateur athlete's standard, self-deprecating answer: "Not as well as I'd like."

We follow her back to lane eight, bordered by lane seven on the left and a wood-paneled wall to the right, and watch her team bowl.

Doris, Sue, Edy, Rita, and yet another Rita have been bowling together for more years than they care to count for me. I don't ask their ages, but they are probably old enough that it's no longer impolite to ask . . . old enough that the number is a status symbol representing endurance and wisdom rather than loss of youth. The other women's shirts are identical to Rita's, only instead of yellow they are turquoise with black collars, each woman's name stitched above the breast pocket on the left front. A leather cigarette case, red lighter, and black ashtray occupy the table behind their lane, where they gather to sip their drinks and smoke between turns.

At a number of points in history, bowling and games like it were outlawed by the powers that be: England's Edward III is said to have banned it to keep men focused on archery practice, and in the mid-1800s it was banned in New England because the sport encouraged gambling. Not ones to contradict mid-nineteenth-century Puritans, my five new friends play a brand of poker while they bowl in which for every spare or strike (a "mark," in bowling nomenclature) a player rolls she gets to draw a card. Unlike the deck of cards we'd seen downstairs, fortunately, these aren't X-rated. At the end of each bowling game, the player with the best hand of five cards wins the pot.

Some would say the side gambling helps elevate the bowling, providing an incentive to roll a strike, which earns the bowler two cards, and not to give up on a spare, which earns her one. The more strikes and spares, the better the score; the better the score, the better chance at having a poker hand that takes the cash pot. Others would say bowlers need a game of chance to distract them from the game of skill they came here to play . . . something that just might afford them a small but important victory despite how many pins fall their way. Doris, Sue, Edy, and the Ritas take their poker almost as seriously as they do their bowling, which is to say it's mostly for fun, but you'd better not fudge the scores. And with good reason—the stakes are high: twenty-five cents a game.

Edy wins on this night. Change has to be made to pay her.

★   ★   ★

All of this is "old" Grand Rapids, still very much alive and bustling, but with a sense that its time is passing. The Clique and Wenger's are the kind of bowling establishments I had set out hoping to find. The minutes we spend in double-decker bowling heaven pass too quickly, but pass they must, for there's one more spot to visit tonight. It's time to buck the Beaver.

On my prior visit to Grand Rapids, I was unable to appreciate the fact that the Buckin' Beaver had a bowling alley attached to it. Tonight we arrive too late to bowl but discover that the bowling crowd is still around, though it has largely moved into the lounge area for karaoke. We observe from the bar with a High Life for me and a White Russian for Tim, and the cries for attention emanating from the stage to the tune of "Brick House" or an overly emotional performance of "I Will Survive" begin to depress me. This is one of those all-too-common karaoke scenes in which those partaking have missed the joke. For them, singing along to a Muzak version of "Da Ya Think I'm Sexy" is a creative outlet and there's nothing funny about it. They reek of the codependency and deep psychological issues that lead people to call tough-love radio shows. The karaoke machine is a gateway drug, the emcee an enabler to these people's attention addiction. It is a powerful demon that drives someone to close their eyes and clench a fist in the air to add impact to their rendition of "Wind Beneath My Wings." But enough of the karaoke. After all, I have demons of my own, and there's a mechanical bull around here somewhere.

"Tim, we're going in." The two of us beeline for the lounge door and enter a different world, one dominated by flashing lights, heavy beats, and an entirely different kind of dysfunction. As with Kevin before him, I lose Tim to the foam-covered dance floor and proceed alone to the back of the room, mount the bull, and again am face-down on a beer-soaked rubber mat in under two seconds.

Too inebriated and bruised to think better of it, I begin talking to a halter top–wearing girl I'd seen bowling earlier who is now having a smoke next to the dance floor. I ask why she isn't dancing and offer her a drink.

"I'm just sitting out for a minute," she says with what I interpret as forced-passive angst, "and I ain't drinking because I'm pregnant with that asshole's kid." She uses her cigarette to gesture toward the asshole.

"Why is he an asshole?" I ask before I can stop myself.

"He knocked up my friend a while back, too. Treated her real bad."

"And then you slept with him anyway?"

"Yep, I guess so." Then a long drag on the cigarette and a deceptively thoughtful-looking gaze at the exhaled smoke. "I guess so. . . ."

A far cry from Edy's joy at winning $1.25. I wonder how this young lady bowled?

"Shoot! I missed him," Tim says, crouching to look into the space between a counter and the wall.

Back at Tim's warehouse, a mouse has just scurried away from the loaf of bread that Tim was using as bait to catch . . . a mouse. At four in the morning. He rigs a clap mousetrap with peanut butter and declares that he'll have this one by the time we wake up. "There were two, and I caught the other one yesterday." Right. There are probably only two. When it comes to vermin, isn't the rule more like ten for every one you see?

Regardless, Tim is gracious enough to give me his bed—some foam padding rolled out on the floor with an Army surplus sleeping bag—while he curls up on the couch.

I sleep like a man too tired to be afraid of mice.

Indiana ★

I'VE never much cared for Indiana. Between having to drive through any time I wanted to travel between my mother's home in Columbus and my home in Chicago, the general lack of scenery, Notre Dame football, and a particularly watchful state police force, it's long been high on my list of states I'd willingly trade to Canada in exchange for natural resources. To help pass the time, I invented a fun little game to play whenever I drive though the state: at any random point once within Indiana's borders, turn on the radio and press "Seek" until you come across a John Mellencamp song. Without fail you'll find one before the dial returns to the frequency at which it started. Guaranteed. Make a bet with your passengers about it. It is as if there is a state law that Indiana's favorite son's cigarette-addled voice must always, on some frequency, be audible.

As I cross into Indiana from Michigan after my night on Tim's floor, "Authority Song" welcomes me to the Hoosier State. On cue, a highway patrolman falls in behind me, where he stays for a hellish fifteen miles while I drive 64.5 miles per hour. To pass the time, I reach for the atlas and try in vain to find my destination phonetically.

"I've got a place for you to stay in Pee-roo," Ron Burkhart, my friend Brian's father, had said on the phone. When he said "Pee-roo" he seemed to briefly speak another language, like when Alex Trebek pronounces a Spanish word on *Jeopardy!*—easily rolling the *r* in the middle of "Nicaragua" with machine-gun-like repetition. Ron wasn't rolling the *r* like Trebek might have, though. He just said "Pee" and "roo."

"Where was that?"

"Pee-roo. It's about eighty miles north of Indianapolis." All six syllables of "Indianapolis" came out fine. Perhaps Ron has had a small stroke that's affected only his ability to speak the name of the town in which he grew up. Regardless, he and his buddy Jim Palmer were excited to return there to show me around.

"We can stay at Jim's mother's house. She still lives in Pee-roo."

It has been a week since I spoke with Ron, and I am supposed to meet him at a bowling alley in Pee-roo this afternoon. Unable to reach him by phone, I stop into a gas station just north of Peru, Indiana.

"Do you know of a town called 'Pee-roo'?" I ask the attendant, holding out my atlas turned to the Central Indiana page.

"Pee-roo's about six miles down the road," he said, pointing to Peru on the map and all but adding "moron" onto the sentence's end.

"Of course."

I quickly adjust my phonetic expectations and pull into the parking lot at Homer's Sports Bar and Riverside Fun Center. I find Ron and Jim at the bar.

"Welcome to Pee-roo," says the bartender.

"Any trouble finding the place?" asks Ron.

"Nope. It's right there on the map, plain as day. 'Pee-roo.' Just like it sounds." Having quickly adopted the local dialect, I share my Miller High Life news and we have a round.

Lee Holmes, owner of Riverside Fun Center, has rolled out the red carpet—the first real celebrity treatment I've received. A banner reading "Riverside Fun Center Welcomes Mike Walsh" hangs above the shoe rental counter, and he's arranged for the local paper to come out and cover my visit.

Ron and Jim are clearly enjoying the fact that we're making a ruckus in their hometown. They invite the reporter to dine with us, filling her with wild hyperbole in hopes that something will appear in tomorrow's paper that will get people talking. I take comfort in the hope that should any of their salacious fabrications make the final edit, the *Peru Tribune* will be too small to make its way to Miller Brewing

Company's attention. I eat my pork tenderloin sandwich and watch the two homecomers revel.

In three hours at Riverside Fun Center there isn't a single person Ron and Jim have seen that they didn't know or at least have a friend in common with, despite having lived away from Peru for decades. (You're still pronouncing it "Pee-roo" in your head, right?) The thirty lanes fill up with a weeknight league and assorted Peruvians who've come to socialize. Among the crowd is Bruce, coach of the Peru High bowling team, and Marla, a middle-aged, fairly reserved counselor at one of the local schools. Thinking she might add something scandalous for Ron and Jim's newspaper article, we try to get some dirt on the school counselor.

"What was the strangest thing you've ever done in a bowling alley?" I ask her.

"One time I mooned my friends," she replies after a minute of thought.

"All right!" I say. "Nudity in the bowling alley."

"Well I had shorts on under my pants or I wouldn't have done it," she replies indignantly. Peru, apparently, is a family town.

She declines to give a repeat performance in our presence, despite Ron and Jim having traveled such a great distance to be here.

Eager to show me some more midwestern hospitality (perhaps not taking into account that I'm from neighboring Ohio), Ron and Jim take me to their old hangout, the Korner Lounge. The sign out front reads: "Korner Lounge. Kary Out. Kocktails. Kold Beer."

I follow Ron and Jim inside, pulling the door shut behind me. Big mistake.

"Don't you go closing that door on me, boy! What do you think, you own the place? Trying to start something?!" This is the bartender's way of welcoming us to the Korner. Apparently she had propped the door open to let the breeze in; I had thought Ron opened it on our way in, and so I was closing it out of courtesy.

For the first time all night, all three of us are speechless, absolutely thrown by the unexpected fierceness of her words, backed up by thick arms and a generally gruff appearance. There is not a hint of jest in her voice, and she stares me down until I return the door to its propped-open position.

Upon taking a look around, I can understand her wanting to keep things just so for the whopping two patrons already populating the bar. Still, it seems a strange way to greet potential paying customers. We opt not to pay much, wrap up the night, and make for Jim's mother's home, where Jim kindheartedly takes the couch for himself so Ron and I can each have a bedroom. In the morning, Jim, his mother, Betty, and Ron reminisce about growing up in Peru.

"You couldn't have picked a cornier place," Betty says upon learning what I was doing in town.

"Well, I heard the bartenders were the friendliest in the country." We recount the incident at the Korner, and Betty offers an explanation.

"She probably recognized Jim and knew that he was one of the cheapest guys in town." Betty laughs, and we laugh with her.

"We live long here," adds Betty, who is eighty-six. "We go slow and easy . . . nobody's in a hurry. We're long livers."

"We thought Peru was near the center of the universe—if not *the* center," Jim observes, noting that fashions would just be getting hot here ten years after they'd already died on the coasts.

Ron talks about the house in which he had grown up, how he and his brother used to pull each other and their friends up and down its main hallway on a rug. "That hallway seemed like it was a mile long."

I sense in Ron a longing to recapture that perspective. To be able to look at the world and be filled with wonder and awe at the simple things. When hallways are mile-long playgrounds and the bed is huge and tall and the space beneath it is populated with monsters. When staying up until ten is something you brag to your friends about at school the next day.

I'm grateful to Peru for giving me a glimpse of that just before leaving for my own hometown on a crisp, sunny autumn morning.

Making my way south to I-70 and the straight-east shot to Columbus from there, I test my Mellencamp theory. Three stations into the "Seek" process the song is "Small Town," the singer's anthem to places like Peru. Appropriate on every level.

For the next twenty miles a state police cruiser follows two cars behind me.

The time arrives for my conference call with Russin and his clients at Miller. I field it from my mother's house in Columbus, unsure of what their expectations are. It quickly becomes clear that they've grasped the spirit of the trip and aren't keen to appear overbearing. If anything, they seem noncommittal, requiring me to do a little more selling than I'd expected.

"This is really just to understand the opportunities, Mike," explains one of the voices on the phone. "We're not even sure it's something we want to get involved with at this point, but it seems like an interesting prospect."

Gulp.

"That said," someone else picks up, "we think the right angle would be pretty subtle and organic. You're a High Life guy leading the High Life, but it's just a part of your style, not some contrived sponsorship."

"I couldn't agree more. I think it would lose something if it were 'the Bowling Road Trip Sponsored by Miller High Life,'" I reply. "The media would lose interest if they smelled a PR stunt."

Heads are nodding on the other line, and though the call doesn't conclude with a million-dollar sponsorship deal, it sounds promising.

"Thanks for your time, Mike. We'll talk things over here and get back to you soon."

Now twenty months after my father's death, as I wait for my mother to arrive home from work, I notice she still has the folded American flag, along with the crucifix, that adorned his casket during the burial ceremony on the pillow on what had been my father's side of the bed. I begin to be concerned that she's wallowing in her grief by keeping these reminders in such a prominent place.

I hang the "Riverside Fun Center Welcomes Mike Walsh" banner from Homer's Sports Bar across the kitchen cabinets in hopes that it will cheer her to see how popular I've become. She responds with mock scorn for my inhibiting the pathway to real cheer: "Michael, how are we supposed to get into the liquor cabinet with that sign in the way?"

Over homemade pasta with shrimp in pesto sauce (and Maker's Mark Manhattans, having ceremoniously torn through the banner) we talk at the kitchen table, sharing stories about my trip so far and speculating with excitement about what might lie ahead and how much fun Dad would be having with this. I consider bringing up the shrine on her bedroom pillow and suggesting that it might help to put away such reminders, but as we talk I realize that I'm in no position to judge. Speeding down the highway, talking with strangers, and checking off states are my versions of a flag and crucifix on display, in many ways more overt and prominent since I've changed the course of my entire life to observe them. The time will come to put these things away, and it will be clear to each of us at our own pace when that is. For me it appears at least another forty-five states away.

Kentucky ★

JEFF Bridges is stoned beyond mellow, shuffling about in a bathrobe and clear plastic sandals. John Goodman is waving a gun and screaming profanities in a rant about unchecked aggression. Steve Buscemi is having a heart attack in a bowling alley parking lot, and Julianne Moore is flying through the air suspended in a harness, splattering paint on a canvas. Naked.

These are the scenes my mother happens to witness each time she passes through the TV room later that night, as I'm doing homework for tomorrow's trip to Kentucky. My attempt to explain the plot of the 1998 film *The Big Lebowski* is futile: "See, that guy's The Dude. A porn producer's henchmen peed on his rug. The loud guy is an angry Vietnam vet who's on his bowling team and is helping him get a new rug. Now, the porn star who's married to the wheelchair-bound millionaire was kidnapped, but not really, by a group of nihilists who cut off her toe and sent it in to her husband as a threat when the ransom money turned out to be a bag full of dirty underwear . . ."

"Oh. Well, now it all makes sense."

". . . only it wasn't really *her* toe. . . ."

To be sure, it's a difficult movie to understand, especially if your sense of humor isn't aligned with its dark, desultory sensibility. Even harder to understand, however, is why someone would create a festival in its honor, let alone why I would change my schedule and drive five hundred miles out of the way to attend it.

Promising to be something of a poorly attended but more drunken *Star Trek* convention, the First Annual Big

Lebowski What-Have-You Fest was born from a half-joking "wouldn't it be great to have a *Big Lebowski* party?" conversation between two friends passing time in a booth at a tattoo convention in Louisville.

Big Lebowski fans to the point of rarely completing a sentence without tossing in a quote from its dialogue, Will Russell and Scott Shuffitt are about my age and, as I'd done in hopping into Mom's Honda, decided to follow a quirky idea to wherever it took them. Tonight it's a small twenty-lane bowling alley in a tough Louisville neighborhood filled with strip clubs and liquor stores. When I arrive some forty-five minutes into the party, I find the two bemused at the crowd's size.

"We thought we might only have thirty or forty people," Will tells me.

There are more than 150 people here, pilgrims from as far away as Buffalo, New York, and Tucson, Arizona. They have come for such party highlights as a *Big Lebowski* movie trivia competition, a dress-as-your-favorite-character costume contest, and a bowling tournament. They have come to shout movie quotes at the top of their lungs while downing White Russians, The Dude's signature drink.

Well, at least they can have their trivia, costume, and bowling contests.

Will and Scott's uncertainty over the number of attendees they would attract and their modest supply of funds led them to rent the cheapest bowling alley they could find. This turned out to be Fellowship Lanes, owned by a local Baptist church and, despite the neighborhood, staunchly prohibitive of serving alcohol or even allowing it to be served. It is that rare breed of bowling alley that has no seedy lounge attached. So there would be no White Russians.

Further, a handwritten sign at the entrance reads: "No Cussing," which rules out about 80 percent of the movie's quotes, including such favorites as, "They're a bunch of fucking amateurs," "This is what happens when you fuck a stranger in the ass!" and, most certainly, "Nobody fucks with the Jesus," though the Baptists might agree with the sentiment, if not the phrasing, of that one.

Such limitations might have daunted a more worthy endeavor. Not so Lebowski Fest. An organic, pointless gathering of like-minded fringe culture enthusiasts, it would need little more than attendance to pull it together. Attendance they have.

All twenty lanes are full, and Scott is making announcements over a barely audible PA system encouraging those bowling to let newcomers bowl with them so that everyone gets a chance.

I join a man dressed as a very convincing Stranger, Sam Elliott's cowboy hat–wearing narrator in the film, and his son, who is dressed as John Goodman's Walter Sobchak. As we roll, it emerges that Walter, who's really a fifteen-year-old named Matt, opted for Lebowski Fest over his high school homecoming dance tonight.

"I thought this would be more fun," he says. Recalling my own high sophomore year homecoming dance, I suspect he's made the right choice. Having introduced his father to the R-rated, f-word-filled film, Matt then convinced him to chauffeur him all the way from Oxford, Ohio, some three hours. His father, Dale, is by far the oldest attendee.

"I put on the hat and vest so he wouldn't be the only one in costume," Dale tells me. As it happens, several others have dressed up as various characters from the film, though Bridges's lead character, The Dude, is conspicuously absent.

The group that traveled here from Buffalo also includes some high school students, seniors, who were allowed to miss school on Friday based on the fact that they were taking a trip to "visit colleges." While they were "visiting" Ohio State University, i.e., getting drunk with a friend who attends there, their car was towed and they spent a day scrounging for the money to retrieve it. Their perseverance in making it to Louisville nonetheless wins them the cotitle for Farthest Traveled along with the group from Tucson, whose distance traveled was actually greater by some thirteen hundred miles.

Celebrating a faithless film in a Baptist bowling alley surrounded by strip clubs is a group of friends who call themselves The Jew Crew due to their common religious heritage. (Actually, it's unfair to call the movie faithless. John Goodman's character is a Polish Catholic who converted to Judaism for his ex-wife, whose Pomeranian dog he cares for while she's on vacation with her new boyfriend, Marty Ackerman. Got it?) Shortly after I sit down with them a number of Crew members, comprised of several couples, begin participating in a time-honored bowling alley tradition upon which the Baptists might frown: public displays of affection. I mentally play back the signs at the entrance but can't recall whether fornicating existed alongside cussing on the banned activities list. Surely it was implied.

Feeling a bit puritanical, and lacking someone with whom to publicly display my affection, I move on from this scene to the snack bar, where even the proprietors are having fun.

"How are things going tonight?"

"Great!" replies a potbellied gray-haired man behind the counter. "We sold all one hundred and twenty hot dogs we bought for the night." At only seventy-five cents a wiener, hopefully the volume compensated for the margins.

In a room off the main bowling area, Will and Scott administer the trivia contest. The questions cover material from well-known dialogue to obscurities that only someone who'd spent considerable amounts of time watching and rewatching the movie instead of helping cure cancer would possibly know. For instance: What color was the nail polish on Bunny Lebowski's toe? Who was the man in the iron lung? What amount did The Dude write a check for at Ralph's?

Passing out sheets of paper facedown to participants seated every-other-chair around a conference table, the duo reminds the test takers, without a hint of irony, "Don't forget to put your name on your paper." One of the participants wears his bowling wrist guard for the exam's duration. At the quiz's end, it's clear that Will and Scott will have to work harder on generating obscure questions: of the more than thirty who took the test, all scored 100 percent. Ten were randomly drawn from that field and given a second-round test to ultimately find a winner.

The night's culminating event is the costume contest. Everyone ceases bowling and gathers to vote with their cheers for various party-goers dressed as Walter, Maude Lebowski, Jesus (pronounced like the Savior, though in the movie the character is a Latino sex offender), some German nihilists, and porn producer Jackie Trehorn. As the crowd makes its selections, a fifteen-year-old dressed as Jesus wins first, the nihilists second, and Dale, who brought his son here instead of to his homecoming dance, takes third.

The First Annual Big Lebowski What-Have-You Fest is so success-ful that the Second Annual will be listed in *SPIN* magazine as a can't-miss event; the event's growth into new cities and bigger bowling alleys will go on to be written up in *The Wall Street Journal*, the *LA Times,* and the London *Guardian.* It will grow to—and I mean this as a compliment—*Star Trek* convention proportions, only without the nerdy sci-fi trappings. The fests, built around a film with a cult fol-lowing, will develop a cult following of their own, counting among its members those who've attended one of the events. A cottage industry of T-shirts, posters, and bumper stickers will be born. Among the bet-ter sellers will be T-shirts that simply read "ACHIEVER" on the front, and photos of Lebowski Fest fans wearing them all over the world will begin to crop up. College symposiums will convene to dis-cuss the plot twists and character nuances. None of this will add in any way to my mother's understanding of the film.

And though this is all yet to occur and there is little reason to ex-pect that it will, a comment from Scott senses something intangibly special about the event. Standing at the back of the building and sur-veying what they have wrought, he turns to Will.

"For the first two hours," he says, "I just walked around smiling."

It is the end of the night and only the die-hards remain: a handful of Will and Scott's friends and the Buffalo group, gathered just inside the front door, afraid to step outside lest the party really be over. There is a palpable sense of wanting to hang on. Much like *The Big*

Lebowski's conclusion, there is a feeling of calm, resolution, and con-
tinuation, an acknowledgment that all is basically right with the
world, balanced. Or, in The Dude's own words, "strikes and gutters,
ups and downs. . . ." Time and again as awkward silence threatens to
overtake the group and officially end the party, someone chimes in
with one more movie quote to extend it just a little longer. Plans for
next year are already being discussed. There will definitely be alcohol, though all agree that Fellowship Lanes worked out perfectly in
spite of, if not because of, its quirks. There will be more contests,
better prizes, an actual screening of the movie. A group of people
who hadn't known one another before tonight will reunite like old
friends, perhaps joined by hundreds more, in a spontaneous embrace
of life and *Lebowski*.

To draw from The Stranger's closing monologue, "I don't know
about you, but I take comfort in that."

Pennsylvania ★

I keep a list, a mental one, of unforeseen disasters I fear will happen on this trip. By no means do I consider this neurotic: hours and hours of solitary driving—wheel time, as truckers call it—leaves plenty of time for the mind to wander into such unpleasant realms. The bright side, in this case, is that it enables me to develop easily executable contingency plans, should any of my worst-case scenarios come true. The list of disasters varies with the day, my mood, and geography. Driving through heavily wooded river valleys, for instance, adds "hearing banjo music and being told I have a pretty mouth" to the disaster list. (Contingency plan for that: call Burt Reynolds.) As I drive from Louisville, crossing back over Ohio en route to Pittsburgh, today, the list looks like this:

UNFORESEEN DISASTER	CONTINGENCY PLAN
Mom's Honda has significant breakdown	Learn mechanic trade, work as mechanic until I've earned enough to hire a mechanic to fix car
Run out of money altogether	Sell plasma, sperm to get from state to state
Run-in with an ex-girlfriend and her new boyfriend as I'm digging under the driver's seat for enough change to buy the cheapest thing on Taco Bell's menu	Ask new boyfriend if he can spare a couple of bucks, explaining that it's the least he can do for my having taught her how to love
Bowling injury	Is there such a thing?
Mom's Honda is broken into, all possessions stolen	Overestimate value of possessions, collect insurance fraud check and live easy for months

Despite my Boy Scout–esque preparedness, never did it occur to me to include "Find self staring down an ass-kicking in the middle of a Pittsburgh bowling alley" to the list. I guess you can't plan for everything.

It all starts innocently enough. Playing the wide-eyed tourist, I approach a young woman in the midst of a late-night rock-and-bowl session and begin asking her questions. It's dark: black lights are the only steady source of illumination. The only other light comes in brief, kinetic bursts from the strobes, lasers, and spotlights pulsing to the beat of very loud music. I find that I have to get very near the woman to ask her questions. Then I have to lean in yet nearer to hear her answers. And then I have to go, right now, because there's a hulking, tattooed man charging toward us. His dense, shaved head appears eager to butt something.

This isn't hard to figure out: I'm talking to his girl. Time to play nice, bring him into the conversation, act innocent.

"How's it going?" I ask, fear peeking through my forced cheerfulness.

(With hostility) "Fine." As in, "Fine. What's it to you, pencil neck?" With the back of his thick left arm he gently pushes his girlfriend away, leaving his thick right arm free to generate a fist that dangles menacingly at its end, in easy striking distance of my face.

"So, are you guys on a date?"

"None of your business." (Walking away, nudging the girl before him.)

(Calling after them) "Do you go bowling a lot?"

(With still more hostility) "None of your business."

"Oh, I see. So you're saying it's none of my business. Carry on then."

I can tell by the crazed *Full Metal Jacket* look in his eye that this is a man with whom I could reason, if I were armed and he were being held down. Enormous pectorals stretch the dingy ribbed fabric of his tank top. This is a T-shirt style morbidly called a wife beater for the sort of ill-tempered, insecure, violent type most commonly seen wearing it, typically while being arrested for a domestic disturbance on the TV show *COPS*. Hanging from his shoulders are gigantic, monstrous . . . how to describe his arms? Pythons? Pipes? Guns? What's the term these days? Walsh pounders?

Earlier in the trip I'd have left muscular enough alone, but I've practically got a major sponsor now. *I've been all over the news. People are paying attention to this trip, i.e., I'm too important for this guy to hurt me. I'm the guy who's bowling in all fifty states, dammit! You'll talk to me if I say you will! Maybe I'll make out with your girlfriend while I'm at it; you can watch, whimpering from the scoring console.*

"Listen, I'm really sorry to bother you," I say, keeping the scoring console between him and me at all times. "I'm just asking questions because I'm traveling to bowling alleys in all fifty states." His fist clenches. "And when I'm done, I might even write a book about people I meet along the way."

At this point a new song comes on the sound system. It's "Escape," also known as "The Piña Colada Song." The rock-and-bowl lighting calms to an almost pleasant sequence featuring the smooth, dreamy effect of a mirrored, spinning ball. I am momentarily stunned as I try to adjust and reclaim my bearings in the changing environment. Everything has slowed down for a moment. The chorus plays, dreamlike, in my ears. "If you like piña coladas, and getting caught in the rain . . ." Then Cro-Magnon maneuvers around the console and gets right next to me in a move so swift and surprising I nearly gag as my fight-or-flight instincts fail me to the point of paralysis.

"Well, why didn't you say so?" he asks. "A book? No shit?"

"No shit," I whisper, trying to find my breath.

I flinch like an abused dog as he swings one of his massive arms toward the back of my head. Only after some thirty seconds do my muscles release their tension as I realize he's just put his arm around me, like a brother, and is spilling his life story to me.

Unfortunately, my adrenal gland had pumped so much of its contents into my bloodstream as it prepared me for a mad dash out the door that I am unable to remember any of his musings for posterity, though I do seem to recall that some of his more important life moments were depicted on his body in tattoo. I can only hope he doesn't read this book and come deliver me an ass-kicking for not paying enough attention to him.

I emerge from the bowling alley unscathed and return to my friend's home, where I'm staying during my time in Pennsylvania, nearby. Little did I know there was an ass-kicking awaiting me there.

My host, John, had been a client of mine before I quit to go bowling. While he is more than gracious to offer me a night's lodging, part of his agenda is to punish me for abandoning his business. His chosen torture devices are a deck of cards, dozens of beers, and incomprehensible rules to a drinking game that he apparently devised to guarantee my loss. After an hour or so of being made to drink because "aces are high this round" only to learn that I would have to drink because "no, remember? Aces are *low* this round!" I make my way to the guest room drooling and incapacitated at 2:00 A.M., less than primed for my 5:30 wake-up call.

Just twenty minutes into my early-morning, hangover-hampered drive to New York, as I pull over to vomit at the base of an exit ramp I reflect on the lessons of Pennsylvania and amend my mental disaster plan for new eventualities:

UNFORESEEN DISASTER	CONTINGENCY PLAN
A steroid-infused Neanderthal catches me talking to his best gal	Tell him I'm writing a book about him and hope he's as literate as the steroid-infused Neanderthals in Pittsburgh are
I've drawn an ace and my opponent says he has a higher card	Just drink. And stop drawing aces.
Get overcome by nausea at 75 miles an hour	Hope I've still got that empty Big Gulp cup in the backseat

Lessons that may well prove useful in a city that never sleeps.

★ New York

LEAVE it to New York to put a velvet rope in front of a bowling alley and charge twenty-dollar cover on a Monday night. This is Manhattan. This is Bowlmor Lanes. Enter the stainless-steel lobby, reach for your wallet, and hope they let you in.

The bouncer, a six-foot-four, three-hundred-pound bald black man who makes my antagonist from Pittsburgh look like an eight-year-old girl, grudgingly takes my money and that of a handful of my friends who drove all the way from Ohio on a mini–road trip of their own just for this night. We're all way too tired and intimidated to gripe about the price. Rather, assuming the attitude of contemptible commoners who are deemed worthy to enter a hot new club, we practically thank the man for fleecing us. *We made it! Now act cool . . . don't screw this up. . . .*

Having seen bowling alleys all over the country that bend over backward to appear friendly and inviting, family businesses that offer discounts to draw customers and yet still struggle to fill the lanes, I wonder if they've just got the formula backward. They should opt for the counterintuitive: create an exclusive, blasé, elitist air about the place and people will flock to your bowling house. Under its current ownership, Bowlmor has cultivated that very image to great success: in 2001 it was the highest-grossing bowling alley in the *world*. Surely the raised-cost expectations that accompany every transaction in New York contribute to this. After all, it can't hurt to draw customers from a population well-conditioned to paying too much, a population perhaps suspicious of all things reasonably priced. Still, I'd like to see a struggling forty-lane operation in small-town Iowa throw up a velvet rope manned by a dismissive, spiteful bouncer to see how business does.

The gated elevator that carries us from Bowlmor's tiny lobby to the fourth-floor lanes grazes slowly past halves of bowling balls and pins embedded into the cement wall between floors, the diamond-shaped gaps in the metal gate framing them as we slowly ascend. The attendant lets us out at the fourth-floor bowling level with all the enthusiasm and contempt of a carnival ride operator on too little sleep, barking some direction about where to get rental shoes or telling us not to stare at the beautiful people or something. Our twenty-dollar cover doesn't kick in for another hour—that's for bowling from 10:00 P.M. to 3:00 A.M. We grab a high table in the bar with a side view of the lanes, stare at beautiful people bowling with cool detachment, and order ten-dollar beers. This is shaping up to be an expensive night.

My older brother Pat calls my cell phone. He's in New York by chance and has just come from a business dinner. Through the phone, I can hear Pat arguing with the hulking bouncer downstairs.

"Twenty dollars? For bowling? You're kidding, right? But I—" Then to me: "Michael, did you pay twenty dollars to get in there?"

"Pat, just pay it and come in. He's a bouncer—you have to fear him."

Pat, to the bouncer, overestimating the reach of my recent publicity success: "I'm here with the guy who's bowling in all fifty states. He's my brother; there's probably a list or something, right?"

I can hear the bouncer's blank stare in reply.

"Um, Pat?" I'm panicking now. He's going to get us all kicked out. We *are* commoners. We *don't* belong here. They're probably sending security now: no questions will be asked; there will be no chance to disavow myself and my friends from my blood relative breaking the unwritten social rules downstairs.

"You must have the wrong number—" I hang up and hope it's not too late. Five minutes later Pat enters, having paid full price for himself and for a friend of our sister Regan who arrived during the showdown with the bouncer.

The house lights turn off, black lights turn on, the DJ begins spinning house and techno music, the pins glow neon at the end of each lane, and it's our turn to bowl. We each give the shoe guy one shoe and limp over to our lanes.

On the surface, this is really no different than rock and bowl or Xtreme Bowling as it happens in bowling alleys everywhere. Bowlmor does a better job of hyping it into a chic club affair in its marketing, but essentially it's still just bowling under black lights and disco balls with music too loud to hold a conversation. The difference, aside from the pricing and attitude, is that even with the lights on, the Bowlmor doesn't look like a bowling alley. Designed with the goal of creating a feel of "sophisticated whimsy," translucent tabletops, curved walls, art deco chairs, circular windows between the lanes and the VIP room, and illuminated kitsch artwork on the cubism-inspired green, pink, yellow, blue, purple, and red walls set the place apart from your average Earl's Lanes & Pro Shop. Showcases full of pins signed by models, movie stars, and *Saturday Night Live* cast members remind you that you're in trendy Greenwich Village and imply that this place is on an upper level of the social stratosphere. People who look to be underwear models and fashion mavens fill the other lanes trying hard to look bored and unimpressed, a skill my group has no capacity for (or interest in) mastering.

The ten of us must be one thousand dollars into our bar tab by the time I stop noticing these details. Even at Manhattan prices we've managed to get amply snookered: Pat's somehow gotten louder and more belligerent. My friend Morgan has stumbled into a new nickname—Staggerhouse—as he lets the weight of the bowling ball swinging like a schizophrenic pendulum on his arm dictate his direction toward the foul line. Kara, at 102 pounds, has wisely stopped accepting refills from the pitchers that seem to be arriving three-at-a-time every time one pitcher is drained to half-full. No one has the slightest idea of the score, nor the growing tab.

Milling around on the sidewalk outside the elevator lobby at the night's end, Staggerhouse makes sure that each girl gets a good, long hug good-bye. And another. Pat has long since departed to rest up for a 7:00 A.M. meeting. The beautiful people file out in groups behind us; Staggerhouse looks to be pondering spreading the love to a couple of the models when JP, who lives here and might have a reputation to uphold, shuffles us into a cab headed in the right direction.

My friend Charlie in Chicago had introduced me via e-mail to her friend Eric, who works at *The Caroline Rhea Show*. Rhea had recently taken over Rosie O'Donnell's show; it was a daytime talk show format, and I'd been pitching Eric on the perfect guest: me. He'd championed me to his producers unsuccessfully, but I wanted to meet him and thank him for his efforts. Not that my graciousness was without selfish purpose: in my call to him I ask if I might be able to see a taping while I was in town, thinking it would give me the opportunity to make my case in person.

"Sure," he says. "We're taping at two o'clock tomorrow; why don't you come for that?"

I'm staying at my sister Regan's apartment in Hoboken. My friends who'd driven up—Morgan Lewis, Gabe Flynn, John Ross, and Jason Barger—are already in the city sightseeing; I leave Regan's place to join them as soon as I finish catching up on some planning for the trip after they leave tomorrow. As I emerge from the 33rd Street station after riding the New Jersey PATH train into Manhattan, my phone rings. It is Eric.

"Mike, we were wondering if you could be *on* the two o'clock taping tomorrow instead of in the audience?"

Though I consider feigning insult at being asked a day before (clearly another guest has canceled at the last minute), I think my response ends up coming out something like, "Oh-my-gosh-thank-you-so-much-you-won't-regret-this!" rather than with the cool nonchalance with which I announce it to the guys when I meet them at a bar just off Broadway.

While I am there, a producer calls me and pre-interviews me. His name is Jason, and for him the conversation is part information gathering and part narrative creation as he prods me for anecdotes that he thinks will play well with the show's audience. By the end of the call I have the feeling this is more a test than a pre-interview and that it's Jason's job to frighten the show's guests into being entertaining. Phrases like, "Whatever you do, don't bomb—I'll get fired" and "Are you sure you're up to this?" keep coming from Jason's end of the phone.

I pass the test, I'm still booked, but it's all working too well. A nagging feeling follows me the rest of the day, as I think they'll call any minute to cancel: "Carrot Top had an opening after all." Nonetheless, I use the news to encourage Miller to make a sponsorship offer.

"Russin," I say on the phone while we're in line to see the David Letterman show, "what's Miller's feeling on sponsoring me? I'd love to mention Miller in my appearance tomorrow, but I need to have some indication of whether or not they're in. Think you can get me a Miller T-shirt to wear?"

"At this point Miller is in, but don't plan to start saying anything until we've got a contract and we've hammered out the terms and the talking points."

More good news as far as I can tell. We spend the evening watching Letterman tape (the show's highlight being a Tony Orlando walk-on to plug his new book) and going to dinner in Hoboken. For good measure the night before my first national syndicated TV appearance, we get bombed and karaoke until 2:00 A.M. before capping the night with drunken, girlish laughter at the day's events over a slice of pizza. Gabe, John, and Jason, who were going to drive back first thing in the morning, change their plans to be my entourage for the show.

★ ★ ★

I'm predictably hungover and ill prepared. The car the studio sent to pick me up arrives late. Rain and a newly implemented traffic pattern in Manhattan conspire to delay my arrival at the studio even further; by the time a security attendant whisks me and my "entourage" into the correct elevator and then to my dressing room at NBC Studios in 30 Rockefeller Plaza, I've completely sweated through the armpits of my light blue shirt. The dark, wet half circles are growing larger and more visible by the minute.

As the rest of my entourage wanders around the eighth floor peeking into *Saturday Night Live*'s studio, Regan and I are left alone to the paper plates of fruit and cheese that have been provided in my dressing room. I'm in the midst of throwing a mock hissy fit about the accommodations ("Where the fuck is my Cristal? This is unprofessional!") when Jason walks in carrying a stack of street sign–sized cue cards in his hands like it's an assault rifle and begins rapid-firing the questions Caroline will be asking me. He then tells me the right answer to each; I'm surprised at how little I know of my own story.

"No, you're doing this because you used to drive the Wienermobile," he corrects me. The intimidation from yesterday's pre-interview continues, only now I can see him rolling his eyes and hear more clearly his muttering about me screwing up and getting him fired. Among the more frightening revelations (aside from being given suggestions of the "correct" answers to questions about myself) is that I, not the show's host, will be leading the interview.

"Assume she doesn't know anything about you," Jason says. So much for the whole "I saw your new movie; it's great!" banter they reserve for real guests. "She'll have these cue cards, but it's your job to lead her from one to the next with your answers."

"You mean *your* answers."

"Right. Just don't screw up. Practice some more and I'll be back to run through it again in a minute."

My shirt's getting wetter. Morgan, John, Gabe, and Jason arrive with the news that they'd just been talking to Tony Orlando in the dressing room next door. None of us would have known who Tony

Orlando was if he were singing at our wedding, but since we'd seen him on Letterman the night before it was like he was an old friend. They'd told him how much we'd enjoyed the appearance. He's here to do the same shtick on *Caroline Rhea* today, and I'm sure he appreciated the encouragement.

A staffer comes and takes me to a room marked "Makeup," where a man in a beret attempts to take some of the pastiness out of my face, applying brown "pancake" makeup with a white sponge. He seems surprised at how much it's taking to turn my Irish pallor camera ready. When he runs out for another jar of pancake, I turn to the hairdresser sharing the room with us and ask for some help.

"Can I borrow your hair dryer to dry out my pits?"

"You want to borrow my hair dryer for what?" she asks, as she combs out a wig.

"Dry out my pits," I say, gesturing to the amply moistened fabric where my arms meet my torso. "You're telling me that Tony Orlando didn't just do this, too?"

Tony Orlando hadn't just done this. In fact, neither the hairdresser nor the makeup artist remembers ever having seen *anyone* do that before, which I find hard to believe. Perhaps they don't have as much experience in show business as I do. I return to my dressing room to find my entourage, and Jason, who's waiting to grill me one more time.

"Okay, so you've talked about why you're doing this, now what's the next thing you're going to say?"

I'm rattled. "Um, is this where I talk about the people who invited me to bowl nude with them?"

"Don't say 'nude'! This is a family show. Say 'naked'!"

"Don't worry, Jason. I'll nail it when I'm out there," I halfheartedly assure him as he runs off to attend to something else, shaking his head all the way down the hall.

Tony Orlando comes into my dressing room and we talk like old showbiz buddies. There's something about celebrities, even C-list ones (or wherever Tony Orlando falls these days). His presence is electric. His smile is white beyond belief. He works the room.

"That's great; what a cool idea," he says of my quest. "I do a concert for veterans every year in Branson—you should come. Either way,
call me when you get to Missouri, or Vegas. I'm usually in one or the
other." He leaves me with two phone numbers, then goes and nails his
segment like the consummate pro he is. We suffer through an interview with actor David Arquette and then part of an interview with
TV's Judge Mathis. Then Jason and a stage manager appear to escort
me backstage, using the remaining minutes to attach a microphone to
my freshly dried shirt and frighten me one last time before the band
plays me on.

I'd practiced this in my mind hundreds of times growing up, only
it was with Carson or Letterman and I was a comedian or a rock star,
depending on the year, not some aimless drifter on a hard-to-explain
road trip. I knew the routine back and forth: walk out, shake hands
with the host, lean in and whisper some inside joke known only to
people important enough to belong on TV, tilt your head back in
fake, knowing laughter, then sit down in the chair and dive into the
pre-rehearsed banter.

In this, my first live run, I nail the walk out. I nail the handshake
and the lean-in. And here is where I realize I'm not one of the people
important enough to belong on TV: I have no inside showbiz joke. I
stammer, don't hear whatever Caroline says to me (probably some inside showbiz joke), and I say, "It's nice to meet you, Caro*lyn*."

I said her name wrong. It wasn't on mic—only she heard it, but
only she matters. How insulting! I'm certain that this is her biggest
pet peeve and that she'll hold me in contempt for it. I can feel my
armpits warming back up for another monsoon. As I sit down, I watch
to see if she's going to stop the taping right now, fire Jason and half
the crew, and toss me out onto rainy Rockefeller Plaza.

She doesn't. We have delightful pre-rehearsed banter, even though
I'm the only one who's pre-rehearsed it. We even stray from the script
a bit, though I wish I'd done so more to punish Jason, who I'm certain
is mouthing the scripted answers from stage left. Caroline "surprises"
me with a bowling ball, bowling shoes, and a bowling shirt. (They'd

asked for my sizes the day before and told me to act surprised, so even this emotion is in fact scripted.) Just like they did at the Bowlmor, she asks me to take off one shoe in order to get the bowling shoes. Not realizing she's kidding, I play along and put my right shoe on her desk—grossing her out and apparently creating bad luck according to her superstitions—but she plays along herself and we end the segment as best of friends. "Do me a favor and promise you'll send us updates from the road," she offers before sending it to commercial. I cap it off with the lean-in-and-pretend-to-be-having-more-showbiz-banter move as the applause and music fade into the break. Caroline reciprocates and asks me my birthday.

"April twenty-eighth," I say, slightly puzzled. Maybe she'll send a gift?

"Really? You're a Taurus? That's strange, because Taureans don't usually travel like this."

So *that's* the showbiz banter! It's all held together by astrology. I should have known!

Jason comes over as soon as the break starts and congratulates me with unbridled enthusiasm. Either I was really good or they had really low expectations. Jason's a different person now, and I'm his new best friend. "You were great!" he says, taking the microphone off, and I feel some Stockholm Syndrome–like sense of validation at receiving my tormentor's approval.

We run into Katie Couric on the way out of the building and she almost steals my limo by mistake. I'm a huge fucking star now. Tony Orlando wants to bowl with me, Caroline Rhea knows my birthday, and Katie Couric is stealing my limo. I put Morgan in charge of my schedule from here on out and hand him my cell phone to screen calls. I can't be bothered with these details.

The limo drops us off back at Regan's apartment. My entourage is Ohio bound except for Morgan, who is staying on through Boston. Already failing in his new role, Morgan hasn't even tried to schedule any appointments for me the rest of the day, and my cell phone isn't ringing. The limo pulls out of sight, we walk through the door, and suddenly I'm just a jobless drifter driving his mom's car and crashing on his sister's couch again.

They say parts of New York are a little rough, and the Bronx—a borough whose name, when added to the word "cheer," means "fart noise"—certainly has that reputation. As Morgan and I arrive at the Bronx's biggest landmark, Yankee Stadium, at 9:00 P.M. we know immediately that the "sophisticated whimsy" of Bowlmor Lanes would be hard to find just across the street from the House That Ruth Built, at Ball Park Lanes.

Baseball season has just ended, but the streets surrounding Yankee Stadium and Ball Park Lanes feel like they've been deserted for years. They're dark. Full newspaper pages blow across them in chilled autumn wind gusts: urban tumbleweed. Elevated train tracks loom overhead, blocking any light from above, and every corner or alleyway has that "good place to dump a body" feel about it. I park Mom's Honda under the dimmest streetlight ever installed and Morgan and I sprint to the bowling alley's doorway.

For the first time on my travels, I'm a minority in a bowling alley. Morgan, the bartender, and I are the only white people in the place. There is no music playing, but had there been I have the sense it would have screeched to a halt upon our entrance, calling all eyes to our nervous presence. No one seems particularly receptive to small talk as we take an exploratory lap around the facility. My, "Hi! How's it going?" is met with puzzled grunts and the occasional curt, "Fine," spoken with a tone that implies, *Now fuck off!* Apparently no one here understands why some midwestern tourist is walking around the place like a glad-handing politician. Perhaps I'm the only one who recognizes my newfound celebrity status; I try not to hold it against them. Morgan, who also doesn't recognize my celebrity status, suggests we get down to bowling.

Easier said than done. Even the counter staff ignore us. Standing in front of them with money in hand, we literally can't buy enough of their attention to rent a lane. The three men joke and roughhouse with one another while Morgan and I beg their pardon and meekly try to get their attention. Frustrated with this approach and no longer intimidated by the surroundings, Morgan figures out the local language.

"What the hell's a guy got to do to get on a lane around here?" he barks, and moments later we're lacing up shoes and trying out house balls.

Bowling on the lane to our left is a couple—a black man and a Puerto Rican woman. He's encouraging her on every roll: "That's right, baby," followed by a pat on the ass or a loud lip smooch. When he bowls he pumps his fist proudly for a good roll and blames the ball for a bad one, wiping it down with a towel and inspecting the thumbhole.

On the lane to our right is Ronald, age eleven, who's been bowling since he was seven. His hair braided in cornrows, he's rolling a brand-new ball—the first he's ever owned—and it, too, is giving him trouble.

"My best game ever is a two hundred," he says. Tonight he's disappointed with his 120. "But I'll get better the more I get used to my new ball."

There's a staircase in the middle of Ball Park Lanes leading up to more bowling, though tonight the stairs are roped off and the lights on the second floor are off. I ask at the front desk if we can go have a look. Recalling my experience in Pennsylvania, I add, "Because I'm writing a book about bowling alleys." With that pronouncement, bolstered by Morgan's newfound Bronx street cred, we gain access. "Of course!" they say, calling to one of their co-workers somewhere unseen, "Martin, show these guys upstairs! We're gonna be in a book!"

Martin emerges from nowhere, a skinny black man with a smattering of teeth, wearing a floppy fishing cap and baggy pullover. He's excited and talkative, kind of like a guy who's just downed a lot of beer, which, from the smell of things, is just the kind of guy he is.

"I learned to bowl from my dad," he tells us as he flips the lights on to reveal thirty lanes on both sides of the building's second floor. "And I kept with it because I thought it would help with the ladies."

Martin demonstrates the role he plays during a Yankee home game—keeping any drunken baseball fans downstairs from coming up and interfering with league play—and then demonstrates a drunken fan, flailing himself down one of the lanes, past the foul line, and almost falling.

Following Martin downstairs, we return to the front desk to chat with Sammy and Norada. The three co-workers chide one another like brothers, showing a warmth I wouldn't have imagined when we entered this place. Apparently it's always there; you just have to earn it. Or tell them they'll be in your book. When they're done impressing me, they call into the back room and beckon for an older gentleman wearing a short-sleeved blue piqué shirt.

George Diamantis owns Ball Park Lanes. George is a Greek immigrant who came here in 1969 seeking a better life, and seems to think he's found it.

"I purchased this place in 1977," he says through a thick accent. "It's a lot of hard work, but we have a good business here."

I take his picture and George smiles big but with a distinct twinge of discomfort at the attention. Silver hair wraps the sides of his head; the top is free of cover. In his right hand are two pens; in his left, a wad of cash. "Larry!" he shouts toward the bartender, pointing at us to signal that he's buying Morgan and me a beer.

"Thanks, George. Will you join us?" I ask, curious to hear more of his "American Dream" story.

"I cannot," he says, smiling and shaking his head. "I have work to do. Please, enjoy." George gestures toward the bar with a magnanimous open hand and he returns to the back office and his dream as we make our way to the bar.

Our beers are waiting when we arrive, and so is Larry.

The word "frenetic" comes to mind after spending only a little time with Larry. From the start of our conversation he is in constant motion, keeping the bar clean and stocked and spewing a nonstop stream of stories and observations.

"I know a lot more about baseball than I do about bowling," he admits, a fair enough dichotomy for a man who's spent the last twenty years working behind a bar that, though it's inside a bowling alley, is physically closer to Yankee Stadium than to the lanes. He talks incessantly, with every story seemingly conjured from thin air with little more than nods and smiles needed from his two-man audience to keep him going.

"So I'm pouring a beer right here—the tap is running—and all of a sudden a guy literally falls out of the ceiling above me. I see him, but I don't believe it. He's hanging from some electrical wires looking as nonchalant as a guy could look having just fallen through a drop ceiling. He's just dangling there, holding real still like he thinks no one'll notice him if he's not moving. I can't believe it and my tap's just flowing; the beer's pouring all over my hand. The guy finally falls, hits the ground, then gets up, runs like hell toward the bowling lanes, and heads for the exit . . . only he ends up running into a closet. The door opens and he runs back out, catches my eye, and I yell at him, 'Pay attention!' He freezes, crouched right where he is, looking at me like I'm about to tell him the secret of life. 'The door is *that way!*' I yell, and he takes off. Turns out he was homeless and had somehow been living in some open space between the first and second floor.

"Nixon was in here one time," Larry tells us, switching gears. "Swear to God, I was standing right here—the place was totally packed before a ball game—he came in that door, looked around like he might want to bowl a line, saw the crowd, and turned around. 'I'll come back later,' he said, then left and broke his promise. Never came back. He was wearing a blue sport coat; it was a Sunday afternoon game and they showed him on TV in the crowd during the eighth inning. No one believed me that he'd been in here until they saw it on TV. Reminds me of the time Mickey Mantle and Whitey Ford came in looking for Billy Martin. . . ."

Describing a scene all too familiar to me, Larry tells of a night that changed his life. It was 5:00 A.M. He was watching TV—some kind of late-night theater: the girl was a robot; the plot was missing. The minutes were ticking away and he felt he was getting dumber as each passed. "I have no life!" he exclaimed to himself, and stopped watching TV for good, right then and there. "It's the one-eyed devil," he proselytizes to Morgan and me. That the day's (year's?) highlight for me had been taping five minutes of blather for a sporadically syndicated TV show gives me some small amount of shame.

Morgan and I are joined by my college friend Brian Himmelsteib as we make our way out of the city. Before we can catch the ferry from Long Island to Connecticut en route to Boston, he and Morgan shoot pool while I'm interviewed at Coram Country Lanes by a trio of ten-year-olds working with a reporter on a biweekly kids' section that appears in *Newsday*, Long Island's main paper. I'm not sure what kind of omen it is that I arrived in New York to be interviewed on nationally syndicated TV only to depart being grilled by fourth graders, but they're a far cry more friendly, if slightly less thorough, than Caroline's Jason.

★ Massachusetts

AFTER grabbing a last-chance slice of New York pizza on Long Island, I park Mom's Honda on a ferry and head with Morgan and Brian to the bar and drink a beer to celebrate crossing Long Island Sound.

In Boston we help ourselves to my friend and former Hotdogger Mike Ballog's fold-out couch and inflatable mattress, and drink a beer to celebrate that. Mike is a native New Englander (from New Hampshire, the Granite State) and has that region's hard-fought pride in its sports teams. On hearing Morgan and I had just bowled outside Yankee Stadium, he takes us to Boston Beer Works for dinner, in the shadows of Fenway Park. We order pint after pint of their Bunker Hill *Bluebeery* Ale (served with a spoonful of real blueberries and a lot better than it sounds) and then cross the street to Family Fun Center with plans to drink a beer to celebrate something, anything, there.

Fierce rivalries aside, and beyond rather disparate World Series records, there are two major differences between this across-from-a-major-league-ballpark bowling alley and Ball Park Lanes in the Bronx.

The first is that Family Fun Center doesn't have a frenetic, story-filled bartender, a circumstance that we will revisit in a moment.

The second is that Family Fun Center doesn't offer tenpin bowling. Rather, it offers a unique-to-New England (and Canada) form of bowling called candlepin.

As its name suggests, candlepin pins are shaped like

candles—narrower targets than traditional bowling pins. There are still ten of them, they're still arranged in a triangle at the end of a sixty-two-foot wooden lane, and candlepin alleys still tend to reek of cigarette smoke, but here the similarities to tenpin bowling end. The candlepin ball is roughly the size of a shot-put, is made of wood, and weighs only about 2.5 pounds. It has no finger holes. Because the key implements (ball, pins) are smaller in candlepin than in tenpin, they're less likely to knock one another over to produce higher scores. Two rule differences compensate for this: in each frame the player gets not two but three rolls to clear the pins, and it is permissible to use "deadwood."

"Deadwood" is the term for pins that have fallen but remain on the pin deck. Unlike in tenpin bowling, the mechanical sweep doesn't clear fallen pins in between rolls, so there are often leftover pins on the pin deck after a player's first roll. A pin lying prone in front of three standing pins can be hit with the ball and knocked into the standing pins, allowing a player to score points from spare combinations that the small ball would otherwise be unable to pick up on its own.

The biggest difference between tenpin and candlepin, however, is velocity: you can really chuck a candlepin ball. It may not help your accuracy, but there's something very powerful about the release gained from getting a running start and hurling that little ball with intent to destroy the wall of pins down the lane. Perhaps this aspect of stress relief underlies why this version of bowling has remained popular in the densely populated, traffic jam–riddled Northeast.

As the four of us and assorted friends who've come out for the night begin to burn off stress, the lack of a story-filled bartender becomes quite apparent, not for a need for stories but for a need for beer.

"We don't have a bar," the woman behind the counter says. Everyone stops what they're doing; jaws drop in disbelief.

We huddle up and Ballog, who always delivers in the clutch, comes up with a plan and enlists me to help execute it. After intense negotiations across the street, we return with several one-gallon growlers of Bunker Hill *Bluebeery* goodness, a dozen plastic cups, and enough blueberries to make a pie. All are happy, with the possible exception of the woman behind the counter at the front desk, who becomes nervous about the legality of our improvised refreshment center. We do her the favor of dispensing of the evidence efficiently and stumble out having added a ninth state to my bowling epic, and a new kind of bowling to my repertoire.

After another two days of sightseeing, during which most of the sights include the words "pub," "tap," or "tavern" in their names, I leave Morgan at the airport and Brian at the train station, and leave Mike's apartment only slightly worse for the wear. Filling up the gas tank and stocking up on nacho cheese–dusted chips for the drive to Vermont, it falls from my wallet; I'd all but forgotten it was there.

In the days following my father's death, I had taken inventory of the things that people said about him—the things about him that had added up to a packed house at the funeral home and a mile-long procession to his burial. Wanting to live up to the precedent he had set, I summarized it into a list of character traits to emulate and actions to take if I wanted to earn a similar reception at my life's end. "Write people notes," it begins, because so many people mentioned a kind word Leo had sent them at some point or another. "Praise others," it says because he was quick and genuine with compliments. "Give people credit," because that's what he had done—literally with his business to help other businessmen get started, and figuratively with his optimism. "Pray," because he was prayerful. "Fish." "Read." "Listen."

I stuck the list to the back of a ticket stub from the last baseball game I'd gone to with my father and both of my brothers, and laminated it to carry in my wallet as a sort of quick reference guide. It was meant to be a constant reminder, so much so that I had actually included on the list the words "Look at this list daily." And here at a gas station cash register I'm seeing it for the first time in months. If it's true that you're your own worst critic, it's all the more so when you're falling short of even the meager goals you set for yourself, laminate, and carry in your wallet. Sitting behind the wheel, I give it another full read and act on the two items on the list that seem most relevant and achievable for me at this moment.

"Embrace humility."

"Drive (fast)."

THE drinkathon that began in Pittsburgh and spilled into Manhattan, Hoboken, onto Long Island Sound, and into Boston, along with the near-constant activity of the trip's first thirty days, has left me incapable of doing much more than sitting and staring. My tongue is swollen with dehydration, my entire body aches with a chronic hangover, and my credit card and checking account balances are at odds with one another. In all, a helpful reminder that my attempt to buck responsibility and live without consequences has, in the end, its own set of consequences.

It is my good fortune that my lifelong friend Owen De-Hoff is studying at Dartmouth's Amos Tuck School of Business in Hanover, along the Connecticut River that divides New Hampshire and Vermont. For the next four days I will be taking him up on his standing offer to crash on the couch of the Vermont farmhouse he and four classmates occupy along with a Bernese mountain dog named Fitch. I arrive and quickly settle into an easy routine of strolling about vibrant New England countryside in the height of its autumn transformation. Apart from keeping wood burning in the furnace and making sure Fitch—a black, white, and brown furry mass the size of a Volkswagen—doesn't carry off any children from the neighboring elementary school, my daily stimulus level is refreshingly limited.

I wake at around nine o'clock every day to Fitch's enormous snout wedged beneath my head and lifting it completely off the pillow to inform me that I will now be letting him out into the yard. He is a persistent alarm clock, and has no snooze button.

The Caroline Rhea Show with my appearance airs on my first day in Vermont, and my in-box floods with e-mails from new fans, old high school classmates, and, at last, a formal offer from Miller. They are offering five thousand dollars, support from their public relations agency, and a supply of High Life T-shirts and hats.

In return, I would agree to drink Miller High Life exclusively, wear the High Life logo and mention the product during interviews, and give them advance notice of my itinerary so that they could arrange for media appearances along the way.

This is unbelievable. Someone is offering to pay me thousands of dollars to drink beer and say things like "I like Miller High Life" while wearing a beer T-shirt similar to one already in my wardrobe. And they'll handle the one arduous task I have left in my life, pitching the media, for me. Not to mention that any number of dollars is a lot more than zero, my current income. Naturally, I respond with tentative arrogance.

"I'm not sure I'm comfortable with this," I say on the phone while standing in the farmhouse yard tossing a stick to Fitch. This happens to be the only place where my cell phone gets reception, and the idyllic setting inspires a relaxed confidence. Acres of lush green field and dense forest reframe my perspective, jostle my priorities, and give me a perception (however false it may be) of detached upper-handedness. Fitch's demands (*throw the stick again, please*) seem much more immediate than those of my potential sponsor. Though I definitely want (and desperately need) Miller's sponsorship, my recent successes and newfound serenity make me push it.

Further, it doesn't hurt that I spent last night at a bowling alley being counseled by a bunch of students at one of the country's top business schools, all of whose undergrad degrees came from universities that wouldn't have even opened the envelope containing my application. The bowling alley nearest Dartmouth's campus happens to be connected to a strip club, making for an odd combination of sport and leisure. While we primarily stayed in the bowling half of the building, at some point our waitress's shift ended and we had to get our beverages from the strip club's bar ourselves. Never have I seen men more willing to buy the next round. While this made it hard to have sustained conversations, their collective perspective on my offer is, "Hold out for more."

"Never accept the first offer," one of Owen's classmates says, fresh from a recent negotiations course. "They're willing to go higher. Remember, they're a multi-billion-dollar company. The money means less to them than it does to you."

He has a point on both fronts, though the bigger factor for Miller will be the return on its investment—not whether they can afford to throw a little more cash my way.

"It just seems like I should have an expense account if I'm expected to be buying beer at all these bowling alleys," I counter, as if this would be a new element in my nightly routine.

"We'll see what we can do," is Russin's response. "It's important to us that we help you complete the goal of getting to all fifty states. I'll call you tomorrow once we have a chance to talk it over."

They are being way too nice. At this point I'd expected him to point out that I'm without any income whatsoever, not a celebrity by any stretch of the word, and, generally, lucky to be talking with them—let alone getting more money just for drinking beer and wearing a T-shirt. All of which would be true, which makes me fully prepared to back down and take their original offer at the first sign of their pulling back.

Instead of pulling back, they increase the offer to $8,500, plus airfare to Alaska and Hawaii. I feel like I've won a game show. That a sponsor is willing to fund my trip is a minor miracle. That it is a brand that so perfectly fits with bowling backed by people who so fully embrace the spirit of the trip is a major one. We agree to the terms, and after ten states, I've finally landed an official sponsor who is not my mother.

We grill swordfish steaks and fresh asparagus for dinner to celebrate my last night in Vermont. We'd have celebrated over Miller

High Life, but they'd recently stocked up on a competing product, so that would have to do. I work through my guilt with the justification that I'd not yet actually *signed* anything.

Early the next morning, well rested, fed, and finally funded, I depart for Brunswick, on Maine's seacoast, a leisurely day's drive through wooded hills and gently winding roads. There, for the first time since Kentucky, and practically for the first time on the trip, I will be walking into a bowling alley knowing no one.

A plaque on the wall next to me is titled "Brunswick Area Bowling Association Memorial." It comprises forty-five individual rectangular black metal nameplates mounted on red fabric and framed under glass. They are arranged in nine rows of five, and each is engraved in gold with the name and year of death of a BABA member. Wilbur Ryder—1982. Fred Longley—1989. Guy Allenwood—1993. Bob Decker—1997. Ralph King—1999. All bowlers who have left this life, honored with a lasting presence here at Yankee Lanes. The memorial hangs in perhaps the only space in a bowling alley that allows for a moment of reflection: right next to the window to the snack bar where one awaits delivery of their serving of nachos and a pitcher of beer.

Jake Wilson's a big man with a round, red face that says he is younger than his center-parted salt-and-pepper hair suggests. He's the manager here at Yankee Lanes, a role that at most bowling alleys also entails the duties of bartender, coach, psychiatrist, and, often, minister of sorts. In my case, "regional tour guide" also applies. Leaning on the front counter—still piled with worn vinyl shoes from the after-school crowd—he gives me an orientation to the geographical bowling environment in southeastern Maine.

"You're lucky to have found this place. There are only eleven tenpin bowling centers in this corner of Maine," he says as he circles their locations on a map. "Most houses here are candlepin bowling only."

While I enjoyed my candlepin bowling experience in Boston, I feel it's a bit truer to the goal of the trip to stick to traditional bowling. Having somewhat randomly picked Brunswick, a town of twenty-two thousand that lies twenty-five miles up the jagged Maine coast from Portland, Jake is right: I am lucky to have found this place.

"You really should talk to Gull," Jake goes on as he gets to the business of rotating rental shoes in and out of service with a quick spray and a "what size ya need?" "There's a guy who's lived a great life and has spent a fair amount of it at this place. Interesting guy, Gull."

Gull is Ron LeClair's nickname. He earned it during pot games as a young man. As is common among more serious bowlers, he and his teammates would each throw a few dollars in the pot and roll a game or two for money before a night's league play began. Call it wagering for fun, but the fun tends to dissipate when the same guy keeps walking away with your money. And so it was with Gull. Invariably he would swoop down (like a seagull . . . see?) and win the pot with a come-from-behind rally. Unlike his waterfowl nicknamesake, Gull is a thick, powerful-looking man with skin and temperament toughened by fifty years laboring as a lobsterman. I find him at the far end of the building. He is surrounded by his teammates, men he has clearly known for years.

Though I'm now eleven states into my trip, I still don't find it particularly easy to approach a group of strangers in the midst of recreational activity and strike up a conversation. I've also learned that when a league meets every week for nearly six months, the bowlers expect to see the same people every week . . . and no one else. Such a routine of familiar faces gets established that an outsider stands out like a five pin left on an easy spare.

Surely more practice playing the conspicuous outsider will make me more comfortable in these situations, but tonight I've got my work cut out for me. Gull's team and the team they're competing against on the next lane take their bowling seriously, and have little time for me. I'd heard that New Englanders have a terse, matter-of-fact manner—especially those from the southeast part of Maine, or "Down Easters" as they're known elsewhere in the state. Harsh winters and nor'easters

off the Atlantic must breed some efficiency with language for survival's sake. As if to prove it true, Gull, this fountain of stories and
deep pool of personality, according to Jake's description, dismisses my
introduction with what a casual observer might call a hostilely put, "I
like bowling. It's been fun."

One of Gull's friends overhears me explaining what I'm doing and
tells me he saw me on *The Caroline Rhea Show*. Before I even have a
chance to start feigning humility he's already turned his back to me in
order to watch the next bowler.

The choreography of bodies taking turns in a crowded bowling alley is a constant, confusing jostling as players make their way to and
from the approach, maneuver around the hip-high scoring console,
pause so as not to distract the current bowler, stumble over stray shoes
and empty ball bags, walk sideways to shimmy between another
bowler and the house ball rack, and step around the legs of a teammate seated in the L-shaped set of plastic chairs to climb the steps out
of the settee area before being thrust into the carpeted viewing area.
Trying to make friends with any of this group makes me feel like a reporter jockeying for position to get a quote from the high-powered
lawyer on the way down the courthouse steps. No one has time for
more than a short burst of conversation, because it's suddenly their
turn or because "Bob's working on three strikes here and I've got to
watch."

And every time I do get a moment of Gull's attention, whatever it
is he's saying is lost on me. Maybe it's the High Life I've been making
friends with at such a rapid pace. Or the way that the din of crashing
pins is combining with the blaring sound system to make any conversation a challenge. Whatever it is, I can't understand a word of what
Gull is saying, and at times I'm not entirely certain he isn't threatening me. When he speaks, the words come out quickly with an increase
in speed and volume at the end, making much of what he has to say
sound like a question . . . or a challenge.

"What the crawn canchoo take bahn a bowln, *don'tyou*!?" he expresses.

"Yeah, I guess one would have to . . . right?" I reply, cowering as I brace for a blow to the head. It doesn't come. Thank God it's his turn to bowl again.

As the bowling continues, Emile Racine sidles over to me and gives me reason to relax a bit. Emile is a ringer for Ronald Reagan in both looks and "well, shucks" folksiness, his thick, black hair touched with gray only around the ears. At seventy-one, Emile has been bowling for more than two of my lifetimes and has the energy and enthusiasm to continue for another two.

"I worked as a machinist for Bath Iron Works for forty-three years," he says. He wears a blue polo shirt, his name embroidered on its breast and a silver pin on one collar depicting a bowler in midstride. Emile's hands shake slightly and constantly—a trait he attributes to the beginning stages of Parkinson's. He works part-time at a car rental company, "for bowling money," as he puts it.

He runs down a long list of tournaments and medals he's won in seniors competitions, state Olympics, and national opens over fifty-seven years in the sport. I can almost see his age regressing as he re-counts important dates in his bowling history: he's fifty-five with steady hands and no gray, entering his first seniors' tournament. Then he's forty, laughing with Gull and the guys over cold beer and a game, his kids at home but on his mind and in the stories he's telling his buddies. Now he's twenty-five, just married to Simone, a lifetime still ahead of them and bowling in their first couples league.

"I've got four kids and eight grandkids," he says enthusiastically, re-turning me to the present and listing all of their names. It's hard to discern which set of accomplishments—bowling or family—makes him prouder.

Gull, seeing me chatting it up with Emile, limps over to show me a scar on his left knee. "That scar's from the titanium kneecap I got put in *lastyear!*" he tells me. *Which scar?* I think to myself. *There are so many to choose from.* I take the fact that he's partially disrobing as a sign that he's warming up to me, though it's the last thing I fully understand him saying over the next twenty minutes of sporadic conversation. As the league session ends and he's getting ready to leave, Gull turns to me and says something that sounds a lot like, "I'll see you tomorrow, then." Noting confusion in my face, he comes over and gives me directions to his home, where apparently I've already agreed to come the next morning at nine to see the view of the bay where he lives. While I'm still afraid I'll be killed when I show up, I hear something about how I'll enjoy meeting his wife, Jeanie, and I promise to make the appointment.

One of the e-mails I received after my *Caroline Rhea* appearance was from the Sterling show on 610 WTVN, the powerhouse AM station in Columbus. In addition to the hometown angle, the host, Sterling, just liked the idea of the trip and wanted to interview me on the show tonight. My sponsorship contract newly inked, in between conversations with Gull and the gang I had spent some time on the phone with Russin hashing out the Miller talking points I'll deliver, which essentially boil down to "I'm living the High Life," and if it seems appropriate I should work in something along the lines of "and what goes better with bowling than the Champagne of Beers?" In all, it seems innocuous enough, and I manage to convince myself that I've not sold out or compromised the trip's independent spirit. Very much.

"On the phone with us is my new hero," Sterling says by way of introduction. "This guy, he's from Columbus, quit his job to go travel the country, hang out in bowling alleys, and go to all fifty states. Where are you and what are you doing tonight, Mike Walsh?"

"I'm in Brunswick, Maine, eating lobster, bowling, and living the High Life," I reply, hoping my shameless plug doesn't sound too contrived. It goes unnoticed, and the interview, a full five minutes covering my dad, Bowling Spice, and a few highlights to date, ends with Sterling restating that I'm his new hero and insisting that I call in and give updates throughout the trip. I hang up, thrilled to have established an ongoing media contact, especially one that Mom and my family can tune in and hear, and return to mingling about Yankee Lanes.

On lane nineteen is a girl in her early teens. She is bowling alone, using a custom-drilled ball made of one of the newer materials to be approved by the American Bowling Congress in Milwaukee. She wears a wrist guard and, when I first see her, is busy wiping her ball down to rid it of the lane oil it picked up on her last roll. Apparently, either she is a serious bowler or her parents bought her all the best equipment the way some parents buy their kids figure skates and lessons only to have the children lose interest when they learn it's hard to skate backward. The girl contemplates her approach, steps toward the line, and delivers a strike that would have intimidated my friends at the ABC in Milwaukee. She is a serious bowler.

And I'm seriously creepy looking. I realize this as her father comes to check on her and I'm standing behind his teenaged daughter holding a camera and a notebook. I introduce myself to him and learn that Jamye, who is thirteen, is practicing for her Saturday morning league. Her fifteen-year-old brother is on her team, though he's opted not to practice tonight. Curious as to what drives a teenager to the bowling alley alone on a Friday night, I ask her father if it's okay if I speak with her, reiterating that I'm a jobless drifter from across many state lines.

Jamye is a quiet, cute girl with the same auburn hair as her dad, only hers is long and thick where his is beginning to thin. She's understandably a bit shy given that there's a strange man twice her age asking her questions and that she's at possibly the worst of all ages—the Age of Awkwardness. I remember very clearly when I was her age: I'd just rounded the corner from cute little redheaded boy to Malachi-from-*Children-of-the-Corn* ugly. Freckles turned from novel markings to conspicuous disfiguring blemishes in my mind. Sharp metal braces mangled my face into a perpetual gaping-mouthed-dumb-guy look as I was unable to close my lips over their medieval workings. Pimples bubbled up from nowhere and hair sprouted in unusual places. I began to smell bad. Though Jamye is doing far better than I was at her age, there's still nothing fun about being thirteen: even the smallest social interactions are wrought with far-reaching implications for your place in the caste system of adolescence. There's a microscope put to your most glaring shortcomings, and everyone else, though they're going through exactly the same thing themselves, appears to have it all together, to be flawless. For certain, the last thing you want is to have unsolicited attention put on you.

Despite this, or perhaps sensing that I'd gone through a Malachi stage and therefore possessed some empathy for the age, Jamye humors me with conversation. She tells me she's a freshman at the high school down the street, and I mention that it looked like there was a football game there tonight.

"There is," she says. "It's the homecoming game; there's a dance right after it."

"Did you think about going to the dance instead of bowling tonight?"

"No, not really. My friends were going in a group, but I've got youth leagues tomorrow morning and wanted to get some practice in."

Bowling is in Jamye's blood. Her dad isn't there to just give her tips; he's there bowling a few lanes down with his mother. Three generations carrying on a tradition that began decades ago.

Having now covered both ends of the demographic spectrum between young Jamye and youthful-but-rather-old Emile and Gull, I begin to pack up, thinking that I've soaked up all the Down Easter culture and ambiance I could hope for from one bowling alley. My good-byes to Jake said, I turn for the door and am spun completely around by a huge incoming wave of girls dressed in what I quickly recognize as the unofficial college coed uniform of the day: tight black shirt cut just above the navel and tight blue jeans cut just below the waist. Adrift in a sea of midriff and suddenly remembering what it's like to see women near my own age, I decide to stay for just a little while longer. Jake shakes his head in my direction.

It strikes me quickly that though I'm not old in relative terms, my twenty-seven to their twenty-one makes me closer to Emile than to them in their eyes. Whatever fantasy I'm having of being invited back to their dorm for lingerie-clad tickle fights and back-rub circles quickly disappears.

Watching (not leering, mind you) as they bowl, I notice a different kind of bowling, and indeed a different mood throughout the building. Gull and the guys are heading home, as are Jayme and her family, and now bowling is a party instead of a sport. They're rolling the ball between their legs, hurling the lightest ball they can find down the lane as fast as they can without even a nod toward accuracy. They have special hand-shakes and high fives that they exchange in recognition of strikes and gutterballs. Nothing really matters; they have infinite lifetimes ahead of them. None of them is working on becoming a better bowler or trying to increase her average, and no one is too concerned about making her turn on time if there's a pitcher being poured. It's kitschy, not competition. There's even an undertone of good-natured mockery toward the sport in their manner. References to cult bowling movies like *Kingpin* and *The Big Lebowski* mask what the social constraints of their current life stage insist they've got to be too cool to admit . . . that they're actually having a good time bowling. But as an informed observer, I can see. They are.

The next morning, I drive to Gull's house and meet his wife, Jeanie. After I look at photos of their children and of Gull's old lobster boats, he takes me down to the dock where his briny wooden traps are stacked, latent in his retirement, rectangular frames wrapped with wide mesh that once provided diners with crustaceans and Ron's family with a livelihood.

"Amazing what the sea can do to a thing," he says, pointing to a fist-sized orange rock with smooth, rounded sides. "That started out as a brick," he explains. Just a few years of tumbling in the surf had taken the sharp-angled building block and softened its contours.

Next he picks up a mussel from the rocky beach, showing me the sticky mess of roots the mollusk grows to hold its place in the seabed, explaining how they're harvested by dragging a specially designed trap behind a boat, or by hand with a rake of sorts.

Stories of Ron as a high school football star with his sweetheart, Jeanie, at his side paint a picture of the two in youth: Ron buying his first lobster boat in 1954 and naming it *Jeanie* . . . the newlyweds spending evenings up the road at Yankee Lanes before the kids began to arrive . . . Ron stowing the lobster traps after a day's work and rushing over to the lanes in time to swoop in on and win yet another pot game, before his bowling buddies became accustomed to this inevitability and gave him his nickname. A lifetime passes quickly in the oral history Ron and Jeanie recite to me: the variables of life: kids, grandkids, losing their parents, and the constants: lobsters, the Atlantic. And bowling.

New Hampshire ★

Plus, she's single and very cute. A
tall blonde with blue eyes.

So ends an e-mail from my friend Anna Marie, who is
concerned about my finding warm, welcoming places
to stay on my trip. She's describing her friend Melissa,
who lives in New Hampshire and has agreed to take me in
for the weekend. Recalling that I made the decision to stay
at Tim's warehouse in Grand Rapids based on a far less
encouraging e-mail, I open a message from Melissa. Apparently Anna Marie has been similarly generous in her
description of me.

"New Hampshire is land-locked, except for this gor-
geous little stretch—sixteen miles to be exact—of Atlantic
Ocean coastline," Melissa writes. "The Seacoast, my
friend, is the place to stay in New Hampshire . . . Anna
Marie gave you a good reference. Feel free to give me a
buzz if you need a place to crash during your Great American Bowling Adventure."

Now, I may be being optimistic when I read into this
that Melissa has a burning crush on me already. I'd certainly been overly hopeful with Bowling Spice, whose far
more overt innuendo actually meant "let's go bowling
sometime." But I've been driving around alone for a long
time talking to old sea captains and being shunned by college girls. Why wouldn't this turn into a romantic weekend with a tall, cute blue-eyed blonde in a New Hampshire
hamlet?

It is with this in mind that I ring the doorbell at
Melissa's address, just off Portsmouth's quaint main street

with shops and a town square, the autumn leaves just beginning to scatter across lawns.

The door opens and I make a mental note to thank Anna Marie. Melissa stands almost eye-to-eye to my six feet. Blond hair bounces just below chin-length. Soft blue eyes combine with an inviting smile to say either, *I'm a friendly person who's letting you stay in my guest room* or *Let the animal sex begin.*

"Here's the guest room," she says, showing me to a very sexless space with a desk and a twin bed. Apparently that's what her smile was saying.

We pass the afternoon with conversation and college football on TV. Over dinner and drinks at an Irish pub we have what could pass for a first date. It is on one hand free of awkward first-date tension given our common friends and that we've already spent the afternoon together. On the other hand, there's the knowledge behind everything we say that we're going home together—even if it's to separate bedrooms. As first dates go, this one would rate high: intelligent conversation (mostly on her part), witty banter, and a sort of intangible connection that comes from having midwestern roots in common. My more sensitive side appreciates meeting and getting to know Melissa; my instinctive, animal side still sees a glimmering hope that the bed in the guest room won't have to be remade.

Her friends John and Courtney join us for candlepin rock 'n' bowl at Bowl-O-Rama. The pulsing music, darkened lighting, and beer-filled pitchers speed the warming process, as does the bowling itself. Someone suggests we compete as teams, husband and wife versus houseguest and hostess. Drawn together as allies, Melissa and I are now united against a married couple. That practically makes us a couple, right? I sense an opening, if ever so slight, of the floodgates. Mirroring John and Courtney's behavior, celebratory high fives begin to linger, our skin touching for slightly longer than necessary. The "attaboy" pat on the ass emerges as a tongue-in-cheek congratulatory gesture. And it's all perfectly safe because it's just part of the game. It's not flirting . . . unless you want for it to be. . . . "Atta girl!"

We move to the lounge after bowling for more drinks. Melissa sits on my right, the four of us packed around a small high-top table. A densely mustachioed man named Carl begins talking with us and soon reveals himself to be mentally off-kilter, relentlessly injecting himself into our conversation. He is fidgety and has an air of antagonistic paranoia.

"You're not bowling in all fifty states!" he says in a loud, conspiratorial tone, accusing me of concocting this story to impress the pants off of Courtney and Melissa. *Well, you're half-right. . . .*

Time passes and Carl becomes more and more agitated; his ranting drifts further and further away from logic. What began as the four of us humoring him and having fun at his expense has evolved into discomfort: the joke has gotten old, and the lunatic is sounding loonier. Melissa shifts a bit closer to me out of necessity as Carl invades her space. Backed by John's six-four frame and 230 pounds ("John—I'll take the mustache, you go for the body"), I dispatch Carl with a discreet but firm suggestion that he leave our presence at once. Thankfully, he does so. I'd have hated to have to stand by and watch John pummel him.

This manly performance, aided by a raised blood alcohol level, apparently impresses Melissa, whose own raised blood alcohol level has lowered her inhibitions. Suddenly we are holding hands underneath the table, hidden from John and Courtney. We wouldn't want them to get the wrong idea, that we're just going to jump into bed having only met a few hours ago. Melissa is a nice girl with a reputation to uphold, after all.

We all return to Melissa's living room for a late-night drink, the married couple on the couch and the vagabond bowler wedged next to the tall, cute blonde on an oversized chair. The hand-holding is no longer under the table, and John once again has my back.

"Come on, Court, we should get home," he says, and the two depart amid my insincere pleas for them to stay.

Alone now but for the awkwardness of the situation, Melissa and I agree that putting in a movie is a swell idea. On the couch now, pretending to watch at first, feigning interest as hands move from holding each other to gently stroking hair, sliding over hips, smalls of backs, and necks. And then we're kissing. And then I'm above her, propped on elbows, fumbling with her top, this beautiful woman whom I met not twelve hours ago. Feeling supremely confident that I've overcome any "nice girl" tendencies that Melissa started the day with, I make my move.

"It's pretty late," I say. "Why don't we go to bed?" I suggest with no designs on sleeping.

"It *is* late," she agrees, pulling her mouth away from my tongue, which had just reentered it. She walks toward the guest room and switches on the light. "If it gets cold in there, there are extra blankets in the closet. See you tomorrow."

To my last pained protest and suggestions that we "could just cuddle," Melissa responds with an almost apologetic shrug that says, *What kind of a girl did you think I was?* I attempt to shrug back, *But think about the kind of girl you* could *be, with just a little effort.* This is hard to shrug. I sleep alone.

Twelve states and I've progressed from shaking hands with Bowling Spice to almost-heavy petting with a pre-arranged sure thing. I'm as much a lady's man as I am a bowler, it seems. Hoping some aspect of my game will improve with time, I set out the next morning to make quick work of Rhode Island.

Rhode Island ★

IT'S important to have goals, and my goal for Rhode Island, geographically the smallest state in the Union, is to spend the least amount of time possible there. It's nothing against the state—indeed, I know nothing about it and have no opinions of it whatsoever. It's just that I've dallied aplenty on this trip and this is an opportunity to make up some time. If all goes well I can be in, bowl, and be out of the state in less than one hour.

Unless I get lost.

I drive into Providence, circle downtown, pass through Brown University, and, not seeing the bowling alley I'd hoped fate would place in my path, stop at a gas station for directions to the nearest one.

I listen intently to the attendant's directions and commit them to memory before getting back behind the wheel: There's a bowling alley two miles up Route XYZ next to the barn that burned down in the fire of '86. Take exit Somethingorother, follow the curve in the road to the fork in the path, and *damn it*! Why didn't I write that down?! The clock is ticking.

Another gas station yields simpler directions.

"Down that way," a Pepsi truck driver tells me, pointing up the road. "Half a mile."

I'm now forty-eight minutes into my stay in Rhode Island; it is unlikely that I'll get shoes, bowl, pay, and clear the border in time to beat my self-imposed sixty-minute mark. Feeling as defeated as such an insignificant failure can make me feel, I slow down and roll two lackluster games before returning my shoes and paying the bill. By force of habit I mention my project to the woman behind the counter.

"You should talk to Spaghetti," she says.

Of course I should.

Walter Paul Menders, or Spaghetti to everyone he knows, is bowling this Tuesday afternoon in a seniors' league on a team called the Mustangs. He is dressed in a light blue polo shirt with a ballpoint pen clipped between the two buttons. His thick, square glasses cover a third of his face, which is constantly beaming beneath a crown of white hair.

"Where's the union? I'm not on strike," he quips after leaving several pins standing on the first ball of a frame. He is the unassuming, enthusiastic epicenter of the league.

"I used an angel hair to get that spare," he proclaims, holding his thumb and forefinger closely together to show how close he was to missing the pin he needed to hit to make the spare. His friends and teammates laugh appreciatively at his antics, if not for their cleverness, then for their familiarity.

"They called me 'Pickles' in the service," he says when I ask him why he's called Spaghetti. Feeling like I've inadvertently walked right into an Abbott and Costello routine, I ask why they called him Pickles. This diverts into another story before I am able to get the genesis of either nickname, and I turn to his teammate Bruce Anderson for a reprieve and some answers.

"How long have you known Walter?" I ask Bruce.

"Who?"

Who's on first . . . "Walter Menders," I clarify.

"Who? Oh, you mean Spaghetti."

Bruce wasn't playing me: almost no one calls Spaghetti anything but Spaghetti. Both men had been in the Navy, Bruce on submarines from 1944 to 1962 and Spaghetti in Africa in the early fifties. They met each other long after their military service, and have another shared vocation that proves as strong a bond on the lanes.

"I used to make five cents a game as a pinsetter in Williamsport,

Pennsylvania," Bruce says with apparent pride in having paid his bowling dues.

"I used to set duckpins and chase the loose change people would throw down the lanes as a tip," Spaghetti says separately with the same pride. Having served as a pin boy is a badge of honor that bespeaks a lifelong connection with bowling and, given that automatic machines have been ubiquitous for nearly half a century now, the credibility that comes with advancing age.

Spaghetti, who is seventy-eight, met his wife in Africa while he was in the Navy.

"She was fourteen and only spoke French. I was twenty-four and only spoke English, but we fell in love," he says. "Her father trusted me. They called me Paul because 'Walter' was harder for them to pronounce." Presumably "Pickles" would have been too difficult to explain, given the language barrier.

"We'd ride around on a '42 Harley that Eisenhower's troops had left behind after the war. We took our honeymoon on it."

Imagining my own father's reaction to a twenty-four-year-old foreigner showing up on a Harley to take his fourteen-year-old daughter for a ride in the African countryside without a common language between them, I gain tremendous respect for Spaghetti's ability to pull this off. But how long could it last?

"We've got twelve children, twenty-eight grandkids, and four great-grandchildren," he says, pulling out his wallet to prove it with pictures.

"And this, this is my pacemaker card," he says, showing me a piece of paper explaining to medical workers and metal detector operators that he's got some gadgetry inside his chest. "I've got seventy-nine months left on the battery."

That will put him at over eighty-four years old when it needs to be replaced. I suspect from his boundless energy he'll outlive another battery or two before it's all over.

Two hours and five minutes after entering it, I leave Rhode Island, grateful to have spent a little longer there than I'd planned. Maybe I can make up the time when I get to Delaware.

★ Connecticut

DAVID Petrie is my godparents' son, which I believe makes him my godbrother, a title that probably doesn't hold any legal obligations but works fine for the purpose of explaining who I'm bowling with at Rip Van Winkle Lanes in Norwalk, Connecticut.

Like the rest of the men in his family, David is imposingly tall; the sixteen-pound ball looks tiny in his hand, just as his fiancée, Paige—who actually is tiny—looks tiny by his side. The two, along with some of their friends, arrive as league play dwindles down, and we are all placed on lane two. A foursome of tall, stunning blond girls with heavy European accents occupies lane one to our left. I introduce myself with characteristic smoothness.

"No way! You're from Europe? So am I! Well, a few generations back anyway."

Though their English is quite good, the fact that they don't appear to have mastered sarcasm and colloquialisms works in my favor and they don't dismiss me out of hand like they really should.

"Anne, Toft, and Line ["Lee-nuh"] are from Denmark," says the tallest, most stunning, and most blond, dressed in tight blue jeans and a tighter shirt unbuttoned to reveal her rather dramatic cleavage. "I am Andrea from Germany. Ve are all au pairs for ze families weeth children."

I'm in love: beautiful foreign babysitters out for a night of freedom away from the pesky kids and their rich parents who boss them around all day.

Toft joins in: "It is Andrea's, how do you say? Birthday. We are celebrating."

Indeed. A cake, party hats, and noisemakers rest on the shared table alongside our pitchers of High Life and recently unfrozen pizza. In the spirit of hospitality and diplomacy, I make an effort to talk with them between bowling turns. I want to learn their impressions of the United States, whether or not they get homesick, what the likelihood of all four of them taking me back to one of their employers' mansions for a romp in the hot tub might be.

"I don't *entirely* hate Americans," Line says. So far, so good. "But when I first moved here I had to care for a three-years-old spoiling brat who gave me a bad impression."

"Spoiling" instead of "spoiled." I think to correct her but stop when it dawns on me that maybe she intended to say the kid was *on his way* to becoming spoiled.

"No, I don't really miss home too much," says Andrea. "I am thinking of moving here permanently after my au pair program is finished."

"I don't understand this word 'five-some' how you have used it," says Toft after I take their picture for them wearing party hats and holding up American flags.

"Never mind," I say, knowing full well this time they're merely pretending that language is a barrier.

I sleep alone, of course, at David's apartment on a beanbag the size of a Volkswagen, which I determine must be a special order available only to the men of the Petrie family. Instead of buxom au pairs I am visited intermittently through the night by his golden retriever, Dallas, who, though a striking blonde, isn't much of a kisser.

I depart Connecticut for a night in Boston with former co-workers Charlie and Rich, who are in town with a former client, Tim. Tim, in addition to buying me dinner and giving me the extra bed in his hotel room, is one of the people who took me up on my postcard-from-all-fifty-states offer. On the TV when we return from dinner is

a rebroadcast of my *Caroline Rhea* appearance, making those postcards all the more valuable.

I circle from Philadelphia west to Hershey, Pennsylvania, to be a
guest in the home of Chris Sands, a friend from college who'd won
several awards in our fraternity along the lines of "Most likely to cause
significant property damage." With a beautiful wife and a newborn, it
is eerie to see the dramatic contrast between the Sands I knew seven
years ago and the one before me now. Joining him on the porch to
hand out full-size Hershey's candy bars of every variety (make no mistake: Hershey is the *only* place to trick-or-treat) to the neighborhood
kids for Halloween, Chris even demonstrates his corporate responsibility.

"What's your favorite candy?" he asks each trick-or-treater, keeping
a careful tally to report back in to Corporate the next day.

From Hershey I return to Regan's apartment in Hoboken to map out
the next few states and pick up some things I'd left there during my
first visit to make room in the car for Morgan and Brian. It's a brief,
one-night stop, as I'm eager to get on to Washington, D.C., with
plans to make quick work of Delaware, Maryland, and Virginia. I
load the car and begin the drive, though not without a strange feeling
that I'm forgetting something.

New Jersey ★

How could you forget to bowl in New Jersey?" Amy Farrar, my host while I'm in D.C., asks, laughing at me.

"That's a good question." I largely blame Regan, not for neglecting to take me bowling there over the ten days I've stayed with her on this trip but for her refusal to acknowledge that she lives in Jersey, as shown by her insistence that it not be printed in our father's obituary. Mentally I was always in New York, even if geographically I was mostly in New Jersey.

This trip's entire foundation is the accomplishment of a relatively simple goal. Lest I forget, it is my main topic of conversation every day: "What are you doing in town?" "This is my brother Mike; he's bowling in all fifty states." "Hi, I'm bowling in all fifty states; will you go out with me?" The goal so permeated my activities that while in New Jersey I was even booked on TV shows to talk about it, though those shows were taped in New York. It would seem impossible for me, single-minded in purpose as I supposedly am, to travel to a state and not bowl there. Yet here I am in Maryland plotting a day trip to bowl in Delaware with a stop in New Jersey on the way since I somehow missed it during the week and a half I've recently spent there.

I arrive at a bowling alley just across the Delaware Memorial Bridge and am rather directionally confused after driving through parts of Maryland, Delaware, and Pennsylvania to get here. Complicating matters is the fact that the bowling alley I've ended up at is called Penn Bowl. At the front desk:

"Hi, just to be clear before I bowl, what state am I in?"

"New Jersey."

"The entire place is in New Jersey?"

"Yes."

"And I won't accidentally cross a state line if I bowl on the wrong end of the building, will I?"

"Do you want to bowl or not?"

"Yes. Sorry. It's . . . been a long drive."

"Apparently. Here are your shoes; you're on lane seventeen."

"But why is it called Penn Bowl? You're sure this isn't Pennsylvania?"

"This is Pennsville, New Jersey. Lane seventeen is that way."

On my way to lane seventeen I stop for a moment to watch a group of senior citizens bowling in their weekly league. It has become one of my favorite things about bowling that on a given weekday, morning or afternoon, there is almost always a group of seniors on the lanes. There is no doubt from the seniors I've met in this setting so far that it's an invaluable part of their lives, that they cherish the ability to gather, socialize, exercise, and compete. But as I think more about it, if not for senior citizens, there would be little reason for bowling houses to turn the lights on while most of the population is at work or in school. The seniors are an important customer base for bowling alleys during the daytime operating hours. Perhaps this bodes well for bowling's future: while senior citizens make up approximately 12 percent of the U.S. population today, they are projected to grow at a faster rate than all other age groups by 2030 as the Baby Boomers enter their twilight.

What's more, the seniors tend to welcome an outsider like me. They're willing, often eager, to talk to a new person, someone who hasn't heard their stories before. It can be a lonely existence after your children move away and your spouse dies and you're less able and have fewer opportunities to leave the house. In my more self-righteous moments I see myself as a goodwill ambassador to the lonely seniors of bowling, magnanimously providing an ear for these forlorn souls. In my less self-important moments I realize I'm the lonely one, that I'm grateful for someone to pay attention to me, a stranger wherever I go, and I typically learn something from them.

After a short time one of the group I'm watching here at Penn Bowl turns to me after exchanging suspicious whispers and glances with a fellow bowler and says, "You won't learn anything from watching us."

Very well then. There's a toddler down by lane seventeen; I think I'll go bowl my game and see if he can give me any pointers.

Jason is three and is bowling with his father. Each roll is a triumphant struggle for the little blond boy. With both arms supporting a blue ball twice the size of his head, Jason waddles up to the line and turns his whole body from right to left as he releases the orb, his right arm following through and sending it side-to-side against the bumpers. I attempt this approach once and my ball careens into the gutter; Jason is unimpressed.

I finish my game and drive back across the Delaware Memorial Bridge to make Delaware the second of three states I'll check off the list today.

★ Delaware

AT a gas station just across the river from New Jersey a kindly man named Ed, speaking with a sort of drawl-slur I can't quite place, gives me his three-minute biography in response to my question, "Is there a bowling alley around here?"

"Yep, I just moved back here from Florida. Grew up here, though, on the other side of town 'til I was sixteen; then the family moved down there. Always wanted to come back. My sister's still down in Florida—she likes the weather. But not me, I like it up here. Just after I got married . . ."

I'd begun to think he had horribly misunderstood my question, or mistaken me for someone who was on a tour of gas station parking lots instead of bowling alleys. Then he suddenly concludes his story by saying, "Bowlerama. Three lights up on the left," and then driving off.

At Bowlerama I speak with Jerry Stewart, owner of Stewart's Pro Shop.

"Bowling centers like this aren't doing so well anymore," he says. "Twenty years ago, all seventy-four lanes would be filled here every night with leagues from six to midnight. Had a waiting list to get into a league. It's nothing like that now."

This afternoon Bowlerama certainly seems to support the *Bowling Alone* thesis. Aside from a guy who's bowling in all fifty states there are only two other bowlers here. They are bowling, out of necessity, together.

The pair of men are on lane thirty-one and their names are Bob and Bill. Bill has been blind since birth.

"I learned to bowl at a school for the blind in North Carolina," he says between frames.

Anyone who has ever seen a blind skier on the slopes shouldn't be surprised to learn that the blind also bowl. And while skiing may be the more dangerous of the two sports, bowling is no small feat for the blind: it requires a kind of visualization—imagination, really—to be able to aim at the pins, to picture their formation and guess where the ball will go. Maybe when all ten are standing it's not as daunting, but what about picking up a lone pin on a spare? I briefly hypothesize that if bowlers with sight regularly leave pins standing at a frame's end, perhaps being able to see the pins isn't terribly important. Soon enough I'll debunk my own theory.

When a bowling house hosts a blind league or tournament it may not seem considerably different from any other bowling event—until you look under the tables and chairs. There an army of Seeing Eye dogs watches and does its best to support the bowlers. Helpful though they may be at daily activities, the dogs aren't generally allowed on the approach, and they're useless when it comes to counting pins. So, as with skiing, bowling requires the assistance of a sighted person. For Bill, that person is Bob.

"We met in 1963," Bob says. The two were working at a YMCA as masseuses, and have remained friends for the four decades since.

"He and I bowl on Tuesday nights with a blind league," Bob says. "There are twenty-four bowlers in it, and each team of four has one sighted bowler."

"We call that one the scorekeeper," Bill adds as he picks up his ball for his next frame.

He guides his approach to the foul line by gently touching his left hand to a specially made temporary rail he sets up in line with the left gutter. Approximately waist-high and running most of the length of the approach, the rail's legs are held in place by ballast easily found in a place like this: bowling balls.

The sighted bowler does a little more than keep score. He's also the one to tell his teammates what their ball is doing, how to adjust to the

ever-changing lane conditions, and, most important, which pins remain standing.

"You've got the five-seven-ten," Bob tells Bill after his first roll, calling the still-standing pins by number.

Bill lines up to roll his spare using the rail and the visualization of
what his target looks like to adjust his approach. He walks up to the
line and releases the ball, then waits to hear the result. He doesn't
need Bob to tell him.

"Only got two," he says, shaking his head as he returns to his seat.

I get some shoes from the counter, grab a ball, and roll my
Delaware game. In an attempt to understand what it is like for Bill, I
bowl one frame with my eyes closed. The first roll yields a respectable
6. On my second roll I cross the foul line and slip on the lane oil,
nearly falling on my tailbone. I open my eyes to regain my balance,
and bowl the rest of my game with them open.

My score is 127. Bill rolls a 143.

Maryland ★

BEFORE bowling in Maryland, my third state of the day, I attend a taping of CNN's *Crossfire* at an auditorium on George Washington University's campus. Amy, who mocked me for forgetting New Jersey but is making up for it by allowing me to sleep on her futon and generally loiter at her home, works at the political debate show. It is currently hosted by a rotating mix of well-known commentators: former Clinton aides James Carville and Paul Begala on the "left" and pundits Bob Novak and Tucker Carlson on the "right." As with most of these shows, the hosts and guests try their hardest to take polarizing and contentious views on issues for the sake of dramatic TV, but here, even on the day after the 2002 midterm elections in which Republicans took control of both the House and Senate, the atmosphere is more chiding than charged. During last night's election coverage show with all four hosts in attendance, Carville, shamed by his party's performance, clowned around, putting a trash can on his head, to the panel's delight. Tonight, Begala and Carlson are the hosts, and Amy introduces me to them following the show.

"Oh, you're the bowling guy," the bow-tied and youthful Carlson says as he and Begala stand in a dressing room removing brown pancake makeup off their faces with baby wipes. "Amy told me about that. Great idea."

"Thanks," I reply.

"Now we just need to get him to bowl in the White House," Amy chimes in. We'd earlier discussed the fact that while the District of Columbia wasn't a requirement

121

for the fifty-state challenge, bowling at the White House would be a worthy capstone.

President Truman had bowling facilities installed in the White House during his administration, though most people credit Nixon with it, largely because of a single photo. Aside from the obvious reasons, Nixon's presidency is memorable for certain images of him that have become iconic capsules of an oddly surreal time. The two-fingered "I'm not a crook" wave. Boarding Air Force One after resigning. Looking uncertain and uncomfortable shaking hands with a drug-eyed Elvis who arrived wearing an enormous gold belt, an open high-collared shirt, and an ornate double-breasted jacket draped over his shoulders. And the photo of Nixon bowling.

Perhaps the lesser known of the Nixon images, it nonetheless became symbolic of his connection to the blue-collared masses. Though some allege the photo was staged for exactly that purpose, Nixon was a card-carrying member of the American Bowling Congress, and I suspect when he stepped into Ball Park Lanes before that Yankee game he really was hoping to get a few frames in. A poster-sized print of the Nixon bowling photo hangs in The Dude's apartment in *The Big Lebowski,* and reproducing it on T-shirts has become a cottage industry.

Since Nixon's administration it doesn't seem that the White House bowling alley got a lot of use. Carter didn't seem like the type. Reagan had his ranch. Someone told me that the during the Clinton years it was used for storage. One doubts the Bushes are a family that bowls together, but perhaps. A contact at the bowling manufacturer Brunswick said that they'd recently refurbished the lanes at Camp David under Bush 43. So maybe W. is a bowler. Regardless, Begala doesn't see my getting into the White House lanes as an easy task.

"It's a pretty closed administration," he says. "We would have let you, though," he adds, ribbing Tucker. "We" in this case is the Clinton administration, and Begala's use of the first-person pronoun suggests he once had the access and power to grant such a wish. He gives me the phone number of a friend who is a political advisor to President Bush, a generous and thoughtful thing to do.

In gratitude for Amy's hospitality, I take her bowling.

Strike Bethesda is owned by the same people who own the Bowl-mor in Manhattan, and consequently it has the same vibe: retro-mod furniture, low lighting, lots of video screens, and pulsing club music. The only apparent thing missing is the swell of beautiful people. Or really any people at all—apart from us the place is completely empty. This is probably because it's the night after an election in Washington and everyone is burned out from victory parties or wallowing in loss, but the cooler-than-thou ambiance rings a bit hollow when there's no one to be cooler than.

The next day I place my call using the number Begala gave me the night before. A receptionist answers and I think at best I'll get transferred to Begala's friend's voice mail.

"Who may I say is calling?"

"My name is Mike Walsh . . . um . . . Paul Begala suggested I call about a project I'm working on."

At this point I'm actually *hoping* I'll get his friend's voice mail. I'm suddenly nervous as hell and certain that my call will spark the opening of an FBI file on me. For better or worse, my dropping of Begala's name elicits a more direct response: his friend takes my call.

"So, you're a friend of Paul's?"

"Well, sort of—I mean, I met him through a friend and he suggested I call to see if you might arrange for me to bowl in the White House."

A long pause, then: "Why should we let you bowl in the White House?"

I spend the next thirty seconds stammering one of the worst explanations I've ever given of my trip, attempting to frame it in terms that seem electorally important, as if letting me bowl at 1600 Pennsylvania

Avenue will help them two years from now. When I finish, there is another long pause.

"Why don't you put something in writing and we'll see what we can do?" His tone is polite, but behind it I sense a distinct, *This guy isn't even worth opening an FBI file on,* in his voice.

Putting my White House bowling dreams on hold for the moment, I opt to spend the last night of my stay in the nation's capital bowling with an ex-girlfriend and her new boyfriend. Virginia is for lovers, huh? I'll see about that.

Virginia ★

BEFORE I started falling in love with every woman I would lay eyes on while riding the El to work in Chicago, I was in love with a girl named Jesse, whom I met in high school. We had a wonderful relationship for five years and then, my anti-commitment instincts kicking in, I decided to call it off . . . not ready for the next step . . . haven't really dated anyone else . . . need to see if there's something else out there . . . I think that chick on the El was digging me. . . .

As is always the case when a guy tells his girlfriend "we should see other people," she soon found a new boyfriend while I floundered, dateless, for long enough to revive my mother's hopes that one of her sons might enter the priesthood.

In fact, Jesse had been with the new guy almost since we broke up. She'd spent almost a year with him in South America and then the two of them moved to Virginia; their engagement is rumored to be just around the corner. I needn't remind the reader that I am unemployed, single, and driving my mother's car, my only possessions in a rented eight-by-six storage unit somewhere in Illinois. I ponder this reality while waiting at Bowl America to bowl a few games with Jesse and Bill, or Bob, or Biff, or whatever his name was. Brian?

Brett has an exam on the evening we scheduled to bowl and will be arriving late. This gives me the opportunity to spend some time with Jesse and talk through whatever it is we might have to talk through. Aside from her ridiculous contentions and views about U.S. social and economic policy and my ridiculous half-fact-based refutations of them, our conversation is pretty amicable. We talk about my dad, whom she adored as well, until it starts to get tearful, then move on to our breakup until it does the same. I'm struck at how easily we fall into our old conversation patterns, how quickly we jump into semi-faux insults that would have seemed flirtatious if not for the history and biting truth now behind them. But mostly we catch up on each other's family and relive the occasional memory. Each story she tells seems to be an unfamiliar (to me) reminiscence of something that we once did together, ending with, "Oh, wait. That's right. I did that with Ben." (Beau?)

She asks about my love life. "Why did you and the last girl break up, anyway?"

"A lot of reasons I guess. On my end the usual poor communication, fear of commitment, always looking for the next thing—typical guy stuff."

"That is not typical *guy* stuff!" she argues. "That's typical *Mike Walsh* stuff."

"Let's stop talking now and bowl."

When we were together, Jesse and I would bowl now and then, and to my recollection she never beat me. (She, of course, remembers a time when she beat me but then remembers that it was actually Brent.) We'd place bets on the outcome of our bowling, the wager usually taking the form of harmless favors young lovers will put on the line in a bet—loser makes dinner for the winner and such. We'd cuddle and hold hands between frames. We'd let the competition serve as a pretext for congratulatory ass-patting and lingering high fives. I know that when Brock arrives I'll be witness to this same sort of display, something I'm not looking forward to but medicine I have to take.

Though I'm underconfident about being with Jesse in the presence of my replacement, at least I'll be able to maintain my bowling superiority and thus prevent total emasculation by keeping my undefeated record. I recognize how pathetic it is that the only pride I can salvage here comes from the unfair advantage gained from having bowled in seventeen states in the past few weeks, but one must use the advantages one has. Home court advantage may be hers, but relative to her I'm the Michael Jordan of bowling.

Jesse beats me 180 to 136.

Bill arrives, along with several of Jesse's other friends, and we have a mostly awkwardness-free game over beer and Bowl America's good (and good for you) cheese steak and fries dinner.

It's a pretty lively group for bowling: yelling to disrupt one another's concentration while bowling quickly turns into physical distraction in the form of sneaking up and grabbing the bowler's ass on his or her approach. This is all innocent and fun until one of Jesse's friends jokes about how she's going to go grab Bill's ass while he bowls and Jesse answers in saucy jest, "It's a nice ass. Trust me."

When I finish dry-heaving in a corner, I return to find the two of them in a close whisper, holding hands in the chairs behind the scoring area. Any taste of crow in my mouth fades as I see how happy she is and how well they work together. Jesse had mentioned they were talking about marriage in "when," not "if," terms, and it strikes me as entirely right.

The next five days I spend with my godparents, Mike and Joanna Petrie, on the Eastern Shore of the Chesapeake Bay in Maryland. This is one of the most distinctive places in the United States. Historically and currently, the Eastern Shore's fortunes go the way of the bay. As much as the migratory waterfowl remain plentiful and stick to their southbound route along the eastern flyway, the hunting guides will be busy. As the mussel harvest goes, so go the mussel fishermen. A good blue crab season means a good year for the trawler who wakes me each morning at sunrise as he makes his first pass along his crab line, capturing the jimmies and sooks in a long-handled net that he sneaks under them just before they see him and let go of the chicken wing he tied to the line to lure them.

We set some crab pots off the dock and collect a handful for lunch. Boiling them outdoors and dusting them with enough OLD BAY Seasoning to coat a whale, we dine on a picnic table covered with Kraft paper, cracking the shells with a thick wooden dowel and dipping them in melted butter. Mike holds court, in a way only a six-foot-six man with a booming voice and a knack for storytelling can.

"Your dad used to complain about his job at Honeywell before he started Columbus Temperature Control," Mike says. "We'd go for sandwiches and he'd bitch and moan about how they never listened to his ideas and sent him out to sell products that weren't right for his customers and so forth. Then he'd pull out this dog-eared yellow legal pad with a bunch of hieroglyphics on it—that was his handwriting, you know. I don't know how he could read it, let alone anyone else. Anyway, over the course of about a year that legal pad kept getting more full—but not any more legible—and sure enough it became the business plan for CTC."

Back in the guest cottage I look over my own yellow legal pad, the one on which I'd begun hashing out this trip. Until Mike told that story I'd had no idea my dad's major shift in life course had begun on similar parchment. I review the list of states in the margins and count thirty-two left to go.

North Carolina ★

VIRGINIA Dare was the first person of English descent
to be born on what is now U.S. soil. Her birth took
place in August of 1587, on Roanoke Island, tucked between what is now North Carolina and the barrier islands
that line its shore called the Outer Banks. Her parents had
come over to establish a permanent settlement in the New
World under a charter granted to Sir Walter Raleigh by
Elizabeth I. The expedition of 121 people included Virginia's grandfather John White, who hesitantly returned
to England for supplies deemed crucial for survival amid a
harsh winter and hostile Indians. By the time he
returned—delayed by a war between Great Britain and
the Spanish Armada—three years had passed. He found
Roanoke completely deserted, with no sign of Virginia,
her parents, or any of the more than one hundred settlers
he'd left behind. On a fence post the word "Croatoan"
had been carved, referring to what is now Hatteras Island,
the home of the Croatoan tribe. A hurricane kept White
from exploring that island, blowing the fleet he was with
so far off course that they deemed it more efficient to return to England. He never again saw any of the settlers,
including his granddaughter Virginia. Nor did anyone
else, at least so far as the historic record is concerned.

The fate of the Lost Colony of Roanoke is subject to
much speculation. In the early 1600s the settlers at
Jamestown, spurred by clues suggesting the Roanoke
colonists were nearby, sent out search parties that found
no sign of them. Explorers in the early 1700s reported en-
countering people on Hatteras who had white skin and

spoke a form of English and had gray eyes—not brown like the rest of the inhabitants—living among the descendants of the Croatoan tribe. Some evidence suggests the colonists made it to the southern end of the Chesapeake before being killed by suspicious Indians. Another account, from the late 1800s, tells of a strange people who spoke Anglo-Saxon living in a small village in southeastern North Carolina, whose family names were similar to those of some of the Roanoke colonists.

As time passes it's unlikely we'll learn the true fate of these pioneers, whether they were wiped from the earth, moved on to settle elsewhere, or assimilated with an Indian tribe. The possibility remains that Virginia Dare lived on, that she bore offspring, that ancestors of this first daughter are among us.

They are not, however, at Nags Head Bowling Center on this rainy November night, unless the offspring of British nobility devolved considerably over five hundred years to become the drunkest bunch of locals on this historically significant archipelago. The twenty-four-lane center is only about half-full, and judging by the number of empty pitchers and glasses, it's about half-full of beer. I've apparently just missed a party, though a handful of people appear convinced it's still going on.

Among them is a family of redheads, all of whom—brother, sister, husband, wife—have the exact same haircut: a glorious flowing mullet, falling past the shoulders in a curl in back and feathered over the forehead in front. The loudest of the family is eager to tell me something important about life, or at least trying to get something straight for himself.

"An honest man's words," he begins, slurring heavily, spit bubbling on his lower lip, pointing at me emphatically. "No, wait. A drunk man's as honest—no, hold on. Hold on. An honest man's drunk . . . ah, fuck. . . ." He drifts off and returns to his table, chin on his chest. Just when I think he's about to fall asleep standing up with a pitcher of beer in one hand and a burning cigarette in the other, he startles and charges back at me with the revelation that was eluding him: "A drunk man's words is a sober man's thoughts!"

They sure is, I think, then get some rental shoes and find a lane. While I'm bowling, alone, someone comes up to me and asks why I'm not bowling with my family. Puzzled at first, I realize he's assumed that because of my red hair I must be with the Mullets. I decide to stop drinking for the night and to get a haircut as soon as time permits.

The next morning I drive to Greensboro, which is in the north-central part of North Carolina, almost three hundred miles due west from the Atlantic coast. At a bowling alley there, I talk with a woman named Janet, who also speaks for her friend Becky, whose laryngitis prevents her from speaking too loudly. Becky is bowling from a three-wheeled electric scooter, the kind they advertise on TV as being so liberating for little old ladies—only Becky isn't a little old lady. She is perhaps in her early fifties and exudes energy despite being physically restricted and vocally challenged.

"I've got multiple sclerosis," she explains in a whisper.

Janet assists: "About two years ago, Becky started losing her balance and was going to quit bowling. We suggested that she bowl in the chair, but she really didn't want to."

Janet looks at her friend, smiling, and adds, "But we made her do it—we'd have missed her too much."

Becky's eyes light with her smile. "I find such camaraderie here," she whispers, barely audible above the bowling racket. "These people make me so happy."

During a stopover in Raleigh-Durham, I make a call-in to the Sterling radio show in Columbus, which I find to be an easier way of updating my family there than making separate calls to each of them. Perhaps overcompensating for not having gotten Miller a lot of media exposure yet, I throw in a few more, "And what goes better with bowling than the Champagne of Beers?" than are necessary.

"All right, I get it," Sterling busts me. "Way to get a plug in for the sponsor. Real subtle. What's in it for me?"

I promise him the High Life bowling shirt off my back and am relieved that he hasn't lost all respect for me after I tried to turn his radio show into an infomercial for my sponsor. He invites me to call in again and pumps my ego as he had during my first call with him, closing with, "You're my hero, man."

From Raleigh-Durham I head south to Charlotte and George Pappas's Park Lanes. When I arrive, owner George Pappas is in the midst of teaching a lesson to a group of bowlers who've signed up for his world-class instruction. George was inducted into the Professional Bowlers Association Hall of Fame in 1986 in recognition for a career on the tour that began in 1969 and includes more than ten PBA titles. He's owned Park Lanes for over twenty years and continues to have an active presence in its day-to-day operation. Today's class is about the mental aspects of the game.

Now, there are some ostentatious bowlers on the PBA tour who pump their fists, openly taunt their opponents, and try to inject a little big-time-wrestling energy into the sport as a way of intimidating their rivals. A bowler by the name of Pete Weber is one of them. His father, Dick Weber, is known as one of the best bowlers of all time, and Pete didn't fall far from the ball rack: he is currently one of the top five all-time title winners. When he's bowling in front of a crowd and doing well, he's prone to thrusting his pelvis outward while making a sharp gesture toward his hips with both hands. The move is part air-humping and part gunslinger reaching for his six-shooters, only the six-shooters part is basically just crotch-pointing. He does this while glaring at the audience as if to say, "You want some of this?!" Though jarring, it comes across as a welcome bit of theater and has probably drawn people to bowling who might not understand the finer points of picking up a 6-7-10 split but who enjoy a good show.

George Pappas is no Pete Weber in this department. His presentation is that of a soft-spoken, humble man. He stands calmly at the center of a semi-circle of students—bowlers of all ages—making careful eye contact and giving thoughtful responses to their questions.

"It's important to keep your focus on the frame you're in," he says. "Don't worry about what happened in the last frame or what you're going to do in the next."

I'd expected a PBA Hall of Famer to be giving psych-out tips that come in handy when bowling on TV against a rookie, but George is subtler than that. He's of the "speak softly and carry a good strike ball" school of thought; his intimidation comes from the steady consistency with which he rolls a strike, as he demonstrates to his dozen or so students this morning.

After some excellent onion rings in the Park Lanes restaurant, I catch up with a former client named Lynn, who took me up on the postcard-from-every-state offer. The eighteen I've sent so far are on display in his home office, which happens to be bowling themed. The stack of postcards goes well with the bowling pin-shaped lamp and the ceramic ashtray with a creepy-looking baby holding a bowling ball perched on the edge. To demonstrate that he's one of the bravest men alive, he shows me a recent Mother's Day gift he gave to his wife: a pair of bowling shoes and a white sixties-mod bowling ball bag adorned with brightly colored stitched flowers. Because nothing says "Thanks for bearing our children" like machine-crafted bowling wear. I send him a nineteenth postcard for his collection from a mailbox down the street, making a mental note to call Lynn if I'm ever hard up for romantic gift ideas.

★ South Carolina

CHARLESTON, South Carolina, is arguably one of the most beautiful cities in America. Despite being the site of the first fighting of the Civil War—the Confederate army attacked Fort Sumter on an island in Charleston Harbor in April of 1861—the town itself was spared significant damage. Thus its cobblestone streets and preserved antebellum mansions have become a draw for vacationers and a have made the city a popular wedding destination. This has led, for better or worse, to a booming bar business catering to bachelor and bachelorette parties that flock here for weekends of warm weather and easily stumbled-to watering holes with names like Wet Willie's and Banana Cabana offering generously potent drink specials. On a given Saturday night the streets teem with groups of men dressed in their finest club-going gear having macho drinking contests and forcibly hitting on groups of women wearing matching T-shirts and carrying various penis-shaped memorabilia to mortify the veil-wearing bride-to-be. The dance floors at places like Wet Willie's are filled with people flirting with promiscuity as they down drinks named The Monkey Shine and grind against each other to booming music and swirling lights. The juxtaposition to the quaint, aristocratic town can be jarring.

As I drive into downtown I'm hoping that this wealth of bars means it will be easy to catch the Ohio State football game on a Saturday afternoon before the nightlife starts. For me, watching an Ohio State football game is like spending three hours at home, especially when traveling alone or far from Buckeye territory. Feeling particularly homesick today, I've set in my mind that all will be well if I can just catch the game. Having managed to locate bars in Europe showing not only American college football but Ohio State games, I assume doing so in Charleston's bar district won't pose much of a challenge. Bad assumption.

After a desperate search, slogging from one bar to another in a relentless downpour, frantically asking bartenders if any of the dozen TVs they have will be showing the Buckeyes' game, I've come to the last bar in downtown Charleston, breathless and all but devoid of hope. I'm preparing to launch into a desperate sales pitch if this bar proves to be like the rest. I won't be above crying, buying a round for the entire crowd, anything to get the right game on just one TV.

Using my wet coat sleeve to try to stop the water dripping from my forehead, I see what looks like a man in an Ohio State jersey coming down a set of stairs. As my eyes adjust to the darkness of the bar and the water, everything has a blurry, dreamlike quality. The man appears to be descending the stairs in slow motion.

"Hey, are they showing the Buckeye game up there?" I ask him. In my head my voice sounds like it's also in slow motion, that deep, creepy, slow voice usually used in movies to yell, "Noooooooooo!" before something explodes. As I finish my sentence my eyes finally adjust, time speeds up again, and the man's face comes into focus, prompting me to add, "Brooks?"

"Walsh?" he says, puzzled.

"Brooks Mathews?"

"Mike Walsh?"

Brooks and I went to high school and worked at the same summer camp together for a number of years. He happens to be here on a weekend getaway with his girlfriend, Becky, and they invite me to join them at their table directly in front of a large projector screen—possibly the only one in the greater southeastern United States showing the Ohio State game. Becky is remarkably tolerant of my third-wheel presence and obnoxious cheering as the Buckeyes win in overtime and I spill beer all over the table.

I reluctantly leave Brooks and Becky to continue their romantic weekend in Charleston without me, walking tall after a Buckeye victory and three hours of hometown reminiscing. I stop in another bar, one with the requisite dark dance floor and swirling lights, and quickly realize that my lone, anonymous drifter vibe doesn't play well in a place filled with groups of bachelor and bachelorette parties. For no one's entertainment but my own I approach a pack of women drinking through penis-shaped straws and say, "Sorry I'm late—did you ladies order the stripper?" This elicits laughter and comments about my physique that are just too mean and hurtful to repeat here. I opt to find somewhere a little more welcoming of lone drifters and make my way to Twin River Lanes.

When I arrive, Twin River is in the midst of cosmic bowling, and so the music and lighting are not dissimilar from the place I just left. Instead of bachelor parties and the like, the crowd here is primarily teens and college kids groping each other in the chairs around the scorer's tables and trying to buy alcohol with fake IDs. I feel much more at home.

After bowling ten frames I pull up a stool and listen in to a conversation at the bar. A young, pudgy woman is complaining to the bartender about a petty fight she's in with a friend, but doing so in a Charleston southern drawl so cordial and melodic it makes her griping sound pleasant.

"I do declare, I was just *so* disappointed that my friend Joanna didn't return my call. I am coming to believe that new may-en of hers, Kevin Hollingsworth—of the low-country Hollingsworths—is just an absolutely dreadful influence on her."

At bowling alleys in other, less genteel parts of the country I've heard this same sentiment expressed with slightly less eloquence, along the lines of, "If that bitch don't want to call me back, then *fine!* I just hope she don't expect me to dry her cryin'-ass tears when that asshole cheats on her again."

Charmed, I'm sure.

Florida ★

As Mom's Honda skirts along the Atlantic coast on I-95 from Charleston, through Savannah, Georgia, and south across the Florida border, my phone rings: it is the woman who took over my position at the job that I quit. She is asking where a file that I had long ago forgotten existed might be located. The memory of that project, of the late-night hours spent in the office, of the stress brought on by something so trivial, and the fact that it couldn't matter less to me as I roll down the windows to breathe the coastal St. Augustine air, is liberating. After being of almost no help to her search for the file, I decide to drive down the entire peninsula and to the Florida Keys despite the time and money I'd save by bowling here on the border and getting on with the states. In Key West I will be closer to Cuba than to any state that will help my cause, but the sunset's supposed to be spectacular. Sure it's inefficient and frivolous, but . . . well, that's reason enough.

Jacksonville is my first stop. My hosts here are Amy and Mark Newkirk, a friend from college and her fly-by-night husband. I don't say this to disparage him: he flies helicopters for the U.S. Navy, and our first stop before bowling is the air base, where we borrow a pair of night-vision goggles to fool around with when it gets dark; Mark refuses to let me play with anything more dangerous.

"Can I at least sit in the driver's seat?" I ask when he shows me one of the Seahawk helicopters he flies.

"It's a cockpit," he corrects me. "Sure."

The guys doing maintenance on the engine look a little uncomfortable with my hopping in behind the controls while their fingers and heads are inches from the rotors. Mark assures me that I can't possibly turn anything on but suggests I not touch anything, just to be safe.

The Navy's equivalent to the Army's Blackhawk, the Seahawk is primarily used for detecting and attacking enemy submarines (it can be fitted with torpedoes), for rescue and aid missions, and for troop transport. Navy SEAL teams pack into the empty, seatless bay until there is barely room to breathe and have a rough but fast ride to their clandestine missions. The pilot can set the Seahawk to hover in place while he goes to secure cargo in the back or have a leisurely cup of tea, though Mark says he rarely leaves the cockpit. Sitting in this machine is a dream come true for the little boy in me, though unlike the time I was five years old and got to sit in a fire engine for the first time, I manage to keep from wetting my pants.

A conspiracy that Oliver Stone has yet to reveal involves the fact that the world's largest single bowling alley proprietor is the U.S. military. There's a bowling alley on nearly every base, and an active league culture—though participation is sometimes disrupted by deployments.

After a brief demonstration of the borrowed night-vision goggles in Amy and Mark's backyard (incidentally, these things are so cool that I actually did wet myself upon seeing the illuminated eyeballs of dozens of creatures watching us in the woods behind the Newkirk home), we bowl a game at Jackson Naval Air Station's Freedom Lanes and Gutterball Grill.

"Are you a sailor?" the man at the front desk asks, and for a moment I fear I need military credentials to bowl. And then I hear him mutter something like, "You could sail my ship anytime," and realize he is hitting on me, not screening me. Not exactly what I expected, but at least I learn that "don't ask/don't tell" apparently doesn't apply to the bowling alleys on base.

A bowling alley fits particularly well on a military base, as most of the buildings look like one from the outside anyway—low-slung industrial buildings without a lot of windows. Like a hangar or a mess hall or a barracks, a bowling alley is designed and built for a specific purpose, and so form follows function. There's no need for architectural flourishes, and there are better things to spend taxpayer money on than grand design. Still, the inside is not tangibly different from any bowling alley I've visited, which is the point of having a recreation facility like this on base: to give people who've sacrificed a normal suburban life in favor of one with an increased chance of taking hostile fire a sense of normalcy every now and then. There are families here; there are couples on dates; there are guys' nights taking place. There is a slightly higher percentage of short, buzzed hairstyles than among the general public, and this is the first time it's crossed my mind that if I outscore my opponent he may be inclined to use Mom's Honda for target practice as I leave town. But aside from that, I may as well be on Main Street, USA, with a strip mall with a Gap across the street instead of a hangar with torpedo-dropping helicopters.

The next morning I climb into the cockpit of Mom's Honda and drive south toward Miami.

Miami: palm trees and hot sand beaches with models as far as the eye can see. Miami: Little Havana and the sights, sounds, and smells of Cuba imported with a steamy Latin flair that says "sexy and mysterious." Miami: hip nightclubs and trendy restaurants filled with daring food and beautiful people. Mike Walsh's Miami: an inland bowling alley on a street filled with chain restaurants and low-cost motels.

The bowling alley is called Bird Bowl, and it is as full and enlivened as any South Beach nightclub, though the lights are a bit brighter and, mercifully, the patrons are a bit more clothed. All of the lanes are occupied, so I go to the bar, a circular counter that faces the lanes on one side and curves into a dark, smoky lounge on the other. I sit down on the lanes side and strike up a conversation with a girl sitting on one of the bar stools. Her name is Courtney.

As often happens when I start talking to a female at a bar, a number of people stop by to see if Courtney needs help getting rid of me. While normally I would take some offense at such intrusion, in this case I understand and appreciate the watchful eyes: Courtney is eleven years old.

What drew me to her, aside from her proximity to the beer taps, was that she was playing the flute. Not for entertainment, mind you—the jukebox in the lounge and the conversations and pins crashing on the lanes would drown out any woodwind—but for practice for her middle school's band.

"We have our Christmas concert coming up," she explains. "My parents have their bowling league Tuesday nights, so sometimes I have to practice here or do my other homework." The sheet music she is rehearsing from is propped up on the bar alongside the High Life I'm trying carefully not to spill on it on one side and a video gambling machine of some sort on the other.

What's happening here isn't neglect or the endangering of a minor—quite the opposite. Courtney is far from unwatched here, as the parade of suspicious onlookers asking why I'm talking to her reminds me. (Prior to speaking with Courtney I found her mother on a nearby lane and asked her permission to talk with the first eleven-year-old flutist I'd seen in some forty bowling alleys.) There is a handful of other kids here, some playing arcade games, others bellied up to the snack bar, and all are under the watchful eye of the greater bowling community, especially while their parents are taking their turn.

As it turns out, I'm the one who needs protection anyway. Courtney is an inquisitive pre-teen and quickly has me on the ropes with her own line of questioning.

"Why would you want to bowl in every state?

"Don't you miss your family?

"Don't you have a girlfriend?

"Don't you have a job?

"Why are you doing this again?"

I look for help on the business side of the Bird Bowl bar and find it in Pat Ogden, a middle-aged woman with strawberry-blond hair and a wide, narrow-lipped smile. For twenty-five years she's worked here in some capacity, and she knows everyone, what they drink, how they bowl. Seeing that I'm outmatched and on the losing end of an interrogation, she gives me an out by asking to hear Courtney play what she's been rehearsing. I move to the other, darker side of the bar. There I meet a bearded man wearing a torn jacket and nursing a cola. His name is Rick.

"My father died here in 1989," he says, shortly after introductions. "He was talking and watching some friends bowl when he just slumped over in his chair, without a word, and his heart stopped."

Rick was at home at the time.

"We hadn't been talking—it had been a couple of years—and we weren't on too great of terms, I guess. But at the very moment he died I felt a cool breeze blow through the house. When I look back on it, in some way I think that was my old man making peace with me."

Rick doesn't seem to care if I believe him or stick around to hear more. He speaks matter-of-factly and, despite a tale of hardship, without woe, complaint, blame, pride, or self-pity.

"I spent a lot of years laying carpet, working one hundred hours a week. I went from making zero money to making tons of it. I started doing cocaine to keep up with the work pace. I kicked the habit once only to start it again." He's now been clean several years and here at Bird Bowl is not drinking anything stronger than a Coca-Cola.

Rick and his adult son are currently living together in what Rick calls a room not far from here; his son works at the adjoining arcade.

"I took out a mortgage on the house my parents left me to lend some friends money, and they didn't pay me back all the way," Rick explains. "I don't hold it against them, though."

He tells a few more stories of drug and drink–induced brushes with death, third-story windows he's fallen or been thrown out of, and various things he's stupefied to look back on. With a sense of gratitude for being alive he ends by apologizing for "rambling."

"I'm not even sure how I've managed to stay alive to tell these stories."

His son arrives after completing his work shift, and the two leave Bird Bowl for the room they're sharing. I follow shortly thereafter and find my own for the night.

There is only one road to Key West. It begins off the tip of the Floridian peninsula and shoots through all of the other keys (Largo, Islamorada, Big Pine, and the Lower Keys) at a maddeningly slow pace, before ending on the island Ernest Hemingway and Jimmy Buffett made famous.

Having arrived exactly twenty minutes after the sunset that the gas station attendant in Miami had told me was a "must-see" has perhaps spoiled my perspective on Key West from the outset. Or maybe I'm just cranky from stretching a 160-mile drive into a five-hour marathon due to a road designed for the leisurely island attitude. Or perhaps I'm having second thoughts about adding so much unnecessary time and mileage to my trip by coming here. But really, does an island that measures only 4.2 square miles really need this many T-shirt shops?

It must be a booming business. There are shops selling paintings, seashells, postcards, shrimp cookbooks, jewelry, and other trinkets that would qualify as "souvenirs" if only for the fact that they say the words "Key West" or have some other reference to the island somewhere on them. But the most available product is the 100 percent cotton T-shirt printed with a half-witted proclamation. Store window after store window is filled with them, and racks of them spill onto the sidewalks. The most popular, judging by its prominent placement in nearly every shop window, reads: "FBI: Female Body Inspector." This is the shirt for the man who has never seen a naked woman. A close second in popularity is a shirt that poses in bold black and red lettering the question: "Who Farted?" This is also available on hats and on underwear, though when applied to boxer shorts the phrase is modified to read: "Farting is my way of saying I love you."

Those windows that aren't filled with small-minded T-shirts are

filled with people wearing them, drinking lager and daiquiris and staring slack-jawed as the Duval Street foot and car traffic passes them by.
Rather than let my mood get the best of me, I decide to join rather
than judge them, and purchase a T-shirt and wear it out of the store.
I am warmly welcomed at Hog's Breath Saloon, receiving high fives
from the well-lubricated patrons as they read my new garment's announcement that "I'm with stupid."

There is an arrow below the phrase, and it points downward.

With the hope of getting a less tourist-centric view of the Florida
Keys before I return to the mainland, I stop on Key Largo, where my
friend Gina has put me in touch with her friend Jenny and her fi-
ancé, Marc. Jenny and Marc have agreed to take me in for the night
despite being in the midst of planning the last details of the wedding
ten days from now. After a night in an overpriced motel surrounded
by faceless vacationers, I find their accommodations to have the two
things I need most: a futon and human interaction.

Jenny says she isn't feeling well and decides to stay in for the night.
Marc is playing guitar in a nearby bar, so I go listen to him and meet
some of the locals. (You can spot them by their untainted T-shirts.)
After dinner and a few beers I leave him there and make for the futon,
which is where I'm soundly sleeping hours later when I feel something
alive climbing in with me.

Is that their dog? No, it's not hairy enough to be a dog. I'm too disori-
ented from sleep and beer to think clearly. *Is it—holy shit, it's a person.
The sliding door wasn't locked—is it a vagrant from off the street?* Moving for the first time, I reach out and touch bare skin, though I can't
tell what part of the body it is.

"Jenny?" I say, on one hand hoping it's her ("I'm flattered, but
you're engaged"), and on the other hoping it's not ("I'd really rather
not get killed, seeing as how you're engaged and all"). No answer, but
whoever it is, isn't wearing very much.

"Marc?" I ask, with a similarly conflicted hope and fear. A pair of feet slides onto the pillow under my head, and at the other end of the futon a head comes to rest alongside my feet. As my eyes adjust I determine that my new bedmate is indeed the man I met less than seven hours ago, the man who less than two weeks from now is to wed the woman on the other side of the wall.

Well, this is awkward, I think, chalking Marc's entry to my bed up to inadvertent sleepwalking. I begin debating what course of action I should take. If I wake him, we'll have a really, really awkward moment right now, at 4:00 A.M. Will I have to remind him of who I am? Will he know where he is? What if he's having some violent dream and lashes out at me and we wake the dogs?

I opt not to wake him, hoping that he'll wake and figure it out himself and crawl back to his own bed and neither of us will ever mention it—though he'll always wonder if I noticed he was there.

The walk from his bed to mine must have exhausted him, because Marc falls quickly into a deep, motionless sleep. I take this as a good thing, as it not only delays the certainly impending awkward moment but also keeps him from kicking me in the face. I stare at the ceiling, debating funny things to say if he's still here in the morning and trying to fall asleep. As I settle on, "Good morning, sleepyhead. You sure gave it your all last night," I hear Jenny come out of the bedroom. She leans over the my feet/Marc's head end of the futon.

"Marc? Marc? What are you doing?"

Marc begins to stir, makes a confused sound as he assesses the situation and pieces together how he got here. I'm tempted to sit up and feign horror, covering myself with the blanket and shrieking, "Oh no! She caught us!" but think better of it and instead feign sleep as the two return to their bedroom.

In the morning I pretend to sleep through one of them getting up and leaving for work. The other, I detect, is still in the bedroom. I take a quick shower, drying myself on a towel that I thought had been left out for me but had apparently been designated for the dog, judging by the thick layer of fur that covered it. Dog hair, if you're wondering, is not absorbent. Dripping through my clothes, I scribble a note on a bowling pin and leave it on the coffee table, thanking them for their hospitality and making no mention of strange bedfellows or dog-enhanced towels. Although they were indeed welcoming, I make a mental note to pre-screen any of Gina's lodging recommendations more carefully.

Turning left at Miami, I make a brief stop in Everglades National Park to see alligators up close, then have a swift drive westward on Alligator Alley, the desolate highway that runs through the swampy Everglades and Seminole Indian land between Miami and Naples. A fence lines both sides of the highway, and if you're watching at all you can see gators resting along it, looking for a chance to escape to the roadway and cause an accident.

In Naples I have the quintessential South Florida experience, staying with my retired uncle Sheridan and aunt Alyce in their Naples home. The surrounding neighborhood is all retirees, and when we go to a restaurant I am the youngest person there, staff excluded, by at least thirty years. And I'm dining with the young crowd: it's almost 7:00 when we sit down—the truly old dined at 4:30 and were in bed an hour ago. We dine with a handful of their friends, and our conversation ranges from who's having what surgery when to arguments about which of their friends are still alive. There is no shuffleboard, however, and the nearest bowling alley is surprisingly youthful and crowded when I visit later.

"You think this is crowded," the manager says, "you should see the place during the daytime when we have seniors' leagues."

Of course. There's no time for that, though, as I still have a good five-hour drive to exit Florida, where I've stayed nearly long enough.

On my drive north from Naples, I phone my friend Laura, whose brother Kevin lives in Gainesville, where he is a grad student at the University of Florida.

"Do you think he wants to put me up for the night?" I ask.

Minutes later I've got directions and a couch for the night. To thank Kevin I make him stay up too late the night before an early class, ogling undergraduate women—all of whom look like models due to the university's strict admissions standards—and drinking things with words like "Hurricane," "Gator," and "Swamp" in their names. Kevin makes it through the night and heroically wakes up in time for his class—all without climbing onto the couch with me. Laura moves ahead of Gina on my list of people to recommend housing, and I leave, after eight full days, my twenty-first state.

Georgia ★

THROWING a metaphorical dart at a map of Georgia, I turn off I-75 North and follow Highway 27 toward the town of Americus, county seat of Sumter County and near the birthplaces of Jimmy Carter, Ray Charles, Luther Vandross, and just about everyone else of any repute who came from Georgia. Either the water here is filled with stardust or the locals have a very broad definition of the phrase "from around here."

As I pass the sign denoting the town's border I notice, down a side street, a group of black men standing around a small fire in a gravel lot across the street from a row of closely grouped one-story homes. They're burning the last leaves of autumn, and leafy ashes wisp through the air, caught by a faint, intermittent breeze. I'm not sure what I expect from dropping in on a group of strangers gathered around an early-evening fire drinking cans of beer, but it reminds me a bit of a campfire I might have stood around with friends, watching the glow and sharing a laugh, so I turn left and park a hundred feet from the fire. The men are initially defensive.

"What do you want?" one asks.

"Nothing," I reply, wishing I'd thought of something better. "Just pulling into town on a road trip. What are you guys up to?"

Their defensiveness turns to indifference tinged with mild annoyance, and a speck of confusion about why it is that I've stopped.

"We're burning leaves, having a beer, and are about to go in for dinner," comes the reply.

147

Sensing they're not going to offer me a beer or invite me to dinner (I'd hoped for one or both, though I'm not sure what would compel anyone to invite someone like me in), I ask where the bowling alley is.

"There's no bowling alley in Americus."

"Oh." So much for my metaphorical dart-throwing skills. "Well, then where can a guy go for a beer and some dinner?"

"A white Yankee?" someone clarifies, causing laughter around the fire. Either my Ohio accent or license plates gave me away, I guess.

"Wait a second—do I look white to you?" I kid in return, to more laughter.

"You should go to Pat's Place. They'll treat you good. Up three lights and left on Lee."

The men return to their homes and I to my car, thanking them on the way.

According to a detailed history on its menu, Pat's Place has been a lot of things besides Pat's Place over the years. In fact, though it's always been on the same piece of land, it hasn't always been in Americus. In 1872, the Civil War's scars still quite fresh in the midst of Reconstruction, part of Americus seceded from Americus and called itself Leeton, after Gen. Robert E. Lee. Twelve years later Leeton was reincorporated into Americus. So, when the U.S. Army used the area where Pat's Place now stands as a camp during the Spanish-American War in 1898, it was able to do so in patriotic-sounding Americus, not divisive, secession-evocative Leeton.

By 1969 the plot of land's rich history had shifted to the mundane—if more convenient for purchasing eight-track players—when an electronics store opened on it. Over the next decade it was occupied by businesses called The Yellow Submarine and The Crust and Mug. In 1980 Pat and Judy Spann bought the building and opened Pat's Place that February. Twenty-two years later, it is still very much Pat's Place, as evidenced by the very man's charismatic presence there, hustling food, charming the guests, and bantering with his employees.

"You must be Pat," I reply after the gray-haired man with a thick white beard sends a friendly nod in my direction.

"Yep. Pat Spann." He extends a hand. "What brings you here?"

"I was just driving through," I reply. "Some guys by a fire recommended it."

"Well, welcome to my place. Hope you have a great time."

Having picked a town without a bowling alley, I decide to follow in the U.S. Army's footsteps and set up camp at Pat's Place for the night. Pat, the consummate host, invites me to sit down with his extended family, who are gathered there for a birthday. As luck would have it, Judy Spann's cousin Clare makes up for the town's lack of a bowling alley by sharing a bowling story of her own.

"My first husband was my high school sweetheart," she says fondly. "We were married for ten years when he was killed in a car crash."

Sometime thereafter she was introduced to a Danish man and married him "perhaps too quickly."

"He was always doing things that made me angry," she continues. "One night I went bowling to blow off some steam and rolled a two eighty. The manager came over and insisted I join a league, but I told him I was just there to vent."

"Clare, even professional bowlers don't often roll scores like that," I tell her. "Maybe you should get back together with Sven or whatever his name is and stick it out for the bowling inspiration. You could dominate the bowling tour!"

"Nope. I'm done with him. That's why I came back to Georgia. I've decided I'm only getting involved with men who have at least two names," as in Billy-Ray or Joe-Bob, "and are from south of the Mason-Dixon Line and east of the Mississippi."

It's interesting for me to be called a Yankee, and to hear the Mason-Dixon Line invoked at all, let alone as a dating criterion. As I had learned my history north of it, my perspective is that the Civil War and the events leading to it were terrible and unfortunate, but it's settled now. Granted, we shouldn't ignore that it happened, or have anything but respect for those who fought it. And I don't think Clare was advocating that the outcome should have been different—she was just being humorous about her new rules for dating, like someone who swears off lawyers after breaking up with one. But it's telling, and important to acknowledge, that a line on a map erased some 150 years ago is still used by those on one side of it for self-definition. Outside of this context I doubt I would ever think of myself as a Yankee or a northerner, but I've been defined that way to some extent by my friends around the campfire and here at Pat's. It doesn't seem particularly harmful, nor derogatory. I'd just never seen the fifty states as anything but a unified nation with a largely shared perspective.

On Thanksgiving eve I bowl in Atlanta with Kara Fitzsimmons, my former Wienermobile partner Courtney's sister. Neither of us is angry enough with someone named Sven to bowl a 280, though the amount of High Life we ingest makes it a challenge to know exactly what our scores were.

The next day is Thanksgiving, and Kara's friend extends to both of us an invitation to dine with her family. This spares me the fate I'd feared would be mine when I saw the holiday drawing near: a Thanksgiving Day meal at a truck stop or a Waffle House. Prior to realizing I could make it to Atlanta in time for the holiday I had begun to fool myself into thinking Thanksgiving alone on the road wouldn't be so bad. I'd regale the other lonely souls at Waffle House with travel tales and they'd offer me their cigarettes and show me photos of their kids. We'd play songs on the jukebox and sing along, laughing and sharing fellowship as we realize that, when you really think about it, we all may be having Thanksgiving alone, but we're really *together*. We'd exchange contact information and every year we'd send one another letters reminiscing about the best Thanksgiving ever.

Kara's friend's home is about an hour's drive from Atlanta, and Kara and I stop at a Waffle House on the way for a cup of coffee to go.

I pause to look around at my imagined best friends for life, wondering what could be if I waved Kara on and spent the day here. Would it be as wondrous and inspiring as I imagined? Sitting at the counter is a fifty-something man with gray stubble and a flannel shirt staring too much and too balefully at the nervous young waitress. Three booths are occupied by one person each, and no one is making eye contact with anyone else for the shame of having no one with whom to spend this holiday. The grill cook, who in my morality play would serve us impromptu off-the-menu creations gratis to make it feel a little more like home, audibly sighs at the cheese-covered hash browns he's about to plate.

"Drive. Fast. Get us away from here!" I beg Kara when I rejoin her in the car. Within minutes we arrive to a feast and friendly, if new, faces who shower us with kindness and all the gravy we can manage. And so on this Thanksgiving I'm most thankful for Southern hospitality. Or, as we call it north of the Mason-Dixon Line, hospitality.

★ Alabama

MY first memory of Dean Youmans is his laugh. We were in an Oscar Mayer conference room during Hot Dog High, the rigorous two-week training session for new Hotdoggers. Thirty loud, overachieving extroverts were milling around munching on bacon-wrapped sausage or whatever meat-laden snack was served between the Refueling Your Wienermobile lesson and the What to Say When Someone Asks If You Sleep in the Wienermobile seminar (answer: "It's not a weenie-bago"). In one corner of the room, Dean was telling someone a story about eating a tomato sandwich. As uninteresting as that sounds in itself, you should know that the story had no plot, lesson, funny and/or unexpected twists, nor was there a dramatic climax. Yet the way Dean told it, with a slow southern drawl, his eyes wide as they looked from the mimed sandwich in his hands to the faces of his audience, and his sincere, joy-filled laugh made the story riveting. By the end of it I wanted nothing more than to eat a tomato sandwich, dripping tomato juice on my T-shirt and laughing about it just like Dean did. His ability to speak so enthusiastically of something so simple is born of an uncommon optimism, one that is contagious and unendingly enviable. It is this I look forward to on my way to stay with Dean and his soon-to-be wife, Jill, in Decatur, Alabama.

Though Dean and I haven't kept in regular contact, I give him partial credit and/or blame for my quitting work to take this adventure. When I lived in Chicago, he would come through town working on some promotional tour that took him to festivals throughout the country, or just for a visit in between trips to Costa Rica or Cambodia. For me, listening to his travel stories at night and then sitting in conference rooms or on the phone at work all the next day was another big, metaphoric tomato sandwich. I needed to get out and live such a life as Dean's.

Between bowling and failing to get the grill lit for dinner (a surprise to me, since Dean had spent over a year touring the country in a tractor-trailer shaped like a giant grill and on which he cooked daily), he and Jill share with me their wedding plans—a ceremony at Hemingway House, one of the bona fide nice spots in Key West.

"Bring me back a T-shirt."

Exploring the area surrounding Decatur takes me to Hartselle, Alabama, and Family Lanes. Wes Moore is the only other person there. He is a large, round man in his twenties wearing a black cowboy hat, and his T-shirt reads "Hartselle" across the top and "Pepsi Cola YABA"—Young American Bowling Alliance.

"One time I was working about this time of day and was the only one in here," he tells me. "All of a sudden a guy comes in off the street all out of breath and asks if there's a phone he can use. I point him to the pay phone, and he calls me a 'honky piece of shit,' then runs back out the door.

"The police came in a few minutes later and asked if I'd seen anyone suspicious. Turns out he was being held under suspicion of murder and had just escaped from jail."

It's much quieter in the place now.

"We'll get a decent crowd tonight, but not like we used to," Wes says. The familiar refrain.

It's not just the bowling alley that seems down: the people in the gas station where I stop for a drink and directions and those in the fast-food joint where I grab lunch seem somewhat depressed as well. This is my impression, that Hartselle suffers from "dying small town syndrome," until I come across a couple of ten-year-old kids wrestling in their front yard. As I drive past, the leaf pile next to them springs to life.

"Yarrrgh!!!" three more kids scream as they erupt from the foliage in an attempt to surprise and frighten me. I return the favor by slamming on the brakes and quickly getting out of the car, hoping to evoke sheer terror in them for an instant before laughing to let them know I'm only kidding. Any initial fear they have is quickly overcome when they see my build and realize they outnumber me five-to-one.

"Let me get this straight," I address them. "You're hiding in a leaf pile on a side street waiting for cars to drive by so you can jump up and scare them?"

"Yep," says the ringleader. All are in knit caps, plaid shirts, and sweatshirts, sloppily layered for ultimate range of movement and warmth.

"That's awesome," I say. "I used to do that with my buddy Morgan in Ohio."

They don't seem terribly impressed—they knew it was fun without my saying so. A woman pulls up in a car, mother to two of the kids.

"Are they bothering you?" she asks, just as much to make sure they haven't caused any trouble as to make sure I'm not some kidnapper.

"Quite the opposite," I explain. "Just reminded me of myself when I was their age."

"My brothers used to do that, too," she says.

That night Dean takes me to the Hard Dock Café and regales me with his latest travel stories, each one a tomato sandwich unto itself. I make notes of places to eat and things to see as I retrace some of his old routes. A band is playing wedding reception music, tired classics like "Play That Funky Music" and tired newer songs like Pink's "Get the Party Started," all of which come across rather peculiarly being sung by a woman dressed in a turtleneck and sweater with Christmas trees and ornaments embroidered on it. "She's a brick . . . house. . . ."

A pair of fifty-something women at a table near ours get drawn into Dean's orbit and chime in when they hear him talking about his wedding plans.

"That's just wonderful," the one named Kathy says. "It's the most wonderful thing in the world." She says this despite her husband dying in an accident and leaving her with two teenaged sons.

"I was really ticked off at him for dying when he did," she says. "It was like, 'Now I've got to raise these kids alone, with no one to talk to about it or help out?' I didn't get any say in the matter."

The kids are now in their midtwenties and she's eager for them to move out and move on so she can begin the rest of her life. Talking about Dean's impending nuptials energizes her. "I might get married again," she says.

Leaving Alabama the next day, I hear Dean's laugh one more time as I get in the car. He and Jill are packing for their honeymoon and a life sure to be filled with more of that laughter and unpredictable adventure. Driving north, the golden hills of southern Tennessee at sunset giving the drive an aesthetic that inspires reflection, I call my friend Cam Conway, another member of our Hotdogger class, to reminisce.

"Cam, do you remember the first day of Hot Dog High, when Dean was telling that story—"

"The fucking tomato sandwich!" Cam interrupts. "I wanted one, too!"

Fighting the urge to stop at the first grocery store I see and buy a fresh tomato and a loaf of bread, I continue toward Clarksville to stay in the home of a complete stranger who'd e-mailed out of the blue. Whatever doubts I have about doing so are tempered by the notion that Dean wouldn't think twice about it. He'd just laugh and see what happens next.

★ Tennessee

ANNA Tomlin seemed friendly enough over e-mail.

"If you want interesting locations in which to bowl," she wrote, having come across my Web site in the wake of my *Caroline Rhea Show* appearance, "I think you should choose Clarksville, TN . . . If you come here you may sleep on my couch (very comfy) and can play with my eight-month-old collie. Hope your trip sees many, many friendly faces."

It was one thing to go bowling with Bowling Spice, a mile from my home and in a city I knew well. It is another thing to spend the night in the home of a stranger who tracked you down via the Internet after seeing you on a C-list talk show. This is the kind of idea that wins a guy a Darwin Award when his body is found hacked up and discarded in a shallow ditch somewhere. The idyllic way the Tennessee hills had looked at sunset has changed, and they now evoke images of Ned Beatty in *Deliverance*; banjo music floods the radio. About an hour outside of Clarksville I pull over to inform loved ones of my whereabouts for the night, just in case.

"Mom, write down this address, and here's the number for the FBI office in Clarksville."

"That's nice, dear. How's the bowling going?"

Anna opens the door, her dog nosing around her legs. "Hi, Mike! Welcome to Clarksville. We're glad you made it." Her brother, cooking dinner in the kitchen, smiles and waves hello.

"My entire family knows where you live, understand?"

"Come on in; we're just sitting down to dinner. This is our neighbor, Ben. He's a specialist at the Fort."

Fort Campbell is an Army base just across the border in Kentucky, and is home to the 101st Airborne Division, first put into combat on D-day when they parachuted in behind German lines at Utah Beach. Ben has just returned from eight months in Afghanistan; he'd been among the first wave of troops sent over to hunt Al Qaeda and oust the Taliban from power. He describes his role as a foot soldier over a dinner of meat loaf and green beans.

"You know the guy in the movies wearing a big radio with a long antenna on his back? The one who always gets killed first and then the movie hero uses the radio while it's still on his back?"

"Yeah!" I say in recognition. "The hero just rolls the corpse over and radios in an air strike."

"Yep. I'm that corpse."

His wife, Billie Ann, laughs hollowly at her husband's sardonic description of his day job. She's heard it before, but it doesn't make her any more comfortable with the notion that he is a prime target among targets because the radioman is always near the commander.

"The first time we took live fire was during Anaconda," he says, referring to an operation planned to cut off the head of the "snake" of Al Qaeda and Taliban forces. "We heard a shot, and none of us reacted. We looked around to see who AD'd—accidentally discharged."

Then they heard another shot, and someone noticed a puff of smoke come off a rock nearby.

"Then everyone's reflexes and training kicked in. We all hit the ground, spread out, and began returning fire. The problem with that is it gave the enemy a better idea of our location, and they began firing mortars, landing on all sides of us and getting closer each time as they adjusted their aim.

"We called in an air strike, and the mortar fire became less frequent and less accurate, meaning that we were killing them and that less experienced fighters were firing the mortars. Eventually we overtook them."

"That must be unbelievably exciting," I say, unable to find a better word and slightly in awe of Ben's strength and courage.

"It was. It was pretty grim, too, inspecting the enemy bodies after the fight," he says.

The Afghanistan front of the war on terror has barely been in the news while he's telling me these stories; most of the talk is about the buildup to an impending war in Iraq. "That stuff is still going on over there," Ben says. "Every day. It's a crime that those guys aren't getting the same credit for defending our nation that we got for going over first."

In front of the Christmas tree, Ben lays out his collection of Afghani currency, a scrapbook of photos of his unit, and the bayonet from an enemy AK-47, a grim souvenir that had been designed, in principle, to kill him.

On that note, Anna, her brother Ryan, and I leave to bowl a game at the Pinnacle, a newish bowling alley near but not on the base. After some friendly sibling rivalry on the lanes and a night on the couch (comfy, as advertised), I depart for Memphis.

Ben's stories stick with me, and that night at Billy Hardwick's All Star Lanes I meet a Vietnam vet named Bill.

"I've been shot at, too," he says after I tell him Ben's story. "Twice. Once while I was working at a bar, and once while I was giving a buddy of mine a hard time."

"And he shot at you?"

"He was fooling around with a girl during an R and R weekend away from our base in North Carolina. They were behind a tree on a riverbank and I started throwing rocks and things toward them. Kind of like bothering a dog while he's eating. I learned my lesson."

In Memphis I stay with Dave, whom I'd met in Milwaukee when he was sharing the corporate apartment I stayed in there. Newly relocated here, he's taken no time fully stocking his bar, and we have a punishing night of drinking that starts in his condo, proceeds to Beale Street, and returns entirely too late.

Looking and feeling my best the next morning, I perform my bowling and Miller-plugging routine for a local news camera at Jillian's, a chain restaurant/arcade/bowling alley/club. That night I return to All Star Lanes, where I see the report broadcast on the 5:30 news.

"Recognize that guy?" I ask the bartender when I appear on the screen, feeling particularly large for my britches.

He glances at the TV, checks to make sure the ice cooler he just filled with ice still has ice in it, and puts me back where I belong. "Nope."

The next day is rainy, so I cheer myself by visiting places where famous people died: Graceland, Elvis Presley's remarkably underwhelming home, and the Loraine Motel, where Martin Luther King, Jr., was killed. An odd contrast, to be sure, and not much to offer in terms of cheering, though the details about Elvis's more unusual behavior make it worthwhile. For instance: the King once insisted that he and his entourage be served meat loaf for dinner every night for six weeks. The audio recording provided on headphones during the tour plays down facts like this as merely cute idiosyncrasies and not signs of gross megalomania. Little mention is made of the whole dying-on-the-toilet-while-pumped-full-of-drugs thing. And not one hint of irony or acknowledgment of bizarreness is made at Elvis's scribbling out a rambling five-page letter to President Nixon on American Airlines stationery requesting (and being granted) a meeting to be made an unofficial agent in the Bureau of Narcotics and Dangerous Drugs.

More disappointing than the whitewashing of Elvis's abnormal behavior, however, is that the King's mansion has no bowling alley. I had been fairly optimistic that the estate's caretakers would have let me roll a game if I explained to them my quest to find the America that Elvis so dearly loved. Alas, even the racquetball court has been transformed into a trophy room filled with gold records and show costumes. If ever there was a bowling alley at Graceland, it is long gone with its former owner.

And so I must be long gone from Memphis. South through Mississippi lies the halfway point in terms of number of states, if not time and miles. The Big Easy, New Orleans, awaits.

Louisiana ★

MY experience in Key West has set my expectations for New Orleans low, and the fact that the sky has been dumping rain for the past two hours of my drive adds to my melancholy mood as I arrive alone in another party town.

A cheap hotel room in the French Quarter compounds this feeling. I arrive well after dark, and outside my window a handful of drunken businessmen pretending it's Mardi Gras make the whole town seem hollow at first impression. Wandering Bourbon Street alone only emphasizes this: nothing so empty as buying a red-punch and grain alcohol–doused Hurricane from a stand with no line on a nearly deserted street. "Show me your tits," I mutter to myself, and choke down the too-sweet mixture. This irony cheers me until I hear one of the businessmen from before shout the same phrase with sincerity at one of the only other souls on the street, a woman dodging raindrops with a heavy bag of groceries. The Big Easy isn't always.

The next day, walking up the stairs to Mid City Lanes, I'm struck by the feeling that this is no place to spend an afternoon. I'm even less enthused when I reach the top: it is nearly dark inside, and none of the typical activity of a weekday bowling alley is taking place. No seniors' leagues, no group of locals chatting it up around cups of coffee, not even a lane-oiling machine dressing the lanes for future activity. The woman behind the counter is the only sign of life.

"Welcome to Rock n' Bowl," she says, smiling.

I see neither rock nor bowl, but she seems friendly and sincere enough. I learn that her name is Becky; her brother John Blancher owns the place, which is known to the locals as Rock n' Bowl.

"John bought the place about ten years ago," Becky says. "It was almost out of business, so he got a real deal on it."

Before freeways were built and began routing traffic around it, Rock n' Bowl was on the main drive into New Orleans; it was one of the first sites visitors saw on their way to the party. Between tourist traffic being rerouted and leagues generally falling off everywhere, the place was struggling. Blancher, as Becky tells it, bought the place for a good cause.

"He got it as a place for my parents to spend time and work, and for me to fall back on just after I'd gotten divorced," she says. "But about three months after he bought it, it was looking like he would have to close it. There was just no business."

Then something happened: people started dancing.

John had started booking bands for weekend nights, and people started flocking to the makeshift dance floor between the bowling lanes and the bar. He expanded music to nearly every night of the week: cover bands, swing bands, eighties bands, and country bands. Today is Thursday, which typically means zydeco music that draws the biggest crowd of Rock n' Bowl's week.

With no music and no one to dance with this afternoon, I ask for some shoes, and Becky assigns me to a lane in the middle of the house. The wood on the lane looks like it's been used for target practice, pocked with divots and scars from years of limited maintenance and drunken bowlers. A sign near the lanes disavows Mid City Lanes, its agents, subsidiaries, beer vendors, and affiliates, from responsibility if you bowl with your own fancy, expensive ball here and it gets damaged by the equipment. The pinsetter at my lane's end creaks and shakes like a washing machine trying to pull free of the wall. I search for a ball from the nearest rack, at first trying to find one without any chips or cracks, then, realizing the futility of that exercise, select the one with the most. It is black, and the thumbhole has a jagged edge that scrapes my knuckle with every roll. I bowl my worst game in twenty-five states, an 81, and two things become clear: the music really is more important than the bowling here, and I will have to return later for dancing.

I spend the afternoon walking along Lake Ponchartrain, then at Café Du Monde eating its famous powdered sugar–covered beignets—essentially deep-fried pastries that taste like sin. I have five orders to fortify my soul before returning to Rock n' Bowl. When I arrive there at 8:00, people are already filing in.

Though I'm not at all hungry, I order the gumbo, which John Blancher confidently (if slyly) describes as "the best gumbo you'll ever eat in a bowling alley," and sit down at a table near the stage to eat it. I am not alone for long.

"Do you mind if I join you for a few minutes?" A middle-aged woman with jet-black hair wearing a black blazer with yellow lapels and high shoulders is standing above me; I invite her to sit.

"I'm Carmella," she says, offering her hand. She's not trying to pick me up; the other tables are all full. "Lots of people come here alone," she explains. Apparently the dancing becomes an egalitarian free-for-all in which everyone rotates partners throughout the night.

The band is tuning up; air breathes through an accordion and the drummer taps his snare drum as he tightens the head. The crowd is massing and Carmella and I are joined by her friend Mary.

"I'm an actress," she says, shoulders thrown back with her best smile shooting out from beneath wildly curly brown hair, adding, "It ain't easy lookin' cheap." She also teaches in a Catholic school.

"One time I needed to take off work to play the part of a disreputable woman," she sets herself up. " 'Father Larry,' I told the principal, 'can you cover my class this afternoon? I have to go play a washed-up hooker.' "

Relating the story about how she promised some men they could each take a pair of her panties if they helped her move her furniture, she closes with, "I had to go out and buy a bunch because I don't wear the stupid things!"

The band strikes up and Carmella pulls me to the floor, doing her best to teach me zydeco dancing while I step on her feet. She trades me out to Mary, who talks the whole time but somehow still manages to move her feet faster than I can bruise them. The dance floor's perimeter is lined with women. The few men who've come out tonight are in high demand; they're aware of this and make a conscious effort to give every gal a turn. It's all very congenial, and there is a smooth rhythm among the more experienced dancers despite the hectic pace of the washboard keeping time and the accordion's cajoling melody.

I spin out to take a breather and run into Lucien, a seventy-two-year-old Cajun wearing a plaid shirt and a giant smile. "I never miss a Thursday," he says, grabbing a young woman for the next dance.

I'm told that there's a soul missing tonight, known simply as "Fluff". Fluff has Down syndrome and works part-time at Rock n' Bowl, carrying a towel to clean up the spills of rookie zydeco dancers like myself. A patron tells me, "He usually sits in with the band and keeps rhythm on a washboard. He gets a big old grin on his face that just spreads throughout the room."

Donna is working behind the bar where I met Becky earlier in the day. In her early twenties, she's the only other person I've met who's been to Americus, Georgia. "Of course I've been to Pat's Place," she says.

As we chat, I notice that the bowling lanes, like the dance floor, have filled. This is the real New Orleans—not that rain and alcohol–soaked sliver I witnessed the night before. Neighbors are talking; old friends are reuniting; young people are doing their best to figure it all out.

I reflect briefly on my journey, which is now exactly half over: twenty-five states behind me and just as many in front. I point this milestone out to Donna, who came to New Orleans just a few months ago for Jazzfest and just ended up staying for no reason she can identify. She aptly comments on that, and on my trip, using words from J. R. R. Tolkien:

"Not all those who wander are lost."

The words stay with me, inspiration despite my getting lost in Orleans Parish Friday morning as I begin the second half of my great wander.

★ Mississippi

THE swelling sense of accomplishment at finishing twenty-five states deflates as I study the atlas and realize that this was the easy part. East of the Mississippi the country is relatively compact and, for me, relatively full of familiar faces. Familiar faces willing to house me free of charge, no less. West of the river is a vast, lonely place by comparison. Example: Rhode Island measures thirty-seven miles from east to west—hardly more than a gallon of gas for an aerodynamic, fuel-efficient machine like Mom's Honda. Wyoming, by contrast, stretches 364 miles from east to west. Even with a healthy tailwind, that kind of expanse will call for more than a full tank to cross. This is not to mention the impact distance will have on variables beyond gas. More land to cross means more days on the road, which means more nights of lodging to secure and more meals to consume. And more nights in bowling alleys. And thus more games to buy, more shoes to rent, and more Miller beer to buy with Miller's money.

Miller's check has finally arrived, a much-needed infusion of income. After some rough analysis conducted on the back of a powdered sugar–covered napkin at Café Du Monde I've determined that in an average week—in small, eastern states, mind you—I'm burning money at an alarming rate.

Three tanks of gas: $90.

Meals and sundries at $20/day, conservatively: $140 per week.

One night of lodging when a Motel 6 is the closest thing I have to a friend in town: $35.

Opportunity costs for nights of lodging with friends (bowling, dinners, et cetera) over the course of a week: $100.

Beer: well, this varies and is nearly impossible to track with any reliability, but if we estimate $15/night, libations add up to somewhere in the neighborhood of $105 a week.

I may have inflated the gas costs and understated the beer expenditures, but if those rounding errors cancel each other out I'm still spending $470 a week. That's $1,880 a month. Divided into Miller's $8,500, that gives me four and a half months. It's been two and a half months since I bowled in Columbus on my mother's birthday. Time and money are of the essence.

With this in mind, spending as little time and money as possible in Mississippi becomes my priority. Driving north up I-55, past Mc-Comb, Brookhaven, and Crystal Springs, I select the most appropriate song in my music collection to listen to while driving through Mississippi. It is called "Mississippi." With lyrics like "feeling like a stranger nobody sees," Bob Dylan's writing befits a wandering, solitary traveler with no certain destination. All the more so for a wandering solo traveler without the resources to stay in Mississippi for any considerable duration: each refrain ends with the narrator's deep-felt regret that he "stayed in Mississippi a day too long."

I pull over for gas in Jackson and fill Mom's Honda's tank. Across the street from the gas station is Lawril Lanes, which will cost one cent in gas and forty-five seconds in time to reach. I put $28.60 in the tank, which leaves $6.00 in my wallet.

"How much for shoes and one game?" I ask the teenager at the front desk.

"Five-fifty," he replies.

With two quarters left over for gumballs or a game of Ms. Pac-Man, I lace up and roll a strike. A crowd of at least a dozen girls cheers wildly behind me, leaning over the four-foot wall that separates the bowling area from the rest of the bowling center. There's a certain "Beatlemania" element to their semi-hysterical cheering and I begin to wonder what intangible "it" I have that inspires such enthusiasm.

They are ten years old, but it's flattering nonetheless. They cheer my next roll, which leaves two pins standing. They erupt again when I pick up the spare, and yet again when I leave an unmakeable split in the third frame. I can do no wrong. By now I am playing to the crowd like an NFL player, raising my arms to encourage the noise and all but running to the wall and doing the "Lambeau Leap" into the crowd. I miss the spare and they cheer again.

The girls are here for a school-sponsored outing, part of a phys-ed program or a field trip for a history lesson or such: Bowling and the Decline of Society for Fifth Graders, perhaps. Whatever the reason, my presence provides just enough distraction to make their last minutes here entertaining. And their presence provides just enough reason for me to put on a show.

I make a slow, overly dramatic approach in the fourth frame. Creeping toward the foul line like I'm trying to surprise it, I extend my left arm straight out just like Bill Murray in the movie *Kingpin*, drawing the ball as high above my head on the backswing as my right shoulder socket will allow. I nail a strike. I turn around, take two quick steps, and fling myself to the floor, sliding on both knees to the end of the approach, looking up triumphantly and throwing my arms into the air like a figure skater finishing a routine. I await showers of praise and roses from the adoring gallery.

Only the adoring gallery has disappeared. I can see them walking out the front door to board a waiting yellow bus that has just arrived to return them to school. The realization that I was merely a distraction while they killed time waiting for the bus sinks in as I kneel there in front of the lane. The guy cleaning the nacho station at the snack bar gives me a blank stare, then goes back to scraping away.

I complete my game quietly and without fanfare, take my two quarters, and rejoin the northbound traffic on I-55, piloting Mom's Honda to Memphis and then across the Mighty Mississippi into Arkansas, continuing north toward St. Louis.

Missouri ★

MY niece Katy and her brother Ben, who are nine and five respectively, have been waiting for their chance at me on the bowling lanes since I started this trip. I'm barely able to stretch my legs after the drive to their home in St. Louis before they're dragging me back to the car to drive to Tropicana Lanes for a Sunday afternoon showdown.

"We're going to beat you, Uncle Mike," Ben informs me, which earns him a headlock and a noogie. Katy keeps quiet (and out of reach of my knuckles) but displays a quiet confidence that says she's been practicing.

Tropicana has fifty-two lanes according to the forty-foot-tall neon sign that stands in its parking lot. A large, glowing arrow streaks up one side of the pole and makes a sharp turn across the top, guiding passersby in for a game. "Do you guys want me to beat you on just one of the lanes, or on all fifty-two?" I ask my opponents as we arrive there.

"Just one," Katy slips.

It is no contest. I crush the two grade-schoolers, despite their heavy reliance on the gutter-guarding bumpers. Ben has some trouble lifting the six-pound ball with one hand, and so uses both arms to carry it to the foul line, where he throws himself to the ground as he releases the ball each time. The method provides some momentum, but he still scores well under 100. Katy's rolls are more graceful, but again, no match for my technique and raw strength. Bragging rights and taunting privileges are mine for the duration of my stay.

"Just for that I get your room while I'm here, Ben." To the victor, et cetera.

"Come join me on the road trip for a week or so. We'll do Savannah, Miami, New Orleans. It'll be a blast."

So went my conversations with my friend Owen when I'd stayed with him in Vermont. At the time it looked like his winter break from school would coincide with the time I'd be in those places—the kind of places where it would be fun to spend winter break. As it turns out, the trip's pace has been brisker than I'd thought—good for me and my finances, bad for Owen and his break. Nonetheless, he lands this morning in St. Louis ready to join me for such school break hotspots as Iowa, Minnesota, and the Dakotas. In the unlikely event he has to write a "What I Did on My Winter Break" report upon his return to business school, I put some education on the itinerary by securing a behind-the-scenes visit to the International Bowling Museum & Hall of Fame.

The IBM&HOF is downtown, across the street from the St. Louis Cardinals baseball stadium and practically in the shadow of the landmark Gateway Arch that is a symbol of this city and a tribute to America's westward expansion, a monument known the world over. To keep pace with such attractions, the IBM&HOF went big: it's a three-story, fifty-thousand-square-foot museum. And as it happens, it's closed to the public on the day of our visit. Jim Baer, the museum's director of marketing, has kindly agreed to give us a tour.

We start with the Time Tunnel, known as Tenpin Alley. It is a three-dimensional time line of bowling's history with large graphic presentations on one wall and full-scale dioramas on the other. One presents the findings of the late Sir Flinders Petrie, a British anthropologist, who cites crude bowling implements found in an Egyptian grave circa 3200 B.C. as proof that the sport's origins go back at least five thousand years. Compared with golf, which only dates back to the

fifteenth century A.D., bowling looks like the sport steeped in history
and tradition. Leaving room for future archeological discoveries, one
exhibit speculates that maybe, just maybe, Cro-Magnon man was a
bowler. (Having learned my lesson about maligning bowling in front
of industry luminaries in Milwaukee, I refrain from telling Jim that
I'm pretty sure I saw Cro-Magnon warming up for his league at Tropicana Lanes the other day. I consider it a measure of how much I've
grown on this trip.)

Moving on from Tenpin Alley, we head upstairs to a room filled
with trophies and graphic renderings of bowling's greatest moments.
It is called the Great Moments exhibit. A mural painted on one wall
shows such memorable events as Earl Anthony's breaking of the
million-dollar winnings barrier in 1982 and Andy Varipapa's two
straight All-Star Tournament wins. For a serious bowler these moments might be like the moon landing or the 9/11 attacks: the kind of
event you'll always remember where you were when it occurred. In my
case and certainly Owen's, we're surprised to learn that bowling has
an all-star tournament.

A kiosk in the center of this room houses the Hometown Heroics
exhibit. It consists of an interactive database containing the names of
anyone who has ever bowled a qualifying perfect 300 game. For a 300
game to qualify it must be rolled during official play in a U.S. Bowling Congress–sanctioned league. Should someone bowl a perfect
game, a local representative of the USBC must be notified within
forty-eight hours and the lane conditions verified. The bowler then
gets to fill out an application for a commemorative gift, like a ring or a
watch, from the USBC. By submitting their verified information,
they're enrolled in the Hometown Heroics exhibit. It is a testament to
bowling's popular accessibility that in its Hall of Fame there is a space
immortalizing the sport's average Joes. A farmer in a small midwestern
town who happens to have a good Tuesday night on the lanes can look
up his name and find his score commemorated alongside the great
pros of the game.

The actual Hall of Fame portion of the IBM&HOF is, like most halls of fame, a little dry. The interesting memorabilia and exhibits are all elsewhere, and the fame hall consists of little more than portraits of the inductees. This one is also confusing: there's a separate hall for the PBA/PWBA (Professional Bowlers Association/Professional Women's Bowlers Association), for the ABC (American Bowling Congress—whose membership and inductees overlap considerably with the PBA's), and another for the BPAA (Bowling Proprietors Association of America). There is also a World Bowling Writers section, which makes me think I should maybe be a little more flattering of the sport in my prose. . . .

The basement of the IBM&HOF should be the finale of any visit, under the theory of saving the best for last. Jim briefly shows us the 1930s-era bowling pin–shaped car (a peer of the first Wienermobile, it was used by Ohio-based bowling proprietors to promote the sport), then sets us loose on the four automatic lanes. (There are also four manually set lanes, but with no one there but us we'd have to set our own pins, which no self-respecting bowler would do.)

"Help yourselves to shoes," Jim says before leaving, gesturing behind the counter. "Here's the spray for when you're done."

And we have free reign of our own bowling facility.

We bowl a competitive game, Owen's first since we bowled in Vermont, and then a local news crew arrives. I do my best performance of Miller's talking points, confident that in the land of Budweiser they'll be efficiently edited out. Perhaps the cameraman's King of Beers shirt tipped me off.

Owen and I spray our shoes, say our good-byes to Jim, and vow to make it into the Hometown Heroics exhibit come hell or high water.

The next day I meet with Bill McClellan of the *St. Louis Post-Dispatch*. When I was driving the Wienermobile we met him at a coffee shop and drove to his daughter's school to pick her up. If it is mortifying for a teenager to have a newspaper columnist for a father, there is likely some solace in the fact that most of your peers don't read the paper. Worlds collide, though, when he shows up at your school in a giant orange car with the word "wiener" in its name. She was a good sport, though, and Bill's column about the event was one of the best pieces written during my year with Oscar Mayer.

We meet at Tropicana Lanes for my second visit, and talk over coffee. The resulting column is another good one, though not surprisingly it omits any mention of Miller High Life. It can be hard to sell Miller in Budweiser's hometown. Feeling a little Catholic guilt over not holding my end up of the publicity bargain, I decide to do my part to gain ground for Miller in St. Louis later that night.

My friend Cam Conway takes Owen and me out to dinner and introduces us to Saratoga Lanes, an eight-lane bowling house that opened in 1916—making it the oldest bowling alley west of the Mississippi. It's on the second floor of a streetfront building in Maplewood, an up-and-coming neighborhood dotted with boutique shops selling antiques, designer fashions, and musical instruments. The eight lanes sit side by side on the far right of the room from the entrance, and a handful of pool tables and high-top tables are spread around the near side, with eight-foot-tall windows overlooking the street. A square bar centers the room, enabling the bartender to service the bowlers on one side and those playing pool or waiting their turn on the lanes on the other. Behind each pair of lanes are an L-shaped blue and white bench and a manual scoring table—no electronic scorers allowed at a bowling alley approaching one hundred years in business.

And business appears to be good. There's an hour wait for a lane, which the three of us, predictably, pass drinking High Life. The bartender soon has to go to his reserve cooler and put more of the Milwaukee-made beverage on ice. "We don't sell much Miller beer here," he explains.

By the end of our hour's wait, the crowd has begun to thin and everyone remaining, some twenty people, is drinking High Life. This is what happens at bars often: someone ordering has no particular drink in mind and asks for the first thing he sees. We happen to have a table full of High Life bottles sitting in the line of sight of any bowler ordering tonight, and the appropriateness of the vintage-shaped clear glass bottle catches on. It can't hurt, we observe, that the three best-looking guys in the bar are drinking it.

By the night's end there is no High Life left in the cooler and the puzzled bartender makes a note to increase his order when tomorrow's delivery comes.

The next morning Owen and I depart for the greatest winter break of his life. There's nothing like the Great Plains in December. Small-town Iowa, here we come.

Iowa ★

No one who applies to drive the Oscar Mayer Wienermobile ever does so with the romantic notion that they'll get stationed in the Midwest for twelve months of driving the twenty-seven-foot-long mobile tube steak. I was no exception.

"Can you imagine?" I exclaimed to my friends on campus after securing an interview with Oscar Mayer. "If I get this job, I'll be driving that thing up and down the California coast, going to beaches, learning to surf, going to the Grand Canyon. I've always wanted to see Seattle."

A realist friend of mine then pointed out that there seem to be a lot of Wienermobile appearances in the Midwest.

"California . . . ," I said dreamily, disregarding him and making a note to ask in my next interview if the Wienermobile has storage room for a surfboard.

Shortly after being hired I learned that I would be assigned to the Midwest for the entire year.

My partner, Courtney, and I did our best to take it in stride, but news from the California team was always a little disheartening. The entire fleet of Wienermobiles kept in touch with headquarters and one another via the same voice-mail system used by Oscar Mayer's corporate parent, Kraft Foods. A high-tech system tailored for people in meetings or working remotely in the field most of the day, it was designed for efficient one-to-one communication or leaving messages for a select group of recipients. Naturally, a group of twenty-two-year-old extroverts used it primarily for pranks and boasting.

"Dudes!" a message from the California team would begin. "Just checking in. This afternoon we took a helicopter ride under the Golden Gate Bridge! Hope all's well in Nebraska."

In our replies to such messages, steeped in self-pitying sarcasm, we would brag of how fresh the corn tastes when it's just minutes from being pulled from the stalk. "And you should see the cows. Such gentle creatures." Such was the view from a half-empty glass while employed in the world's greatest job.

We made the most of it, though during my lower moments I'd have to reassure myself that at least I was getting to see the parts of the country I knew I'd never go see on my own . . . unless I decided to go bowl in them during a pre-midlife crisis. And so tonight Owen and I will risk life and limb to return to a place I never thought I'd see again.

The last time I was in Jefferson, Iowa, it was to award a semi-finalist in an Oscar Mayer contest with a ride in the Wienermobile. Jefferson is a town of about four thousand, and after having dinner and walking once around the town square we realized we'd done everything there was to do in Jefferson. Then we spotted a bowling alley.

The bar in front had a few people in it, but the lanes themselves, on the other side of the bar's back wall, were dark and empty as we peeked through the door next to the jukebox into the bowling half of the building.

"Not many people bowling tonight," the woman behind the bar joked as she turned on the lights on the lanes for us to bowl. She was a brunette with a kind face and a welcoming demeanor that made us feel like family despite the fact that the locals were all staring at us, wondering what we could possibly be doing in town. (We'd parked our vehicle a few blocks away.) When Courtney had trouble finding a ball that fit her right, the woman noticed and brought out her personal ball for her to use. It was blue and said "Vickie" on it. Courtney's game improved markedly.

This experience, in this little bowling alley in a tiny, off-the-path town, was one of the catalysts for the trip I'm on now. If a fraction of the bowling alleys I visit across the fifty states are as quaint and inviting, if there are people like Vickie in them, it will be worth having ditched my job and put my life on hold to encounter them.

Tonight, as I attempt to navigate to that same place with Owen using nothing but my memory and an inaccurate map, a dense fog rests on the dark, narrow, unmarked roads between our hotel in Perry, Iowa, and the lanes in Jefferson. About ten feet in front of the front bumper a thick white wall obscures any view of what's ahead. The headlights only make it worse, reflecting off the moisture particles to make them appear impenetrable. More than once I skid Mom's Honda to a halt to avoid tearing into a pasture that suddenly appears in front of us as the road curves sharply in the other direction. Owen, who spent much of the drive from St. Louis talking to his friends who were spending their winter breaks skiing or in tropical latitudes, has been reduced to the same bleak outlook of my Wienermobile voice mails.

"We literally passed a town called Boondocks," he tells one.

"Come on," I try to cheer him. "This is the heartland! The core of America! Embrace it! Look at that farmhouse, the Christmas lights and the smoke from the chimney, it's a real-life Norman Rockwell!"

"Tell me again why we're not in New Orleans right now?"

After some twenty minutes of adding to the inner-car tension by being utterly lost and all but blind in the dark and fog, we find Jefferson. The town is nothing like I remember it, and despite its tiny size I manage to get us lost on the one-square-block town square, spinning off down all four streets before finding the one with the bowling alley on it. Inside, a familiar-looking woman is behind the bar.

"Is your name Vickie by chance?"

It is, but beyond that the place is entirely different. The bar that felt barely open on my last visit is bustling, and the lanes that were dark when I last arrived are furious with chatter and rolling balls.

Vickie vaguely remembers my last visit, and I tell her the nature of my current trip. Owen and I order food and a round of High Lifes at the bar and wait out the league play that's still in full swing on the lanes. While we're waiting for our food, Vickie approaches us excitedly.

"You'd better see this," she says, gesturing Owen and me to get up and look through the service window at the eight lanes on the other side of the wall.

"Larry—in the red cap and gray shirt—is about to roll his twelfth strike."

Twelve strikes in a game is a perfect game, a 300, a ticket to the International Bowling Museum & Hall of Fame. Debates may be had as to where rolling a 300 falls on the sporting feat spectrum—not as hard as pitching a no-hitter but harder than hitting a hole in one—but for most bowlers this is a once-in-a-lifetime achievement.

The bowlers on all eight lanes have stopped and stepped away from their foul lines. The crowded bar has gone quiet, and all eyes are on the tall, muscular forty-six-year-old man in front of lane six. He holds his ball and looks at the pins, checks the position of his feet, and begins his approach. The last eleven times he did this, he knocked down all ten pins.

He does it again. The crowd erupts and swells around him, tousling his hair after knocking off his cap, grown men hardened by years of hard outdoor labor shaking their heads in respectful appreciation. Even Owen and I are high-fiving each other, hugging strangers, and pushing to get close to the biggest hero in town.

"I've been trying to do that for thirty years," he says with subdued pride. His name, for the record, is Larry Gray. "Lefty" to his friends. Tonight, everyone's a friend of Lefty's.

Owen and I return to our seats at the bar just as our meals arrive.

"We're a small town; we do everything big," Vickie says when I remark at the immense portions of our dinners. Indeed: a paradox on a plate, the mini–corn dogs are piled high and spilling off.

Vickie and her husband, John Woodford, bought Spare Time Lanes and Lounge in August of 1997 to do something they loved.

"It's going all right, but it's not easy," John says, setting Owen and me up on a lane after the leagues have gone. "Vickie still works full-time at American Athletic. She makes gym mats all day and then comes over here to help run this place."

The two are outstanding hosts. John has spent the night working the lanes to make sure everyone is happy—and that Larry gets his picture in the paper—while bowling on a team himself. Vickie, in a show of uncalled-for generosity, refuses to let us pay for our meals and our bowling.

If the sense of community is, statistically, gone from America according to the theory of *Bowling Alone,* Jefferson, Iowa, and Spare Time Lanes on Chestnut Street are the exception. Just ask Larry "Lefty" Gray.

AGAIN the Wienermobile casts its oblong shadow on my current adventure. This time it does so by way of a serendipitous phone call from one Russ Whitacre.

Russ managed the Wienermobile program for over fifteen years, practically since the company brought it out of retirement with full-sized college kids instead of Little Oscars at the helm. The job of Wienermobile program manager requires an odd combination of temperaments—part cheerleader, part babysitter, part corporate executive, part air traffic controller, and part drill sergeant, with a little bit of relationship counselor thrown in.

Imagine being responsible for some thirty fresh-out-of-school twenty-two-year-olds driving around the country in quarter-million-dollar vehicles that embody a Fortune 100 company's brand equity. Try sleeping through the night knowing that Mike Walsh is within driving distance of Graceland and has been talking about crashing the gates to get a photo of the Wienermobile on Elvis's front lawn. Try remaining calm when you get a letter, seemingly from a hotel manager, seeking thousands of dollars in damages for a wild party a pair of Hotdoggers threw in one of his hotel's rooms. (The letter was actually an April Fool's joke from me; it nearly got me fired.) Try taking a deep breath and counting to ten when one of your employees gets the high-profile 12.5-foot-tall company car stuck under a twelve-foot-tall bridge in Boston during rush hour—just in time for the evening news and a front-page photo in the *Globe.* For better or worse, the job requires a lot of travel to put out fires and check in on teams to remind them of the more nuanced rules of the road. Like if you get offered a wad of cash to drive a bachelor party around for the night, you should decline it. The upside of all that travel is that it gave Russ an encyclopedic knowledge of things to do, places to eat, and sights to see everywhere from San Francisco, to Saginaw, to Sikeston. His phone call today as we cross the border from Iowa into Minnesota demonstrates that knowledge.

"Oh, you should go to the SPAM Museum in Austin," he says on learning our location. "Just get on Ninety East from where you are. You'll be there in an hour."

Hormel, which makes SPAM, may be a major competitor of Oscar Mayer's, but no one who has spent the last fifteen years managing a program comprised of sending a fleet of wheeled frankfurters on an endless road trip can turn down such an attraction—even if it is providing aid and comfort to the corporate enemy. On Russ's recommendation, and thinking it will add to Owen's "What I Did on My Winter Break" report, we turn right at I-90.

The next time anyone suggests to you that Americans have devolved into a cultural abyss teeming with mass-produced excrement aimed at the lowest common denominator, inform them that we have a museum dedicating 16,500 square feet of valuable farmland to canned meat. And it happens to be an outstanding museum—though one could be forgiven for having low expectations. After all, compared with, say, Abraham Lincoln, SPAM doesn't offer a great deal of rich subject matter on which to build a museum. I mean, how much is there to say about canned meat stuff?

Well, among other things, SPAM was so valuable to the allied forces during World War II that, years after the war he'd led and after he'd served as president, Dwight D. Eisenhower wrote a note to a retired Hormel president. It read, "I ate my share of Spam along with millions of other soldiers. I'll even confess to a few unkind remarks about it—uttered during the strain of battle you understand. But as former Commander in Chief I can still officially forgive you your only sin: sending so much of it." That might be a hard letter to locate at

the Eisenhower Presidential Library, but it's part of a prominent display here. Soviet leader Nikita Khrushchev echoed those sentiments in
an autobiography in which he wrote: "Without SPAM we wouldn't
have been able to feed our army!" A wall of SPAM (some 3,390 cans)
greets visitors on the entrance and sets the stage for the world of
SPAM beyond, a world accented by a SPAM-filled conveyor belt
weaving through the space, by a life-size trivia game hosted by comedian Al Franken, and by a looping video of Monty Python's performance of their song "Spamalot."

Owen and I finish our Christmas shopping in the museum's gift
shop and return to the road and finish the drive to my aunt Ginny and
uncle Earl's home in a near-Minneapolis suburb.

"Your grandmother was a bowler, you know," Ginny tells me over
dinner and a nice bottle of wine.

Dorothy Buckley, my grandmother, epitomized class and embodied grandmotherliness. Living in a modest apartment after being widowed for the second time, she doted on her grandchildren and
great-grandchildren, making them toasted cheese sandwiches on their
visits and faithfully mailing a card and a check for every birthday. She
also had a tough, opinionated side, though, a self-assurance born of
Irish-Swedish genes. From politics to religion to differences in the various types of pasta (they are all the same and don't try to tell her otherwise), she was unafraid of making a stand. It's this side of her that
enables me to almost envision her spending time in a smoky bowling
alley circa 1948, though it's not a very believable vision.

"It's true," Ginny insists, and I take her word for it. Until I see her
bowl.

She and my cousins Stephen, Colleen, Michelle, Katy, and Shawne
and her husband, Alain, join Owen and me at Bryant Lake Bowl for
dinner and a game.

In a trendy Minneapolis neighborhood, Bryant Lake Bowl is part theater, part upscale restaurant, and part bowling alley. The theater part features obscure indie rock, one-man plays, and a weekly book club—hardly bowling alley trappings. The restaurant's menu boasts of its largely organic and sustainable suppliers from local farms and includes such items as smoked trout, chèvre, and fresh fish dishes served at market price. Hardly bowling alley fare, though I must admit the seared ahi was a refreshing change from the processed cheese I've been living on recently. The bowling, though, is vintage.

The rack of well-worn shoes on the wall to the right of the eight lanes is self-service, leaving me to wonder who's in charge of spraying them between bowlers. The first pair I pick up is still warm from the previous bowler, and I feel around until I find a cool pair, as if that will make a difference in the germ count. All of the balls show a good deal of wear, suggesting that Bryant Lake's ownership applies the same zeal for sustainable resources to its bowling equipment as it does to its food. The scoring tables are manual, and the settee area is crowded with nine of us bowling and cluttered with bags and shoes and coats.

We split into teams of some sort, while my female cousins—all of them married, mind you—fawn over Owen's Dutch good looks. The low scores among my blood relatives, particularly Ginny's staggeringly low forty-two pins, give doubt as to whether my grandmother ever did set foot onto the lanes. In bowling maybe nurture wins out over nature.

The next morning, bidding good-bye to Ginny and Earl, Owen and I head west, vowing to make quick work of both Dakotas and Nebraska in order to get him to Kansas City in time for his return flight.

★ North Dakota

MY first visit to North Dakota was during ninth grade and, as it happens, the result of my father's handball mission. He had rented a cabin on Big Pine Lake near Perham, Minnesota, for a month to try his hand at retirement and invited any of us to join him for a few days if we could make the trip. The high school versions of Owen, my friend Morgan, and I had come up with my brother Peter for a week of fishing, cards, and harassing the girls behind the counter of the Dairy Queen. Perham is located in west-central Minnesota and as a town of twenty-five hundred is one of that area's more populous. It was quite the week, especially once we learned that three of the four Dairy Queen girls were finalists in the summer's Miss Perham contest. Every high school boy's dream.

Perham is ninety miles east of Fargo, North Dakota, and my dad had somehow arranged a handball game there. He offered to take any of us along on the drive, and Morgan and I took him up. Like today, even then Owen had absolutely no interest in going to North Dakota. I don't blame him, as I have absolutely no recollection of what Morgan and I did while my dad played handball . . . perhaps harassed the girl behind the counter of the Fargo Dairy Queen?

Having opted out of taking that drive the first time, Owen is paying for it now. The harsh winter that's sure to be in store for the Dakotas and Minnesota hasn't yet arrived, but the land is prepared for it. Fields are brown and lumpy, the remnants of harvested crops jutting out of the dirt at sharp angles that suggest a violent end to the plants' lives. The sky is an endless dull gray-white; a high ceiling provides no visual variation to relieve the eye or attract its gaze. Pine trees clump together in groups at random intervals along the highway. They look bored, but maybe that's just the two of us projecting our own boredom on the terrain. It is an awfully bleak day when bowling trivia is a welcome diversion.

"You know," Owen says, reading from a bowling book that was resting in the backseat, " 'a pin hidden behind another pin can be called a *barmaid,* a *sleeper,* a *mother-in-law,* or *one in the dark.'* "

"That's interesting."

"And a two-seven or three-ten split is called a *baby split—*"

"That's nice."

"—but if it's a two-seven-eight or a three-nine-ten it's a *baby split with company.*"

"What are *bedposts*?" I ask, hoping to stump him.

"That's easy. The seven-ten split. They're also called *fence posts* or *snake eyes.* What's a *bender*?"

"Isn't that what we did with Cam in St. Louis?"

"Nope. It's a ball that curves so much it almost falls into the gutter before cutting back into the pins."

He continues, largely out of good-natured spite for the boredom of the drive. His tone takes on an air of mock fascination as he recites each new fact as though it is opening a whole new world to him.

"*Big ears* is the four-six-seven-ten split. And *Brooklyn* is when you hit the headpin on the wrong side—that's also known as bowling *Jersey side.* But a *Cincinnati* is the eight-ten split. And a *Dutch two hundred* is when you roll a two hundred by alternating strikes and spares for the whole game. And a *Greek church* is a split with three pins on one side of the lane and two on the other. That one's also known as *double nuts with a man in motion.*"

"Why?"

"It doesn't say. A *full hit* is when you hit the headpin dead on, which is likely to leave a split because you're not hitting the *hole,* which is also known as the *pocket.* But a *broom ball,* on the other hand, has so much action that it just sweeps the pins away. And a *leave* is the pins that are left on the pin deck. What's three strikes?"

"A *turkey.*"

"Four strikes?"

"A *four-bagger.*"

"A *buzzard*?"

"I don't know."

"Three open frames in a row. What about grandma's *teeth*?"

"You're making that up."

"It's an unexpected or unusual leave. What about a *Jack Manders*?"

"Isn't that like a Rob Roy, only with bourbon instead of Scotch?"

"No. It's also known as a *field goal,* when you roll the ball between two pins that look like football goalposts. Named for a 1930s Chicago Bears kicker."

"Is that right? Well, if I were going to the *dime store,* what pins would be—"

"The five and ten."

"What about a *lily*?"

"That's the five-seven-ten split."

"And *poison ivy*?"

"The three-six-ten split."

"What's the difference between a *picket fence* and a *rail*?"

"None. They're both a one-two-four-seven or a one-three-six-ten split. What's a *Swiss cheese* ball?"

"I think it was on the menu at Bryant Lake Bowl."

"Wrong. A ball with more than three holes in it."

"What happens when you yank your shot?"

This question summons the ninth grader in both of us, ending the trivia game as we guffaw at the innuendo. After a stop at a Dairy Queen we arrive in Fargo.

We agree to bowl here quickly and get to somewhere—anywhere—in South Dakota for the night. It doesn't matter where; South Dakota is a close second-to-last in Owen's "Places to Visit on My Winter Break" list.

We come upon West Acres Bowl off of the first Fargo exit we see, and Owen bowls his first turkey of the trip while I can't seem to stop rolling Jersey side and leaving a lily. Ten frames apiece later, we exit West Acres Bowl and drive south, blasted by a relentless wind that has gathered momentum over hundreds of miles of the broad Dakota plain to our west.

★ South Dakota

ARRIVING in Sioux Falls, South Dakota, we check into a motel and inquire about dinner and bowling. The desk clerk gives us the coordinates of the bowling alley with a brewpub nearby it. Owen and I opt for soft pretzels, bratwurst, and hamburgers as a prelude to bowling, a choice that nearly adds another half day to our trip.

"We've got cosmic bowling starting in fifteen minutes," the manager at Empire Bowl informs us. "All the lanes are reserved for the night, so I can't let you guys bowl." His tone is unsympathetic.

We weigh our options. We'd made good progress today and would like to get on the road early tomorrow morning. Surely we could find another bowling alley, but that would require more effort, and there were a number of beers we still wanted to try at the brewpub we just left.

After some discussion, Owen heroically persuades the manager to let us get a game in, provided we finish before bowlers with reservations show up hungry for their lanes.

"You've got ten minutes. Ten."

Exactly ten minutes pass, and I can now claim to have bowled in thirty-one states, thanks to Owen's persuasive skills and a complete lack of concern about skill and score.

The bar stool cushions at the brewpub are still faintly warm from our last visit, and we celebrate the fastest game ever bowled by breaking my contractual agreement with Miller and consuming gallons of the local brew.

Nebraska ★

OWEN and I are huddled around our third round of High Life at Parkway Lanes in Lincoln. Having spent twenty-four hours a day together for a week, we've run out of conversation topics, and our surroundings—the High Plains by day and bowling alleys by night—aren't contributing much in the way of subject matter. While he appreciates the bowling aspect of the trip, he's easily bored with it. Where I could spend hours taking stock of the variations in rental balls and chatting up an eighty-year-old woman about the nuances that automatic scoring has brought to the sport, he's not quite as invested. Understandable, and I wouldn't have expected otherwise. It's nice to have someone familiar along for the ride.

Still, there is noticeable tension between us, and I'm starting to recall something I read about the first settlers of the Plains. Homesteaders who came here to earn 160 acres of land by merely staying here for five years found doing so harder than it sounds. The soil, though fertile, was shallow and required new and different farming techniques to cultivate. Trees were few, which meant that lumber for home building was scarce. The first homes were built from sod, miserable square buildings with a doorway framed from wood and likely not even a window to bring in light. A sod roof provided little protection in a heavy rain, and so the inside of the homes would often be damp, along with all the family's belongings. The solitude, particularly harsh winters, and relentless howling wind, paired with such miserable living conditions, would drive some settlers insane enough to murder their families or take their own lives to escape the monotony. Owen and I have not said a word to each other in twenty minutes, and I notice him paying a lot of attention to a kitchen knife behind the snack bar counter. I decide we need our space, and walk away from him without turning my back to join a group of men in their early twenties bowling on lane seven.

As is typically the case with this demographic in bowling alleys, the bowling outing is an exercise in camp: life imitating films imitating life. Their conversation consists almost entirely of quotes from cult bowling movies *Kingpin* and *The Big Lebowski*.

"I'm throwing rocks tonight!" one says, imitating Steve Buscemi's *Lebowski* character.

"Mark it eight, dude," says another, recalling a scene in *Lebowski* in which a gun is drawn over a scoring dispute.

"Sweeter than Yoo-hoo," another says upon rolling a strike. The line is from Woody Harelson's *Kingpin* character, Roy Munson.

"You almost got Munsoned there," one comments on a teammate's nearly missed spare.

The ironic appreciation the twentysomething male has for bowling runs somewhat counter to the bowling establishment's aspirations for the sport's resurgence as a seriously taken pursuit. It embraces the less favorable stereotypes of blue-collar, out-of-shape participants unfit for more athletic endeavors. It skips by televised bowling except to get a laugh or make a drinking game of it. The guys on lane seven here have all entered funny pseudonyms into the electronic scorer instead of their own names. One has on the largest pair of rental shows the bowling alley offers—a size 17—for kicks despite his size 10 feet. But while the pitchers of beer and efforts to out–movie quote one another take priority, the bowling itself is more than incidental.

"We like bowling," they seem to be saying. "We just have to mask that affection with sarcasm so girls don't think we're bowling geeks."

Owen joins me behind their lane and together we join the movie-quoting consortium, suddenly refreshed and tolerant of each other's company after a few minutes apart. We toast the trip on his last night, clinking clear glass bottles of the Champagne of Beers above the ball rack and lacing up for his last series of frames. When it comes to comparing winter break stories with his classmates, he'll be able to say he's survived the Great Plains and bowled in six more states than he'd bowled in just a week ago.

Walking out of Parkway Lanes, I pause and look to the west to ponder my progress to date. Eighteen states remain out there in that vast darkness, and I briefly gasp at the expanse. The states only get bigger and emptier from here.

★ Kansas

IN Kansas City I drop Owen off at the airport and land on the couch of a Hotdogger friend, Chris McCarley, whose apartment is well appointed with the finer things in a twentysomething bachelor's world: a leather sofa, a Foosball table, and a case of Miller High Life. While Chris works, I practice my bank shot on goal and begin the foundation of a beer can pyramid—a beer-amid, in the parlance of college students everywhere—to be completed later. Not a bad afternoon, really. When Chris gets home we check "bowl in Kansas" off my list at a bowling alley near his home. A bowler on the lane to our right catches wind of my trip and is aghast at one particular element.

"You've never bowled in a league?"

"Nope," I say, feeling somewhat self-conscious due to his accusatory tone.

"How can you be doing this and never have bowled in a league?"

"I guess I'm not that big a bowler," I reply, wondering when Chris will get back from the bar to help defend me should the man get any more agitated at my lack of bowling experience.

"That's like people who go to the Super Bowl just to tell people they went, even if they don't like football."

"Well, I do like bowling; this is just the first time I've really—"

He doesn't hear me. "That's like learning to drive on a Rolls-Royce. Or getting to play Augusta even though you've never swung a golf club. Or people who spend twenty thousand dollars remodeling their kitchen but don't even cook." He has a surprising number of examples like this, to varying degrees of metaphoric accuracy, but the point is made: I should have gotten some league experience before setting out.

Though my time in St. Louis checked Missouri off the list of states to bowl in, my lack of recent media pursuit has me feeling a bit short on delivering a return on Miller's investment, so I schedule a morning of bowling on the Missouri side of the border—nearer where the news offices are.

None of the news desks I called to invite to my bowling open house seemed very enthused about the idea of covering it, though, and I'm starting to doubt whether the second half of the trip will be as fruitful for me or for Miller on this front. When no cameras arrive for the first hour I spend at Ward Parkway Lanes, the assistant manager sounds a lot like the staff at Sawmill Lanes in Ohio on the road trip's first day.

"You really think TV cameras will show up?" she asks.

"They have before. . . ." My halfheartedness trails off into noheartedness and I befriend some of the seniors bowling this Thursday morning. Among them is a ninety-eight-year-old woman who, in addition to having bowled in dozens more leagues than I have, has a 189 average.

"What's your average?" she asks.

Just in time for me to avoid answering that it's somewhere near sixty pins below hers, three news crews arrive simultaneously.

"Good talking to you. Gotta go!"

Unaccustomed to juggling multiple crews at once, I do my best to hurry through the taping and hit my message points. The NBC affiliate takes an especially long time, indicating that this will be a longer, more well-produced piece than the typical fifteen-second mention I usually merit as the closing credits roll.

The camera crews also spend a few minutes interviewing the ladies' senior league participants, and when all the commotion is over I've reached folk hero status for bringing such a hubbub to their weekly game. As a result, I get my shot at a road trip first that would surely please my antagonist from last night: I'm invited to sub on one of the teams in official league play.

This is no small event for the league, either, which is comprised entirely of female senior citizens. To allow a young man to sub for a missing teammate could put other teams at a significant disadvantage, upsetting the balance of the season entirely.

"After seeing you bowl, I don't think it will be a problem," Maliea, the manager who is also a member of the league, tells me. "You're on the New Yorker team."

I bring my ball over and assess my new team's dynamics. I'm the youngest on the team, and in fact the entire league, by about thirty-five years. At one end of the table near our lane are Jean and Ann, who are in the midst of a cigarette break. My other teammate, Carolyn, appears unbothered by this despite the fact that she must regularly step away to take hits from an oxygen tank that she has at the other end of the table. Apparently the doctor's orders that put her on the tank said nothing about avoiding smoke-filled environments. That or it's just hard to keep a bowler out of the alley, no matter how reduced her lung capacity is.

As we bowl, we talk. I learn that the team is named the New Yorker for a deli Carolyn used to own. And I learn that Ann is seventy-three and that she lost her husband on this past July Fourth after fifty-three years.

"My refrigerator broke down," she says, "and I was complaining about having to make the decision about how to handle it. My sister said, 'You've been making decisions your whole life.' She was trying to encourage me, but it's frustrating. Do I have to make *all* the decisions now?"

Not an uncommon sentiment. I'd recently spoken with my mother. The ancient, polar bear–sized freezer in our garage had turned warm last week, spoiling its contents and depositing a sizable puddle on the garage floor. She quickly had it replaced, a job that would have fallen to my father had he been alive. The replacement freezer—a smaller, more efficient model that was long overdue anyway—didn't work, either. It didn't work for the same reason that the old one quit: the fuse was blown. After shopping for and buying a new freezer, then arranging for the old freezer to be taken away, learning that the simple flip of a switch would have solved the problem made my mother feel ashamed, frustrated, and angry with herself. But mostly she missed having someone around to make some of the decisions. My father may well have done the very same thing (though I'd like to think his forty-some years connected to the construction industry would have led him to first check the fuse), but he and my mother would have at least shared in the decisions, and in the guffaw.

Maliea's insight about my not giving team New Yorker an unfair advantage is more than prescient. In fact, I turn out to be a detriment to the team: my 110 is our low score. Jean rolls an average-shattering 112; Carolyn—between oxygen breaks—rolls a 118 and Ann a 149. My only consolation is that our team actually ends up winning the game, but what little self-respect that restores in me is quickly stripped away when I find out that Frances Lyons, the ninety-eight-year-old I'd briefly met earlier, crushed my score with a 190 six lanes over. (Incidentally, she doesn't look a day over ninety-two.) No wonder she's so much better than I am, I console myself: she's got seven decades of experience on me. Twenty years ago, about the time I was entering third grade, she came her closest to a perfect game by rolling a 297.

"Good game," I tell her.

"I'm just doing the best I can with the material I've got to work with," she says. She is a gracious winner.

"I lost my husband shortly after being married," she shares. (When someone has lived this long, "shortly" could take on a relative meaning as it does in geologic time, but in this case she'd only been married about a year.) She was living in Kansas City then.

"I had some money, and my sister knew how to drive a car," she says. The year was 1931. "I bought a car, but I didn't know how to drive it. So she drove us to San Antonio. I owned a beauty salon and stayed there until 1946."

At ninety-eight, Frances has outlived most of the rest of her family. Only a nephew, a great-nephew, and a great-great-nephew survive.

"I take a lot of comfort in the ladies I bowl with," she says of the young seventy-somethings around us. "And the fact that I'm still driving."

After being so soundly beaten by a women's senior league, I relish my afternoon matchup: Graham and Avery Bolar (yes, pronounced "bowler"), ages three and five respectively. They belong to Dana and Mark Bolar, friends of mine from college. Even though I bowl this game poorly, Graham is no match for me and I literally beat the pants off of him. Or, more accurately, he just wet his pants and, rather than leave the flashing lights of the video game he'd been pretending to play, he just dropped his pants and aired himself out right there in the arcade. Oh, to be young again.

> My name is Kim, I'm 25 and I've been following your story from the beginning—I absolutely love it!!

Judging from the two exclamation points at the end of the first sentence of her e-mail, I assume Kim means what she says, emphatically. The note's closing, however, is far more intriguing: "And call if you want to stay with my roommate and I while in Kansas! We're just two normal, fun, and cute Kansas girls."

As a matter of fact, I've always wanted to visit Lawrence, Kansas. . . .

Kim's overtures sound a lot like those I read from Bowling Spice back in Illinois, though not as innuendo filled. Darn it. Kim and I exchange e-mails and agree to meet at Royal Crest Lanes at 8:00. I arrive early and make friends at the bar.

"I'm the Black Cowboy," the man next to me introduces himself. His black curly hair cascades to his neckline, falling from beneath a black cowboy hat; his mouth is framed by a black goatee. He is, in fact, black.

"I suppose 'African-American Cowboy' doesn't roll off the tongue as well," I reply, trying to be politically correct. The Black Cowboy, friendly though he is, doesn't have much time for political correctness.

"I spent enough time in jail that I know one thing," he tells me over beers amid poinsettias and Christmas lights that decorate the tiny lounge area. "I don't ever want to go back."

I don't know the protocol for asking someone about their prison experience, but I have to assume that it's akin to asking a lady her age. Without asking the burning question—"What'd you do?"—I glean that the Black Cowboy did his time for having a good deal of success dealing drugs.

"Now I run a car-detailing business," he says. "These employees are a lot easier to manage," he adds, laughing.

"Listen, Black Cowboy," I say, thinking he might be an ally if Kim turns out to be a serial killer—a thought I can't seem to let go of when my first contact with someone is over the Internet. "I'm meeting this girl here who may well be a crazed stalker. You'll have my back if she pulls a knife or a shiv or something, right?"

"Mike?" a woman's voice says behind me. I let out a brief, shrill scream, turning around to find a cute, smiling twenty-five-year-old woman in fashionable rimmed glasses. "I'm Kim." She looks to weigh 110 pounds. The Black Cowboy laughs, then shakes his head and turns away.

Kim's only weapon turns out to be a killer hook on the lanes, and we banter like old friends about bowling, travel, and our families. But mostly bowling.

"I didn't realize how much I was into bowling," she says, "until I was home recently going through some old photos and news clippings—and it was like a bowling history of my family. It was like we'd never done anything but bowl. We each had our own ball, and my mom's team even bowled in state tournaments."

I find myself falling in love with Kim the more she talks and the more the High Life talks. After bowling she takes me to a campus bar (Lawrence is home to the University of Kansas) where strong tropical drinks flow liberally and where every so often powerful fans turn on and a simulated hurricane blows through the bar. There are traditions and rituals associated with this, but I'm too inebriated to keep track of them, and too distracted by the fact that cute Kim from Kansas whom I just met is now dancing on the bar in front of me. Her shirt inches up above her belt ever so slightly and I swoon at the sight of her flat, bare stomach being revealed for mere seconds.

I really need a girlfriend.

This night ends without one; in an awkward moment as we leave the bar it's agreed that I should probably find a motel. If I had asked, she might have offered me her couch. If she had proactively offered it, I've have accepted all too eagerly and probably caused her second thoughts about my intentions. Parting ways is all for the best in the end, as I've got to meet an ex-girlfriend's parents tomorrow anyway.

Kalli and I have spoken and traded e-mails sporadically in the three months since I tried to grope her good-bye the night before leaving on this trip. Despite that behavior, she's supported and encouraged me since then and insisted that I stay with her parents in Waverly, Missouri, if I was ever nearby. It happens to be on the way home to Ohio, where I'll spend Christmas.

I don't know why I think this is a good idea. While I'm sure they're nice people, I've never met Kalli's parents, and so this encounter doesn't have the trappings of a reunion. I try to put myself in their shoes: *Our twenty-seven-year-old daughter dated a guy for about six months. They broke up and haven't stayed in close contact since, and thus he isn't someone we need to be thinking about as a potential son-in-law. And how thankful we are for that, since he just quit his job and is now unemployed and driving his mother's car from seedy bowling alley to seedy bowling alley doing God knows what.* "Sure, Kalli. Send him to Waverly and we'll show him a good time."

I've convinced myself that Kalli's father will invite me into the basement to show me his extensive knife collection within minutes of my arrival to make it clear that he doesn't want me getting too close to his daughter again.

Waverly is a town of about eight hundred about an hour's drive east on I-70 from Kansas City and another forty minutes north on a two-lane country road. It sits on the outside of a bend in the Missouri River, where a Union Pacific train line runs along the southern bank. Apple orchards make the autumn a festive time here, and the flooding river bottoms to the north can keep the springtime unpredictable. I make the last leg of the drive in complete darkness, and the sparsely populated surroundings add to the unease I'm already feeling. For miles not even a farmhouse can be seen on either side of the road. A single, distant light off on the horizon to the east comes and goes from view with no sign of life. No one to hear me scream if the knife demonstration goes awry. At least Kalli will be there when I arrive. I phone ahead for directions to clarify the final few turns. Her mother answers.

"Hi. This is Kalli's friend Mike. I'm about thirty minutes away and just wanted to let you know I'll be there shortly."

"Great, Mike. We'll hold off on dinner until you get here," she says pleasantly. "Kalli should be getting in around midnight, depending on the traffic around St. Louis."

Apparently Kalli left Chicago a little later than expected and now I'll be meeting the ex-would-be-parents-in-law for the first time alone.

Brenda and Dwight, Kalli's parents, are as gracious as can be when I arrive.

"Come on in," says Brenda, showing me to a bedroom in the basement. I see no knife collection, though a gun rack on the wall holds two rather large rifles. I quickly scan the room for ammunition before following her back upstairs.

"It's my cousin's seventieth birthday tonight," Brenda explains. "I hope you don't mind joining us for her dinner."

"That sounds great."

This won't be so bad! A quaint dinner with Kalli's parents and a seventy-year-old woman, a nice, low-pressure meal that will kill the few hours we have to wait before Kalli's midnight arrival.

If only that were the case. When we get to the restaurant, the hostess greets the Hilbrenners and informs us that we're the last to arrive. "Everyone else is in the party room."

Instead of a quaint dinner with a handful of complete strangers whose relative I once dated, I'm being ushered into a private dining room filled with at least forty of them: grandparents, aunts, uncles, cousins, second cousins, in-laws, outlaws, and just about every other relation one could imagine. And none of them has ordered dinner yet. This being a family affair, they've been waiting until everyone is present, and my late arrival has been holding things up. My palms begin to sweat as I scan the faces of people who look rather hungry. Off to a good start.

Fortunately, this isn't my first impression on most of them. As it turns out, many of them happened to have seen me on the Kansas City news broadcasts, a fact that not only saves me having to explain what I'm doing but also happens to be somewhat impressive. It's not every day that someone who was on yesterday's evening news stops into a town of eight hundred to make you wait for your dinner.

More important than my quasi celebrity, however, is the implied endorsement Dwight and Brenda are giving me just by including me in this event. An extended family in a small town can be a pretty closed society. From the outsider's perspective it can be like trying to break into the Mob: it helps to have someone vouch for you. By the end of the meal they've all made me feel like I'm a part of the family. By the time Kalli arrives at midnight I'm able to catch her up on the latest family gossip.

"Your cousin's got a new girlfriend, from Grand Pass," I tell her, showing off both my family and regional knowledge.

"I can't believe you're in my house," she says once her parents have gone to bed and we're alone in her living room. We exchange a long, tender hug before saying good night. "I'm glad you're here."

Several of Waverly's streets were named by Kalli's grandfather A.J. There's Frances Street for his wife, Kevin Circle and Dwight Drive for his sons. After nearly getting stuck in a gulch while showing us his undeveloped land (off-roading with a seventy-five-year-old man behind the wheel of a minivan now ranks as the most dangerous thing I've done on the trip), he points to where he's planning to put Kalli's Corner, currently a densely forested acre at the top of a steep hill.

We spend the rest of the day riding with Kalli's father to nearby towns tending to various vending machines he leases all over the area in a business he, his brother Kevin, and A.J. run. Everywhere we go everyone knows Dwight, knows Kalli. Each conversation includes an inquiry about someone's family member who is ill, how the kids are doing away at college, or how the new car is. The familiarity and inti-mate knowledge people in these small towns have with one another is remarkable. There were more people living on my block in Chicago than live in Waverly and these surrounding towns, and I knew not one of them well enough for this kind of interaction.

That night we bowl in nearby Higginsville, in a building built in 1908. Dwight, of course, knows the owner and checks to make sure the pool table, jukebox, and arcade games he has leased to Higginsville Bowl are in working order.

I'd never bowled with Kalli, nor had I ever found women bowling to be particularly attractive. This changes when she rolls her first ball. I can't take my eyes off of her: her form from behind is flawless—and I don't just mean her body but also the way she bowls, a fluid motion with a thorough follow-through.

Has this trip turned me into some freaky fetishist? I begin to wonder. *Am I really evaluating a woman based on her bowling form? Or is it just the mixture of the old, familiar relationship within the context of my new adventure?*

We drop off Kalli's parents and, after a trip to one more bar where we happen upon the only two of her relatives I hadn't yet met, return to her living room couch and whisper while playing with Cooper, her German shepherd.

"I feel like I'm in high school and am sneaking a boy in while my parents are asleep," she says.

"Why *aren't* you sneaking me in?" I ask, inadvertently moving us into a "talk." "I mean, why didn't we work?"

"I know. It's the most frustrating thing. We had so much fun; we just didn't communicate very well when it came to our real feelings."

"Yeah, I think we both held back a lot, kept each other at a distance." The conversation continues; we're very close now, on the couch with our foreheads nearly touching.

We're not exactly baring our hearts just yet, but here in Waverly, Missouri, at 2:00 A.M. in the glow of her parents' Christmas tree, it feels like we're finally having a breakthrough. We begin kissing, and a flood of familiar comfort and excitement washes over me. This lasts only a few minutes before we go our separate ways, with so much to sleep on.

I barely sleep.

As we are saying our good-byes the next morning, loaded down with iced tea and packed sandwiches, and even a tank of gas that Dwight and Brenda insisted on buying I stand with my back against Mom's Honda and talk sheepishly with Kalli. She has a speck of black pepper stuck in her teeth, her hair is a mess, and she's wearing baggy pajama bottoms and a loose-fitting sweatshirt. She looks beautiful despite it all.

"Where do you think you're going to live when you finish your trip?" she asks.

"I don't know. I really liked New Orleans. Maybe Vermont. . . . I haven't really seen the West yet. . . ." *Chicago, if you'll be there,* I think, but for some reason can't say it.

"I think you should move back to Chicago," she says, surprising me with her frankness, though she softens it with a playful tone.

"I don't know. It might be interesting to see what happens. . . ." My defenses, for whatever reason, are back up. Sobriety, playing hard to get, the nature of a man so noncommittal in all things that his belongings are locked in a storage locker while he drives around semi-aimlessly—anything could be the cause.

I get in the car and begin pulling down her driveway as she waves good-bye, having agreed that we'll talk more often as I finish the trip. On the drive out of Waverly I feel like I did when I dropped her off after our first date in Chicago, smitten again, thinking that something good may come of all this.

My other thoughts on leaving Waverly for the eight-hour trip back to my own family and a respite from the road trip concern small-town life. People in small towns wherever I go invariably ask, "Why'd you come *here* of all places?" New Yorkers take it for granted that people want to visit there, but there's always a sense of surprise and puzzlement among the people in smaller towns that anyone would want to come to "little old" here. Indeed, on the surface I'd ask myself the same question. But spend a few nights in someone's home, see how close they are to their family and how strong the support network is among people who all know one another so well, and the question becomes "Why am I leaving?"

In the end it comes down to a question of "home"—where that is and what it means. For me it means my mother, my siblings, their children.

And this year, home will also mean a trip to West Virginia to bowl in the state that, somehow, I forgot.

West Virginia ★

A lot of my correspondence with people who've been following my progress through my Web site has involved answering the question "What happened to West Virginia?"

A great question in general, but even more astute coming from someone who's observed that I've covered everywhere from the Atlantic Ocean to the Mississippi River except the state that lies against my own home state's southeastern border. So how could I have missed it? Honestly, I just forgot. West Virginia is a victim of poor planning and whimsical destination selection on my part. To be sure, nothing was drawing me to the state, with its reputation for hillbilly backwardness. The upside is that by checking it off while I'm home for Christmas I have the chance to take Mom along on the road trip. Just what she's always wanted . . . too bad I already got her a SPAM oven mitt.

To give her the full Bowling Road Trip experience, I do zero research or planning before we jump in the car en route to Wheeling, some 120 miles from her home. She needs to see what it's really like to get lost and ask strangers where the best bowling alley around is. She'll be so impressed with how I'm using her car.

After getting directions at a gas station I cross my fingers and hope Elm Grove Bowl won't be closed for some reason. Snow flurries have begun whipping around in the air, and the forecast calls for a chance snowstorm. Having to spend much more time looking for a bowling alley could, I fear, get us stuck in Wheeling overnight when we'd planned for only a day trip. Sure, I want to give Mom the full road trip experience, I'd just rather not bunk up with her at the No-Tell Motel—which, at first glance around the neighborhood, looks like one of the finer establishments Wheeling has to offer. Thankfully, Elm Grove Bowl is open and has a lane for us.

I never played team sports as a child beyond the obligatory soccer team someone's dad coached while we all ran en masse after the ball, a clump of eight-year-olds moving as one. Nonetheless, for some reason I've never understood, I am fiercely competitive. I've had to remove myself from playing certain video games in order to save friendships, and have undergone hypnosis to cope with Foosball losses. Today, competing for the first time against the woman who bore and unconditionally loved me for twenty-seven years, I learn the origins of my competitive spirit. Though she'd expressed a desire to better her sister Ginny's forty-two pins in Minnesota, I quickly realize that my mother is really gunning for me.

After helping this seemingly graceful, elegant senior citizen get her rental shoes and pick out a ball, then buying her some nachos and High Life to encourage a sort of mother-son picnic atmosphere, I watch the nurturing soul who made my school lunches for twelve years turn into a bowler out for blood. It won't be enough for her to beat her sister's score: My mother, like anyone else I bowl against, wants to beat the Bowling Road Trip guy at his own game.

Apparently Mother's been reading bowling magazines.

"Looks like they haven't dressed the lane yet today," she comments, a technical observation I am not yet sure how to make myself. "Better start your hook early to avoid coming in light in the pocket."

"Mom?"

On my first roll, in the midst of my backswing, she yells, "Good luck!" rattling my concentration and causing me to send the ball way off target.

"Mother, please, no talking while I'm bowling."

As I attempt to pick up my next spare she kindly, and loudly, informs me that my shoe is untied.

She rolls a 7 in her first frame. "Good job, Mom," I say, holding up my hand for a high five as she's coming off the approach. She walks past, looking straight ahead and nudging me with her shoulder on her way by.

Throughout the game, the intimidation keeps up and her remarks become progressively more elaborate and hurtful, ranging from the technical, "Be sure and keep your elbow in close to your side" to the personal, "I've always liked your brothers and sisters more than you!"

While I don't claim to be a good bowler, there is no way I'm going to let my mother, God bless her heart, beat me. I put up a 111 to her 102 in a closer match than I'd have liked.

"A one eleven?" she taunts. "I mean, for someone who bowls every day that seems really bad. Aren't you learning anything on your trip? Maybe I should take my car back."

After two losses she insists on bowling another, despite my comment that I'd like to rest my arm and back a bit for the second half of my trip.

"What, are your wittle muscles sore?" she condescends, adding with contempt, "I thought I only had three daughters."

The "road trip" portion of our day proves less antagonistic, though it is evenly divided between mother-son bonding and the kind of backseat driving someone who's just driven fourteen thousand miles alone in three months isn't used to. My mother has an amazing ability to blend the two into a single piece of conversation.

"You know, Michael, I'm really getting a lot of enjoyment out of following your trip, though I'd be enjoying it more right now if you weren't following that car so closely."

"Yes, Mother."

"Watch out for that truck. Do you see him? Do you think you'll see a lot of old friends during the rest of the trip? He's got his blinker on."

"Yes, I see him. I think so. On the old-friends thing. I can see his blinker. Yes."

"Your father used to get tickets all the time on this stretch of road, back when he had an office in Wheeling."

"I'm going the speed limit, Mom. Relax."

"No, I was just thinking about your dad. I wish he could be here to see you doing this. He'd think it's wonderful."

"I know, Mom. I wish he could be here, too."

"Watch out for that Chevy."

On the way out of town I stop by to visit the third-grade class my friend Megan Patrick teaches. I've been sending them postcards from every state, and Megan somehow uses the correspondence as a learning tool. Though I try to think of something thoughtful and age appropriate, I'm typically writing the postcards on the dashboard at a rest stop just before leaving a state, and with ten different people to write to I get a little bit of writer's block. A representative note to these kids might read: "Mississippi's great—they're known for their bowling." Occasionally I'll think of some trivia that might spark a classroom symposium. Noticing that a lot of postcards feature the state's official bird, and that a lot of states (Ohio among them) claim the cardinal as such, I wrote on one postcard: "How many states call the cardinal their official state bird?"

In return for my postcards, Megan had the kids all write letters to President Bush asking if I could bowl at the White House. Their request was denied, though somehow I don't think the president actually saw the letters. After I show them a slide show of some of the nondrinking highlights of my trip, one of the kids raises her hand.

"Seven," she says.

"Pardon?"

"That's how many states there are where the cardinal is the official bird."

"Oh, I had no idea."

You learn something every day.

★ Arkansas

RETURNING to the road after two well-fed weeks at home, I am joined in my beeline toward Arkansas by a scarlet and gray, maize and blue ceramic cockatiel that I received for Christmas. As disgusting a color combination as that sounds, it is all the more so to a Big Ten conference fan, for these are the colors of my Ohio State Buckeyes (the scarlet and gray) tainted by those of their archrival Michigan (the maize and blue).

The Bird had started out in the home of our family friends the Robertsons, who lived in Detroit, and at the time it was a rainbow of similarly mismatched tropical colors as painted by an artist whose brilliance, apparently, is yet to be understood. During a visit to Detroit sometime in the 1970s my father commented to Gary Robertson, "That's got to be the ugliest thing I've ever seen." He was being charitable.

Later that year a package arrived at our home, addressed to my father, containing the Bird, a not-so-subtle suggestion of a hand gesture of the same name.

"Right back at you," my father said, painting it gray with scarlet highlights and a large "O-S-U" across its plumage, sending it back to the Robertsons in time for the OSU/Michigan football game.

"No, I insist, fuck *you*," Gary replied cordially, adding maize and blue highlights and the letters *MU* repeatedly inside the *O, S,* and *U* before leaving it at our home during a visit to Columbus, to be found as his car was just pulling out of sight.

And so it went, back and forth in clever, good-natured

fun for decades, an unwelcome surprise between two humorous men participating by proxy in the greatest rivalry in sports. Having the Bird is like being "it" in a game of tag: you dread and try to avoid it at all costs, but once you are it, it's great fun deciding how you'll get rid of it. My father died while not "it," a moral victory for our family. Gary may have outlived Leo, but he carried the shame of being stuck holding the Bird. Sadly, Gary died about a year after Leo, and in our shock and grief we never really considered the Bird. Gary, however, had trained his son Curt well, and seeing me basking in free-spirited wanderlust, he took dead aim and cursed me with the Bird, an albatross around my neck for the remaining sixteen states of the trip.

After a night in the seediest motel I could find in western Kentucky, the Bird and I cross into Arkansas, companions for the rest of the trip.

In Morrilton I leave the Bird in the car and spend an hour or so bowling on lane one at Playland Roller Rink and Bowling Center. A man is refinishing the lanes on the right side of the house. Lane two is occupied by a touching father-and-son outing, if by "touching" you infer a picture of painfully strained communications.

"No! No! No!" father yells at son, who is bowling incorrectly. "Do it like this!"

Father then demonstrates a different way to bowl incorrectly. He admits to me that he's never bowled before, either.

The son, who is about twelve and torn between being an obedient youngster and being the angst-filled teen that puberty is calling him to be, says almost nothing, though he appears to be paying attention. That is, until he rolls his next ball exactly the same way he'd done before. Apparently because it frustrated his dad even more, if the son's ball was heading toward the gutter he would reach down and pull out the retractable gutter guard to knock it back onto the lane. It was bumper bowling with an added element of skill and timing that merely having the bumpers up the whole time wouldn't have required. I admire the kid's ingenuity and subtle rebellion in the face of an overzealous father. Perhaps, though, their relationship would be better served by a game of catch in the backyard.

Robert Huntley is the man refinishing the lanes on the other end of the alley. He and his wife, Shannon, own Playland.

"We met on skates," Shannon says, explaining that she and Robert fell in love after meeting in a roller rink; skating has played a big part in their life for the past eighteen years, and now it does so in a professional capacity: half the building at Playland is occupied by a cavernous room with an oval roller-skating surface surrounded by waist-high walls.

"We moved up here about two years ago to buy this place, from the owners of a rink where Robert was working in Texas," she continues. The couple lives in an apartment on the property with their teenaged son, Andy. There are racks of old brown roller skates, the kind with big orange stoppers at the toe and laces that come up over the ankle.

"A lot of people bring Rollerblades, but a lot still rent the skates," Robert says. "The skating side of the building is supporting the bowling side."

Bowling really is in trouble, I think.

Having shored up the skating business with an elaborate light and sound system, Robert is learning the ins and outs of the bowling business, teaching himself lane maintenance and how to run leagues.

"I'd never bowled in a league before, let alone hosted one. There's a lot to know."

Tonight is the first night of a new league. Among the surprises, even to me, is that leagues not only have presidents and vice presidents and secretaries but also, by rule of the American Bowling Congress, a sergeant at arms—in case anyone gets abusive or a disagreement gets out of hand. During tonight's vote, a woman named Beth with a mildly intimidating build is elected to this position; on paper she's in charge of making sure, among other things, the language is kept out of the gutter.

"I guess they picked me because if I haven't said it, it hasn't been said," she says. Kind of like putting the town drunk in charge of the liquor cabinet.

"Have you ever had occasion to call on the sergeant at arms?" I inquire of Ora and Geneva, a pair of sisters in their early forties who bowl on Beth's team.

"Not in bowling, but we work together and have had to be physically separated from each other at the office," the deceptively mild-mannered Geneva says.

Though tiny in frame, Ora is tough enough to be bowling with a broken hand; I decide a sergeant at arms is a good idea, at least while these two are around.

While their parents bowl, a group of children is content to play with Matchbox cars on a table near the snack bar, scraping together change from their parents to buy a cup of soda and entertaining themselves with imaginative games they are creating on the spot with the cars and boxes of Christmas lights, paint trays, and tools that are scattered about the side of the lanes that Robert is refinishing. They couldn't be happier or more stimulated, using what's around them to generate their own fun. And here I had to quit my job and make a *real* car and a three-thousand-mile-wide country my playground. Either adults are too complex or children are gifted in needing little to gain pleasure from life.

Among the bowlers is Joan, who came to Arkansas by way of an 18-wheeler.

"I was driving a truck and fell in love with a man who lived in Morrilton," she says. "So I moved here."

Sensing a kinship of long days on the road, I ask about her trucking days.

"The thing I liked about driving was the think time," she comments. "You notice the stars more, and the moon when it's full. . . ." She drifts off in fond memories of the road.

I say my good-byes to the Huntleys and drive to the first motel I find, noticing the stars a bit more and wondering what kind of motel charges only seventeen dollars for a room. The answer is on the nightstand: the kind of motel that has a coin-operated vibrating bed. They must make a killing in quarters.

Oklahoma ★

No road trip across America—bowling or otherwise— would be complete without spending some time on Route 66. The road was the first paved route from Chicago to the Pacific Ocean, and along it were born the modern-day motel, the drive-through restaurant, and the establishment that gave Ray Kroc the idea for McDonald's. John Steinbeck coined it the "Mother Road" in *The Grapes of Wrath* in 1939, but its story starts more than a decade earlier.

In 1923 the first civic musings about establishing a national highway system began, and among its most ardent proponents was an Oklahoman named Cyrus Avery. A former insurance salesman and oil investor, he was appointed to the State Highway Commission in Oklahoma that year. Almost immediately he began promoting a Chicago-to-California route that would come through his home state, bringing with it revenue as recreational travelers and commercial vehicles traversed the country. By 1926 the route was established, though it wasn't officially named U.S. Route 66 until 1927. At the time, the vast majority of the nascent highway was unpaved, well-packed dirt.

During the 1930s, as the Dust Bowl ravaged the central United States with rolling clouds of fine black topsoil that buried tractors and would carry dust all the way to the East Coast, Route 66 became a path of exodus. It's estimated that 15 percent of Oklahoma's population left the state over this time, most of them heading west on 66 for California and spawning the derogatory nickname

Okies—the hungry, desperate migrants captured in Dorothea Lange's stark black-and-white photographs from the era.

By 1938 the entire route was finally paved, and as the country's fortunes turned for the better after World War II, 66 entered its heyday. Driving along it took tourists through the Painted Desert, near enough to the Grand Canyon for an easy side trip, and past hundreds of restaurants and attractions that sprang up just to grab one or two of their itinerant dollars. In 1946 Bobby Troup wrote "Get Your Kicks on Route 66," a song that would be a hit for Nat King Cole, Chuck Berry, and the Rolling Stones, among others.

Population growth, an increase in the number of cars and commercial trucks making their way across country, and President Eisenhower's experience in the European theater during the war would lead to the route's demise as a main course across the country. Legislation passed in 1956 called for a new highway system, and by 1970 nearly all of Route 66 was bypassed by humming four-lane interstates. It was officially decommissioned as a U.S. highway in 1985, and while some 85 percent of its course through eight states is still drivable, the ill-maintained Mother Road is gradually returning to the dust from whence it came.

Still, the same sense of nostalgia that keeps some bowling alleys open keeps parts of 66 alive as well. As I pull onto it after a twenty-five-mile detour from I-40 there's no question as to what road this is. Every shop, hotel, restaurant, and service station (even those not of the Phillips 66 chain) along this stretch of 66 employs the iconic black-and-white route marker in its name, or at least in its window. Hardly the efficient thoroughfare it once was, the route itself has become a destination dotted with small towns and quaint-looking restaurants and shops. For reasons I can't explain, I find myself pulling over at an antique shop somewhere outside of Oklahoma City. I am not one who visits antique shops. I do not go "antiquing."

"Antiquing" is what old people, stuffy Martha Stewart types, and annoying newlyweds do as they furnish their home for the first time. Further, "antique" is not a verb. One can't *antique* any more than one

can *lamp* or *Cleveland*. The verbification of nouns like *pencil* (as in "it
in for lunch"), *carpet* (as in "-ing the whole house"), and *table* (as in
"the matter for further discussion later") doesn't bother me, because
they're functional and, more important, not boring. A bunch of rick-
ety old chairs and dusty lace doilies are neither active nor very functional. Or so I think as I walk into Jim Booze's shop, Outskirts
Antiques, in Chandler, Oklahoma.

Jim's a tall, skinny man with wind- and sunburned features. His
red-brown skin is loose around his neck, which has a bandage covering a wound at the collarbone. He greets me as I weave among densely
packed furniture and boxes stacked to the ceiling.

"I got into this business by accident," he tells me. "I never had
much interest in antiques or old furniture until I started seeing them
as time capsules of a sort. These old pieces all have stories."

We're standing in front of a glass-fronted set of shelves from the
early 1900s.

"This one was part of a family's life for generations," he continues.
"It was there for it all—marriages, kids, fights, parties. *Life*."

As he describes this, I immediately think of our kitchen table, a
long rectangle of darkly stained oak that has occupied the kitchen in
my family's home for about a quarter century now. For all of that
time—an entire generation—it has been the center of the Walsh family's universe. The table was there for nearly every meal we ever ate together. Mom and Dad sat at its ends—Dad with his back to the bay
window, holding court for us and whatever guests may have joined us
for the meal, and Mom near the stove, attending to everyone's gastro-
nomic and emotional needs. My brothers and I shared the three chairs
on my father's right and my sisters the three across from us. My seat
was in the middle of the boys' side, to serve as buffer keeping Pat and
Peter from killing each other with steak knives during some angstful
adolescent years. The table was there as we celebrated birthdays and
Christmases and Thanksgivings and Easters—literally hundreds of
events. It was there when the eighty candles on Grandma Buckley's
birthday cake set off the smoke detector. It was there as we mourned

our father's death and prepared his funeral; it held the drinks and sandwiches as we gathered with a houseful of friends and family after his burial.

The table was there when my sister Regan, then eight years old, attempted the magic trick where you pour a gallon of milk into a cone of newspaper and the milk miraculously (at least when a real magician does it) disappears. Regan's milk, of course, sopped the newspaper, a number of dinner guests, and the floor beneath the table; our collective laughter and teasing sent her out of the room in tears. The table was there for the first Thanksgiving after our dad's passing, the first time he wasn't there to carve the turkey, when the tears weren't just Regan's. And it is still there now, the lone witness to my mother's evenings as she sits nibbling on whatever snack she's made herself for dinner, reading the paper and wishing fervently that her husband was in his place at the other end.

Jim silently watches as I relive all of this in an instant, and then shows me some of the highlights of his collection, other pieces, like the Walsh kitchen table, that have stories, that have seen life.

"This is a collection of love letters that date from 1895 to 1910," he says, pulling out a box full of envelopes and papers. There are some eight hundred of them, and Jim seems to have committed each one to memory.

"The woman, really a girl at the time, was high society, and the boy was from the wrong part of town, the wrong kind of family," Jim narrates for me. "But she wrote him for fifteen years anyway. Twenty-one of the letters were written by a friend of hers while the woman was fighting scarlet fever." He shows me; these mainly contain news of her health, and update her star-crossed lover on her body temperature at three different times of the day.

"I did some further research into the couple," Jim says. "It ends happily: they were married in 1910."

I shake hands with Jim in front of his shop, a new perspective on dusty old antiques in mind and just a few more miles on Route 66 to go before rejoining its replacement and then turning south.

That night, in Norman, Oklahoma's Sooner Bowl, antiques and history weigh heavily on my mind. The night's league is comprised mostly of teams of thirty- to forty-five-year-olds, but I opt to go antiquing and sit down with a team named "The Old Guys." The "Guys" are named John, Art, Paul, and Frank, and their ages add up to 305 years. Art carries more than his share of these years, at ninety-two. As his younger teammate Paul puts it, "He's old enough to be everyone here's daddy."

Art, who is so skinny he must weigh something close to his age, walks toward the foul line with his ball by his side, increasing his speed by the time he reaches it, then drops his ball into what somehow turns into a perfect hook.

"I worked for the U.S. Geological Survey until I retired," he says, "in 1963."

I think about this for a moment. In the forty years since this man has been retired, the Beatles invaded America and we figured out how to land and walk on the moon and won the Cold War. He's lived through nine presidents and has outlived 50 percent of the Beatles. I must know, "What have you been doing for all that time?"

"I've been golfing a lot," he says, "and bowling some. I moved down here about nine years ago to be near my daughter. My wife has Alzheimer's and is in a nursing home nearby. She has trouble remembering me, but I visit her every day. We've been married sixty-six years now."

"It must be really frustrating to see her go through that," I say, thinking it an understatement.

"It can be," he replied, "but you know what? I'd miss loving her."

Art's teammate Paul, who is old enough to be my grandfather and yet, as he noted, young enough to be Art's son, is a retired postal

worker. He speaks of a time he worked for the government in another capacity.

"Uncle Sam sent me halfway around the world to get shot at for a
while," he says. "Then I came back here."

The people doing the shooting had been Germans; Paul helped lib-
erate Italy from them during World War II. Today we call that a just
war, though I suspect it must have been a hard thing to believe when
the bullets were flying at the then-young Oklahoman.

"What was it like, going to war?" I ask Paul.

Over the din of crashing pins and announcements that we're approaching the end of league play, Paul puts his finger on the dichoto-
mous nature of being a soldier, something nearly impossible for those
of us who've never served to understand.

"I wouldn't take a million dollars in exchange for the experience
and memories," he says, "but I wouldn't pay a cent for one more second of it."

Texas ★

CROSSING the border into the state known for the saying "everything's bigger here," I drive due south through Dallas and stop in Austin to meet a high school friend whose nickname was Big Daddy long before he ever moved to Texas. He's lost most of the weight since then, but the moniker remains. We drive to Austin's outskirts to visit the Salt Lick, a barbecue joint the size of, well, let's just say it's quite large, and then return to town to bowl a few lines.

The bowling alley's dimensions are in line with those of other states. The adjoining Dart Bowl Steakhouse features "Austin's favorite homemade enchiladas" and Lone Star beer is the beverage of choice—contractual obligations to Miller notwithstanding. A 52" high bowling pin–shaped cutout serves as an amusement park–style measuring stick in reverse: "You must be no taller than this bowling pin to bowl with bumpers." This rule proves to hinder the Big Dad's game, and he puts up lackluster numbers of pins across the board.

The Texas Union Underground, which serves as a student center and recreation facility for the University of Texas, offers informal courses like Couple Massage, Intro to Texas Hold 'Em, and, thanks to a state-of-the-art twelve-lane facility, Beginning Bowling. I watch as a morning class completes its lesson and lace up for a date with the local NBC camera crew.

I flirt shamelessly with Julie, the cute sportscaster who's covering the story for them.

"I keep in shape with a steady diet of High Life and nacho cheese," I say in my best self-deprecating-yet-endearing way, gesturing toward my burgeoning belly that happens to be shrouded in a High Life logo.

We bowl a number of frames for background footage, and Julie proves to be the consummate professional—responding to neither my flirtation nor my obvious attempts to work in Miller talking points, most of which are edited out by the time the piece airs that evening. The exception is the shot in which I'm patting my belly, which on camera comes across as gross and embarrassing rather than endearing and funny. Lesson learned.

After a late lunch in San Antonio with the crew of a Wienermobile that I happened across (they're easy to spot), I mosey over to the Alamo for a quick tour and decide it's time to put Texas behind me and get to New Mexico today.

Not that that's remotely possible starting this late in the day. Despite the fact that San Antonio is nearly in the middle of the state, it's still well over five hundred miles to the New Mexico border. The barren landscape that is West Texas makes that distance immeasurably longer. Not knowing this at the time, and trying to inject a little bit of Route 66–style romance into this leg of the journey, I opt for an old highway, Route 190, that runs parallel to Interstate 10, which cuts across the lower half of the state from Louisiana until it hits Mexico and follows the Rio Grande along the border to El Paso and then into Las Cruces, New Mexico.

What I-10 would offer in term of speed and efficiency 190 promises in intrigue and adventure. As I make my way westward, I begin to realize this may be a promise unfulfilled. The town names that looked so enchanting on my map—Eldorado, Fort McKavett—in their small font size and tiniest of dots representing their locations turn out to be merely stop signs with interminably bland scenery filling the long stretches between them. The landscape is an exhaustively boring composite of sand, unremarkable rocks, grass, and low-lying scrub brush in all directions, which is exactly what I-10 offers, only without the stop signs that might have been towns to impede my escape.

Darkness falls hard and I've made no progress in conquering this giant state; 190 takes on the feel of a ghost highway, nothing visible in any direction beyond the limited tunnel of light projecting from the front of Mom's Honda. The headlamps actually make the darkness on either side darker, a vast emptiness that envelops me. My solitude begins to get the better of me, and I revert to irrational childhood fears about monsters under the bed, ghouls in the closet. Only now my parents' room isn't just across the hallway. In fact, the nearest person is across an untold expanse of threatening landscape that I'm convinced is filled with specters of cowboys who died unavenged deaths and have a strong distaste for itinerant redheads in white Hondas. My cell phone's signal is sporadic, and it's too late to call anyone for company anyway. I begin wishing to see some other traffic to counter the fear my imagination is creating, but when another vehicle does appear I scream, then pray it is not a ghost. And then there are the armadillos.

The first one looks defiant, pausing to look up at me from the middle of my lane as though I've trespassed on its property. Its gray body has the humped shape of an old man, and its eyes are a haunting yellow. I jerk the wheel into the oncoming lane.

The second one is trotting toward me like we're playing chicken. Again, I swerve into the left lane, only to find another 'dillo waiting for me there. The back left tire catches this one. In the rearview mirror I see it spinning on its hard, shelled back, the contact with my Goodyear having flipped it over.

The road continues on like this interminably, making for some tense driving. It's not like they're small—some of these bastards look to be the size of baby bears, and I imagine the damage to the undercarriage from hitting an animal with the root word "armor" in its name could be pretty severe. God forbid I break down.

Running this gauntlet of ghost cars and fearless shelled mammals wears on me and convinces me to stop in the next town I come to, which turns out to be Iraan (pronounced "Ira Anne"). The town is apparently known for its Mexican food and overpriced rooms where they know travelers coming off the ghost highway will pay anything to pass the darkness behind a locked door.

I rise early and keep driving west, the daylight and a change of routes to I-10 making the trek that much easier, though the Texas miles still seem bigger.

New Mexico ★

NINETEEN letters, arranged in an order that is at once beckoning and foreboding, decide my destination for tonight. Their clear-cut, black-and-white, somewhat sinister implication is unlike anything I've ever seen on a map. I need to go there, to say I've been there, to send postcards postmarked from there, to take pictures by the "Welcome to" sign, and to ask the question that everyone must ask the first person they see there: "How did this place get the name Truth or Consequences?"

This is, after all, New Mexico, which rose from the definitive dust of the Old West. Back when it was just a territory, posses chased outlaws here. Cattle were stolen. Banks were robbed. Legends were born and inflated. Billy the Kid is buried in New Mexico, though some dispute that fact: like most outlaws and legends, the Kid's story is shrouded in the mystery and controversy that comprise the nature of all outlaws and legends. Many contend that the man Sheriff Pat Garrett shot in 1881 wasn't actually the twenty-one-year-old bandit who'd killed a man for every year he'd lived but rather an unknown Mexican who was in the wrong place at the wrong time. This, some allege, allowed the real Billy the Kid to escape and live a full, free life until 1950 with the perfect cover: "Nope. I'm not him. He's dead."

I am certain there is rich history like this behind the naming of Truth of Consequences. Were these the words of a renegade U.S. Marshal known for offering criminals a choice between the two just before he dispatched them with his pearl-handled Colt? Was this place a crossroads for wanted men running toward the promise of freedom and tacos in Mexico? A place where gunfighters made their last stands? Where duels on dusty streets were once the only form of law? There is a reason it earned its name as a place where all is laid bare . . . or else. Can one find the answer to this question at a bowling alley? I have a feeling it's as good a place as any.

The bar at Chili Bowl Lanes is dark and dim despite it being early evening; when I left, the sun outside was still quite visible, making its way past Arizona and California on its way over the Pacific horizon. I sit down two stools away from the only other patron in the bar, a young-but-weathered woman smoking bargain cigarettes. She smokes them quickly, as though she doesn't want to let the red glow at the end turn to gray ash. She is drinking chardonnay on the rocks and complaining loudly to the bartender about someone named Toby, who I gather is her boyfriend.

"If that sumbitch wants to go around puttin' his dick in everything he sees, fine! I'll just tell his momma I'm moving back east and takin' her grandbaby with me. See how he likes that!"

Down any hopes of finding Chili Bowl's bar to be an Old West–style saloon with swinging doors and a plinky piano, I opt not to distract the bartender's attention from this woman's tale of woe. This isn't the context in which I want to be regaled with the legend of how Truth or Consequences came to its name. And I fear that Toby's girlfriend will inject too much contemporary drama into the story. I turn to the TV and wait for the league crowd to pour into the adjoining lanes.

The TV, a beacon of brightness wedged into an otherwise dark corner, is tuned to one of the reality shows that have recently become the punch line and storyline of our popular culture. Until now I've managed to maintain only a superficial awareness of the shows, hoping the trend will pass before I get the chance to be made dumber by it. The program in front of me at the moment appears to be about a beefy-looking man who wears a sweater and rides a horse around while a bevy of narrowly caricatured women look up at him anxiously.

Joe Millionaire, perhaps, or maybe *The Sweater-Wearing Bachelor* or *Who Wants to Marry a Guy on a Horse?*

There is little left to write about reality TV shows, and little I would like to repeat here. Their ubiquity, their success, and their debasing shallowness have been lamented quite thoroughly, even by devotees who acknowledge their fandom with a hint of sheepishness . . . a guilty, voyeuristic pleasure. The coincidence of being subjected to an entire episode of one in the town of Truth or Consequences is, however, worth noting. As I'm disappointed to learn from the woman behind the counter at Chili Bowl Lanes, the legend of the town's name has more to do with *Fear Factor* than any Old Western folklore.

"It was named after the Ralph Edwards game show."

Before there were reality shows to give average people their chance to be on TV, game shows filled that role. And before there was TV to make average people into stars, there was radio. In 1940 up-and-coming radio personality Ralph Edwards brought to the airwaves his version of a parlor game: *Truth or Consequences.* Audiences of the day—without the aid of visuals—would listen as contestants answered trivia questions and paid "consequences" for incorrect responses. Kind of a *Let's Make a Deal* meets *Jeopardy.* "Consequences" might include dressing up like a baby or washing an elephant—things that seem rather tame in contrast to current-day game shows on which being buried alive with snakes might be the actual game, not just the consequence. How such sight gags translated into audio humor is difficult to imagine from today's perspective, as is the folksy innocence of it all. Edwards would thrill the radio audience with impish, in-on-it commentary as contestants executed their consequences. "Aren't we devils?" he would ask rhetorically, basking in the hilarity of the bit.

Somehow this lasted on the radio for nearly two decades with great success. As the show's tenth anniversary approached, Edwards called out to a nation of listeners and pleaded for some city out there to rechristen itself in honor of his show. In exchange, the show would make its tenth anniversary broadcast from what used to be Anywhere, USA, but would henceforth be known as Truth or Consequences.

Enter Burton Roach, a New Mexico state senator and manager of what was then the Hot Springs Chamber of Commerce. The town was named Hot Springs for reasons both historical and super-historical. The super-historical: geothermal forces that developed over millions of years to heat and bring water to the earth's surface here. The historical: the area around the springs themselves had long been a neutral territory for southwest Indian tribes. They would gather here for inter-tribal exchange and to make use of the healing mineral water. Famed Apache chief Geronimo was a regular visitor. But by 1950 there were literally dozens of other towns named Hot Springses in the Southwest, all relying upon tourism for income. Roach saw an opportunity to gain publicity and differentiate his town from all the other Hot Springses by associating it with Ralph Edwards's show; he called for a vote on the matter.

The vote passed, though not without some protest, and on April 1, 1950, Ralph Edwards brought *Truth or Consequences* the radio show to Truth or Consequences, New Mexico. At that moment, this Hot Springs ceased to exist.

Memories of this grand publicity stunt now long gone from the national consciousness, the people of T or C are stuck having to tell that story to visitors like me who can't fathom what a phenomenon it was at the time. The ever more outrageous and fleeting nature of our entertainment today just wouldn't translate to something so quaint and civically permanent. Ralph Edwards's harmless impishness lies in stark contrast to the humiliating intent of shows that seek to break up relationships or exploit deep-seated personal fears. There will never be a Joe Millionaire, Montana, a The Bachelorette, Ohio, nor a Temptation Island, Kansas. After all, there are no islands in Kansas.

On lanes eleven and twelve at Chili Bowl, a team of bowlers is wearing royal blue polo shirts with "Sutherland Chiropractic" written in cursive on the back. They slap high-five after each roll in support and celebration with both teammates and competitors and say things like, "Well, that's why they call it 'bowling' and not 'pins falling down,'" when they roll poorly. Rather than swearing, they've taken to yelling, "Aflac!" after a bad frame, mimicking the frustrated duck in the insurance commercials.

A man named Dennis is standing behind the lanes watching his wife, Susie, bowl.

"My feeling is, if you're not having fun you're doing it wrong," he tells me when he learns what's brought me to T or C. "I was an engineer near Anaheim, California, and had a house overlooking Disneyland. Each night I'd sit out on the front porch and watch the fireworks show for free. It got to the point where I could predict the next burst because I'd seen the same show so many times. Anyway, I was confident if I quit work I could always get my job back or find another one, so I made a point of quitting every winter to travel."

"How did you meet Susie?" I ask.

"A couple of years ago I happened to be out at a bar and saw her sitting with her sister. I asked her sister, 'Does she like to dance?' "

"What did her sister say?"

"She said, 'Yes,' so I asked Susie if she'd care to. We've been dancing ever since."

A bowler named Christine who speaks with a slight German accent tells me, "If I go on vacation, my bowling ball goes with me."

"Are you on vacation now?" I ask.

"No, I moved here from Hamburg. Back in 1958 I met an American GI stationed nearby. We fell in love listening to rock and roll."

"You're not Priscilla Presley, are you?" I joke, referring to the fact that Elvis met his future wife in similar circumstances. Christine humors me with a slight laugh and goes to bowl her turn.

Ken and Nancy are the husband-and-wife team that owns Chili Bowl. It was Nancy who shared with me the history of how T or C got its name.

"It's been a lot more work than we had planned," she says of running the business, though it runs in the family. "We have a son in

Texas who runs a very big bowling center there," she adds with subdued pride.

As the center empties out, Ken assembles a number of his personal bowling balls on lanes one and two.

"Come on over, Mike. I'm going to show you how to roll a hook," he says.

Having seen me bowl, he decides it's time for an impromptu lesson.

"Try this one," he says, handing me a blue ball with a duller surface than most house balls. "That helps it gain some grip on the lane," he explains. The holes are designed so that the thumb goes in as far as the first knuckle and the two fingers only to the very tip.

"That will help you put rotation on it when you release it."

Like a father teaching a son to catch a baseball or ride a bike, Ken walks me through improving my bowling—though since we're keeping score he doesn't hesitate to shatter the pins when it's his turn.

By the game's end, he's got me by eighty pins, but I'm rolling a respectable hook. The ball leaves my hand and glides down and toward the right gutter on the first part of the lane, then catches and turns back toward the headpin.

As the last patrons depart, I thank Ken for the game. Preparing to lock up and shut the lights off for the night, he and Nancy walk me to the door, where we stop for a moment. On the wall to our right there is a plaque shaped like the number 1 and a framed news clipping.

"We bought this place to give our younger son a place to work on his game, and to someday take over from us," Ken says. "That's from a tournament he won when he was eighteen, four years ago now. He was killed in a car accident a year later on his way home from a bowling tournament in Albuquerque."

This place that was supposed to be their legacy to their second son when he was ready to take it over, and a place of entertainment and joy in the meantime, is a constant reminder of a tragedy they'd not be able to put out of their minds anyway. I can think of nothing to say in response to this, such an unexpectedly emotional way to end a night of bowling.

Tears well up in all of our eyes as we look around in silence at a bowling center that's become a shrine. Eventually I thank them again for their hospitality, knowing there's nothing I can do to soften their pain, and check into a motel for the night.

★ Colorado

ADDING adventure to my adventure, I spend a night under the stars at Great Sand Dunes National Park to remind myself why I don't like camping. The park's namesake dunes have been formed by wind blowing sand for millennia against the base of the Sangre de Cristo Mountains, which act as a wall preventing the sand from blowing farther east. Covering nearly nineteen thousand acres, at their highest the rolling dunes rise some 750 feet above the ground; their shapes are constantly shifting and changing at the wind's whim.

With a view of the sun setting over this remarkable field of massive, golden dunes, my campsite has a fire pit, a picnic table, and patches of snow in its corners. At once, as the sun finally disappears, the air temperature drops from 40 degrees to near zero, just as the park's ranger had warned me it would. After burning through two bundles of wood purchased at the park's visitor center in a fire that provides almost no warmth, I retreat to Mom's Honda, thinking the time to be near midnight. The blue glow of the digital clock, newly set to Mountain Time, reads 9:30. I spend the road trip's longest night starting the car, letting it run for just long enough to get warm, then shutting it off in hopes of sleeping until daylight. Each time I wake, the clock mocks me by having moved only thirty minutes or so. At 6:00 A.M. I bail out of the park, and I drive with the heat blowing at full blast for an hour until a diner in nearby Alamosa opens.

That night in Colorado Springs, I have my first brush with my own near fame at Bear Creek Lanes: as I bowl, a young man bowling alone on the lane adjacent to mine, getting in some practice for an upcoming league, gets my attention.

"Are you the guy who's bowling in all fifty states?" he asks.

His name is Brooks, and he had read an article about me in *American Bowler* magazine. Okay, so it's not exactly *Vanity Fair* and Brooks isn't exactly groupie material, but I nonetheless let it go to my head. From sleeping in a borrowed car to full-on celebrity in less than twenty-four hours . . . not bad.

The next morning, I return to Bear Creek Lanes. No one recognizes me this time, but a seventy-five-year-old man relates to me.

"I was in advertising, too," he says when I tell him about the job I'd quit to go bowling, and agrees with me that the field can feel like it lacks meaning. "Sometimes you wonder why you're spending so much energy trying to get people to buy things they don't need."

Briefly self-conscious, I put on my green pullover to cover up the Miller High Life logo on my T-shirt.

From Colorado Springs it's off to Denver, where a group of friends from disparate corners of my life ranging from college, Oscar Mayer, and Chicago to work and my current odyssey gather at Sport Bowl, a beautiful dive with eight lanes and walls lined with faux-marble laminate. Sixteen of us take over the right four lanes and drink the place dry of High Life.

Fresh as a daisy the next morning, I drive into the Rocky Mountains and the city of Edwards therein.

The reason for this side trip initially has nothing to do with bowling and everything to do with seeing my former Wienermobile partner, Courtney, and her husband, Bill. Bill had been a Hotdogger for the year before us and then stayed on as an "advisor" to make sure the newbies could handle the job. He then used this position of authority to begin courting Courtney in what might be the strangest venue ever for workplace romance. (The boundaries of good taste and a release I signed with Oscar Mayer prohibit me from making a wiener joke here.) The two were married in September.

Bill, who speaks very quickly, says, "You'regoingtogotoLeadville, right?" to which I reply, "Courtney, translation please?"

"He's saying you need to go to Leadville. It's about an hour up the mountains and has the highest bowling alley in the world."

Bill drives me to Leadville, where, after learning that their Super Bowl party tomorrow night will involve ten-dollar buckets of Miller High Life and self-service nachos (press the button and hot cheese oozes right onto your plate and into your arteries), I decide to return for my last night in Colorado.

Leadville is a tiny town, a mile long and about as wide. The views are spectacular, as one would expect, when the streets are not literally in the clouds. The town has the feel of an Old West mining town, which it once was: silver mines drew some thirty thousand people to 10,152 feet in elevation during the late 1800s, gambler and gunfighter Doc Holliday among them. Holliday once wounded a man in a shoot-out in Hyman's Saloon here.

The crowd at Kristi Lanes, consuming copious amounts of High Life and specialty shots the bartender, Wrae, keeps pouring, at times feels like it might break into gunplay.

"I had to put a kid in a headlock the other night," Wrae, a woman in her thirties who manages Kristi Lanes and apparently serves as its bouncer on occasion, says. She has the temperament for it.

"I've been married twice—picked wrong both times," she says with an odd mixture of grimness and joviality. "I'm not afraid of anything."

Following the game, some bowling, and twenty minutes of unintelligible conversation with an unshaven, quite drunk man who kept leering at young girls, I make my way to the Silver Dollar Saloon. There a man is recounting advice he gave his child about how to deal with a bully at school.

" 'You're seven years old,' I told him. 'Kick his ass in the nuts!' "

I order a beer from the tap. Reading about the place's past—Oscar

Wilde once drank here, and the "unsinkable" Molly Brown once cleaned the very tile floor upon which I'm standing—I say something about how much history there is here. The man who is teaching his seven-year-old about nut-kicking chimes in surprisingly philosophically.

"Every second you breathe is history," he says. "There is no future."

The bartender, Raquel, has a somewhat sunnier outlook as she conveys one of the unexpected pleasures of living nearly two miles above sea level.

"My kids' favorite thing is to chase clouds down the street."

The next morning I chase clouds through Leadville with Mom's Honda, past Kristi Lanes, across the Continental Divide, and north into Wyoming with eleven states left to go.

★ Wyoming

I cross the Colorado/Wyoming border and turn west. The sky, light blue from horizon to horizon, is cloudless. It is a perfect day for a drive in this direction, racing the sun toward the ocean, gaining ground with the Earth's rotation the whole time. As I get farther west, however, Mom's Honda begins to struggle. The infrequency of highway exits along this stretch of I-80 and my lack of urgent car repair funds weigh heavily, and I pull over at a rest stop to look under the hood and pretend I know something about engines. Suddenly I'm faced with a bigger problem: I can't open the door.

That's not quite accurate. I can't open the door all the way. I get it partially open and a giant, invisible hand forces it shut, my left arm folding involuntarily at the elbow.

Holy shit, that's a lot of wind.

Across the parking lot, a pair of truckers are adjusting the canvas straps holding crates the size of Volkswagens onto their flatbeds. "Just double-checking," they tell me when I finally manage to exit the car, pulling my fingers away from the slamming door just in time to avoid injury. "The wind was rattling some of the crates in front loose."

"Of course," I say, though it goes unheard amid the clatter of canvas and whistling air catching the ear at off angles. "Very prudent of you to make sure your cargo doesn't careen off and crush the next Honda that tries to pass you."

To my left is a lone tree, barely rooted in a rock formation, somehow holding on to the ground with its roots, forced to grow with an eastward tilt by the same relentless wind that impedes my progress. Its trunk bends midway at nearly a 90-degree angle. For miles in any direction, it is the only tree of significant size, growing some thirty feet from a pile of rocks. It must be the world's heartiest and most improbable tree.

Mom's Honda is running just fine, I determine without opening the hood for fear of it blowing clear off. There's just a bit of a headwind. I manage to get the door open and slip into the driver's seat before it slams shut with no help from me.

Holy shit, that's a lot of wind.

Jeffrey Lanes in Rawlins is a bit wanting for conversation at first, something I attribute to a life spent speaking in short bursts that can be heard above the wind.

"Where do you go when you're not hanging out here?" I ask a woman bowling on lane three.

"Anywhere."

"Is this the best place to have a beer in town?" I ask the man at the bar cheerfully.

"As good as any," comes his response, dismally.

Then, in a reminder to be careful what you wish for, a stranger chats me up.

"Holland's the best place in the world to be in jail," the tall, lanky thirtysomething man with sandy hair says. There is a certain wistful nostalgia in the way he says it and then looks into space, nodding thoughtfully as if he's thinking, *Ah, prison . . .*

I find myself oddly wishing I had a basis of comparison for his claim. I want to say, "Oh yeah? Ever do time in Canada? Now *that's* good imprisonment." Instead I hold out my hand: "My name's Mike."

"Mike? Clint. Nice to meet you."

That Dutch prisons offer a sort of paradisiacal incarceration was the main lesson of an involved tale about his work experience as drug

runner transporting cocaine for a Colombian cartel. Apparently he'd
been imprisoned in enough countries to have his own broad base of
comparison.

Prior to being jailed in Holland, he'd been held up there by some
Jamaican traffickers in a deal gone bad. Certain they were about to kill
him, he managed to talk the men into allowing him one phone call.
He called his boss in Colombia, who told his captors this: "Your door-
bell will ring in twenty minutes. If my friend doesn't answer the door,
I will hold you responsible."

"Twenty minutes later six Colombians I'd never seen arrived at the
Jamaicans' apartment," Clint says. "They rang the doorbell, guns
drawn, and got me out without firing a shot. Scared the piss out of the
Jamaicans. Scared me, too. No way I'd ever roll over on my boss if he
can dispatch a posse that fast from another hemisphere."

That didn't stop the Jamaicans from eventually rolling over on
Clint to the Dutch authorities, who arrested him and showed him
what a good prison is like. This all seems somewhat unbelievable to
me, and his tales get wilder the more red beers we consume. ("Red"
beer is the en vogue beverage here: beer mixed with tomato juice,
Clamato, or Bloody Mary mix. Filling, cheaper than a proper dinner,
and the tomato's saltiness really dresses up a High Life nicely.)

"My wife and son are down in Texas," Clint says. The latter was
born on a beach as Clint performed the roles of both delivery room
doctor and nervous common-law husband.

He spins brush-with-death stories of miracle spider bite cures he
found among tribes in remote South American villages and heroic
chases running from drug lords. The rant wanders meanderingly until
an intense look forms in his eyes. He turns straight toward me, grabbing his beer glass forcefully.

"It exists. The technology to run engines on hydrogen exists, and
the CIA has been using it in their black helicopters for years."

The conspiracy theorists always get to the black helicopters eventually. It is their proof of concept: an unsubstantiated phenomenon that
explains world events. A plane crashes with an important political fig-

ure on it? Black helicopters caused it, then came and cleaned up any evidence of their presence, made everything look like an accident. Kennedy gets shot: a black helicopter from the grassy knoll fired the magic bullet. An earthquake hits Iran during a politically sensitive time: black helicopters. We're dependent on foreign oil because the CIA is keeping its hydrogen engine technology secret: how else could a black helicopter run so quietly? It all makes such perfect nonsense, and at the conclusion of Clint's hydrogen engine spiel I politely thank him for the conversation and make for the door.

On the way home I stop in the Rifleman.

While it's been a bar for some thirty-three years, past tenants in the Rifleman's space have included a Montgomery Ward catalog store and candy shop during the days when Rawlins was an important mining and railroad town. Tonight there are only three other patrons inside and Beverly, the bartender.

Despite the thin crowd, it would be hard to be lonely here: there are at least thirty-five animal heads, antlers, and stuffed carcasses adorning the walls. A sign on the wall promotes a kind of social responsibility that should be reapplied throughout society: "If you knock a ball off the pool table, you must play fifty cents in the jukebox." I like the notion of rule breakers giving something back to society like that.

One of the carcasses, stuffed and occupying a balcony in the rear of the bar, is a two-headed calf. This fascinates me—it's the kind of thing that I never believed existed, and it's no replica. This is an honest-to-God mutant cow that was part of the way to being twins and instead came out of its mother with one body and two heads. I stand with my red beer and gawk at it, openmouthed, for twenty minutes. On my walk back to the motel I phone a friend who lived in Wyoming for several years and mention the oddity.

"There's a two-headed calf in every bar in Wyoming," he says, simultaneously deflating me and filling me with wonder.

★   ★   ★

On the TV in my room in the Rawlins Inn, President Bush is giving
the State of the Union address. "The first car a child born today
drives," he says, "could be powered by a hydrogen fuel cell."

Suddenly guilty for having doubted Clint's sanity, I sleep fitfully;
the distant rumble of rotors fills my ears.

I arrive in Jackson, Wyoming, just before sunset the next day and
find a charming town evocative of the Old West, with wooden sidewalks above streets muddied with snow and sand spread for traction.
Off the town square is a park whose entry arch is made of elk antlers,
shed by herds that inhabit a nearby elk refuge and Grand Teton National Park. This is appropriate enough, as I learn the only bowling
alley in town is at the Elks Lodge, run by that animal's Benevolent &
Protective Order.

The Benevolent & Protective Order of Elks was founded in 1868,
in New York. Originally begun as the Jolly Corks, a loose group of ac-
tors and entertainers looking for an excuse to drink on Sundays, the
BPOE evolved into a charitable fraternity dedicated to providing such
things as eyeglasses to needy children, artificial limbs to those who
couldn't afford them, and outings for underprivileged children. While
all of that sounds warm and cuddly, it's still a somewhat secretive society. Aspiring members must be sponsored by an existing member
and cosponsored by two more, fill out an application, and then be
voted on by the membership. As with most organizations of this sort,
there are secret rituals and traditions known only to the members.

As I stand in the icy mountain air outside the BPOE lodge on
Broadway Avenue in Jackson's town center, the only tradition I'm
concerned with is one that allows wayward travelers who really need
to bowl to enter the lodge. Though I went to a bowling alley in Rawlins, I didn't actually *bowl* there, since I was so caught up in unraveling
conspiracy theories and discussing the merits of various foreign penal
systems with Clint. Backtracking out of remote Jackson to find a

bowling alley would be inefficient in a state so sparsely populated. A glance at my map shows Jackson as the largest town in northwestern Wyoming, with the next closest population that might support an operational bowling alley looking like Rock Springs—four hours south down a two-lane highway when tomorrow I need to move north toward Montana. As I reach for the buzzer beneath the "Members Only" sign, I'm praying for some benevolence on the part of the Elks.

The door opens and I find myself in a rather dark lobby. To the left is a rather dark bar with about a dozen members who until this moment had been enjoying the privacy and camaraderie of the Order without an outsider's intrusion.

"Hi. Sorry to bother you. I was just hoping I could bowl a quick game."

"The bowling alley's downstairs," says the bartender, eager to get me out. "I don't know if they'll let you bowl or not. Ask for Jim Taylor."

Following his gesture, I find a staircase and make my way down. At the foot is a large red stop sign, foreboding at first, but as I get closer I see it says: "Wet Shoes Off Here" under the word "Stop." It's not to keep nonmembers out—it's to keep snow off the lanes.

"Of course you can bowl," Jim Taylor says warmly, if slightly puzzled by the fact that I'm cowering meekly when I ask him. His gray beard connects to a band of hair that stops at the crown of his bald head, framing a friendly smile. "Just as soon as this group finishes up I'll put you on a lane."

A group of employees from nearby Jackson Hole Resort is finishing up a private twenty-five-year-old birthday party on the lanes. The partyers are mostly transplants from other parts of the county who came once to ski or rock climb or hike and just ended up staying.

"We rent the space out to raise funds to keep the building operating and help us with our charity work," Jim says. "We're busy a lot of nights, actually."

The four lanes are in pristine condition, thanks largely to Jim's passion as their caretaker.

"I guess that's why they keep me around," he says. "I'm one of the only guys who know how to fix the pinsetters."

On one wall a giant bowling ball is painted, with a trail of overlapping red circles painted behind it to imply the motion of a ball rolling down the lane. The opposite wall shields the bowling area from the bar/front desk where Jim is standing while a couple of Elks members are casually watching the bowlers through square windows in the wall. Two L-shaped wooden benches polished to a shine flank the parquet floors on either side of the settee area, and the scoring tables are manual, with built-in projectors. Writing with grease pens on transparent scorecards, the bowlers can follow the action on rectangular screens above each lane—a precursor to the modern electronic scoring console.

While I wait for the group to clear the lanes, Jim tells me a little about Jackson.

"Twenty years ago my arm would get tired from waving as I walked down the street, I'd see so many people I knew," Jim tells me. "There are a lot of new people now, though. You don't see as many familiar faces."

While Jackson's population is only around eighty-five hundred, that's about double what it was as recently as 1990, driven by increased tourism to Grand Teton and Yellowstone National Parks, as well as a migration of wealthy businesspeople and celebrities buying up nearby ranches.

Jim is featured in a painting in the stairway of the Mangy Moose saloon, one of the main hangouts in Teton Village, the slope-side lodging for Jackson Hole's ski area. Wearing a blue tank top that reveals his belly, shorts, and blue-and-red-striped tube socks in cowboy boots, he's running from a moose that is interrupting his picnic with a buxom young lass who's holding a small white dog. It's a ridiculous but locally iconic painting, and in addition to his friendly demeanor, surely people recognize him from it. No wonder so many people would wave to him.

The birthday party group starts to thin out and a lane becomes available. As I bowl I notice a young woman on the lane next to me. All night she has been rolling a wicked hook that just shatters the pins on impact. The sound alone is impressive, different from other sounds of pins crashing in a way that only someone who's spent the last four months in bowling alleys might recognize. She is exponentially better than any of her peers, which I point out to her.

"When I was twelve my mother died in a car accident," she says. "So it was just my dad and me. I was entering puberty and he had no idea had to handle it."

"I can't imagine."

"Like any teenager, I hated him and blamed him for everything," she continues. "Great daughter, right? Being a total bitch while he's trying to deal with losing the love of his life and raising me."

"Well, you wouldn't have wanted to deprive him of knowing what it's like to have a teenager," I say, trying to provide some gentle levity and wondering what caused her to tell this story when I told her she had a good bowling hook.

"Then he enrolled us in a father/daughter league, and it let us spend time together without the pressure of growing up and grieving. Kind of a way to distract us both, I guess. For three hours every week we could let down our guard and relate to each other."

"Do you still bowl with him?"

"Every time I'm home."

Thanking Jim and the Elks for their hospitality, I put my shoes back on by the stop sign and wander the streets of Jackson for an hour before holing up at a lodge. The wooden sidewalk thumps and creaks quietly with each step. The Grand Tetons stand dark and strong in the blue, snow-lit night. Tomorrow my journey into the West continues with ten states remaining.

★ Montana

I N a minitribute to my father, at whose funeral a contingent of Ohio State Troopers wept at losing such a profitable source of speeding ticket income, I had planned to test the limits of Mom's Honda as soon as I crossed the border into speed-limitless Montana. And I do so, passing a hundred at the state line and still climbing, until I see this sign, just after the one reading "Welcome to Montana":

SPEED LIMIT 75

Apparently Montana has done away with its previous law regarding speed limits on highways ("reasonable, as road conditions dictate" is what I'm told the law books said). My tribute ruined, I slow to ninety and follow signs to Historic Downtown Butte to have a look around at what I am imagining will be another quaint Old West town with wooden sidewalks, swinging saloon doors, and rugged, mustached cowboys just in from the drive.

I fail to find anything quaint, much less wooden sidewalks and swinging saloon doors. But I do manage to find rugged. Rugged, along with its close cousins Haggard and Trodden, has set up camp in a bar with no name that, at two in the afternoon with almost no outside light penetrating its filth-layered windows, is completely full. A thick haze of smoke hovers, stagnant, in the two feet of space immediately below drop ceiling panels that have been yellowed by nicotine deposits accumulating over years. The patrons appear to be descendants of cowboys whose cattle didn't much care for them: I can't tell whether it's unemployment or a shift at a backbreaking factory that just ended that has put such misery into the faces, but I know I don't want to catch what they've got. No bar should be this full and pouring so many stiff drinks this time of day. I use the pay phone to make a call and run for the car, breaking the speed limit by twenty all the way to Helena.

In Helena I check into a motel and hit Sleeping Giant Lanes, named for a mountain formation that looks like a giant man lying on his back on the Helena horizon, to have some red beers for dinner. The bar/lounge is bustling like the one in Butte, but it's a more congenial bustle and the right time of day for it—night.

The evening leagues finish up and I approach the counter to get a lane only to be rebuked because "cosmic bowling" is starting in ten minutes and all the lanes were pre-reserved. I plead with the manager, insisting that I can bowl a game in less than ten minutes—"just ask the guy in South Dakota"—but to no avail. So instead of bowling I return to the bar and meet Dave, a thirty-three-year-old who'd just moved back to Helena from Oregon, where he lived a half mile from the Pacific Ocean.

"So you got tired of the ocean and came back home to the mountains?"

"Yeah," he replies. "Fuck the ocean. Too much rain."

How articulate. Fuck the ocean indeed.

On the wall next to the kitchen table in my family's home, there was a framed list that had been a Father's Day gift to my dad one year. Written in calligraphy, each line captured a child's perspective of his father at a different age. "My daddy can do anything," it read at age four. Similar observations follow at ages five and six, but then the child's heroic view of his infallible dad starts to deteriorate with each added year. At age eighteen it reads, "Father? He's hopelessly out of touch." But as the child grows into adulthood he gains a new appreciation for his old man, seeking his advice and, after his father has passed, wishing for another chance to speak with him. "If only I could talk it over with dad one more time," it ends.

I'm reminded of this as I drive from Helena to Bozeman, piloting Mom's Honda through wet, meaty, wind-driven snowflakes that are quickly accumulating in the mountain passes. Jackknifed trucks, wrecked horse trailers, and sidelined SUVs dot the highway on either side and even sometimes right in the middle, causing me to swerve around them. Despite having ignored the sign some miles back that read "Chains Advised Beyond This Point," I'm demonstrating world-class driving skills. For this, I credit my dad.

By the time he taught me, his fifth child, to drive a car, his nerves were amply frayed from the ordeal of having taught the first four. Typically he would take me out for a cruise around the neighborhood before dinner and after having a long, stressful day of work. While this would have been a white-knuckled adventure for most as I accelerated wildly, braked erratically, and checked my blind spot by turning my head and shoulders completely away from the direction in which I was speeding, he rarely even flinched. It didn't hurt that, in ironic defiance of open container laws, he usually brought along a cocktail. It was, after all, just before dinner. I made it a gauge of how well I'd performed whether any of his Manhattan had spilled due to my uneven wheelwork.

In addition to a wealth of advice about accelerating more smoothly ("Pretend there's an egg under the pedal that you don't want to break") and braking more predictably ("Ahem," followed by a look that said, "Maybe you should ease onto that brake pedal a few feet *before* the stop sign") he had one piece of driving advice he repeated all his life. Every time it snowed he seemed to revel in telling people— anyone, not just his kids—that, "The key to not getting stuck in the snow is to keep moving." He'd make a sweeping circular motion with his arm in front of him to demonstrate perpetual motion, and always had a twinkle in his eye as he said it.

In a self-congratulatory moment after narrowly avoiding a fishtailing semi by accelerating around it, I repeat the phrase aloud, making the same motion with my arm. As I reflect on it, though, something bothers me about the twinkle my dad had in his eye and the frequency with which he made that proclamation despite Central Ohio having very few days of annual snowfall. I begin to realize that he was telling a joke. It's not a funny one, closer to folksy truism than humor, but it amused him because he was the only one who got it every time. "The key to not getting stuck in the snow is to keep moving." Of *course* it is! You can't be in motion and immobile at the same time. This was like when something is lost saying, "I'm sure it'll be in the last place you look." Of course it will, because you won't look anywhere else after that.

Despite it not being funny, I begin to laugh at the fact that for decades it was funny to him, and him alone. That he made a point to say it at every relevant opportunity, not expecting or waiting for someone else to catch on, but because it amused him that no one did. Picturing him doing this, with the hand motion and what I now recognize to be only semiearnestness, my laughter gets the better of me, and I have to pull over to the side of the road because I'm nearly doubled over and my eyes are welling up. After a minute, I compose myself, sobered by the realization that I'm in a white car on the side of a mountain highway during a blizzard. I put Mom's Honda in drive and hit the gas to rejoin traffic. Only I don't rejoin traffic. The front wheels spin futilely in the snow, the icy ground and the car's static inertia winning out over gaining momentum. As it turns out, the key to not getting stuck in the snow is to keep moving.

After ten minutes of digging out and spinning the wheels into ruts of increasing depth, I manage to get back to the road and reach Bozeman safely, with a greater appreciation of my father's nuanced way of presenting information than I'd had when I was younger.

The Bozeman Bowl is one of two bowling alleys in town, both of which are hosting the city bowling tournament today. The lounge here is an elevated room separated from the bowling lanes by giant bay windows that allow a full view of the action. The house is full, and it is difficult to move about. A man named Norm is perched next to me at one of the windows.

"My hips are giving me trouble," he says. "Otherwise I'd be out there defending my title." Norm won his division in last year's tournament.

"I'm just here watching my wife, Betty."

Betty is bowling on lane fourteen; we watch her from our vantage point and talk.

"I was drafted in 1944. Navy."

"How long did you stay in?"

"Ha!" he laughs. "Well, I left in '46 when my tour was up. Then I rejoined in '49 because it was a good job and I enjoyed it."

"Did you retire from it?"

"Not quite. I served a total of sixteen years. You need twenty to retire. My first wife left me and I had to quit to take care of my three kids."

"That's too bad."

"Then my second wife died of diabetes."

"That's horrible."

He's silent in agreement. I turn to a sunnier topic.

"How'd you meet Betty?"

"It was 1989, at Willy's Dance Hall. I danced with her, and I guess it's been working out pretty well."

"How's the hip affecting your dancing?"

"We still get out dancing now and then." He smiles, shakes my hand, and hops off his stool with surprising fleetness, leaving the lounge to congratulate his Betty as she comes off the lanes.

After the tournament play ends for the night I get a game in and head to a motel to pass the night alternating between a rancid hot tub and a small TV with three channels. I think briefly about venturing into Yellowstone, just south of Bozeman, but recall my night in the Great Sand Dunes and decide I might not be cut out for a park with erupting scalding water and a healthy bear population. I'll leave for Idaho in the morning.

Idaho ★

IN *Travels with Charley,* John Steinbeck spends several paragraphs discussing the differences in language that states use in their road signage, comparing the "terse form of instruction, a tight-lipped laconic style sheet wasting no words and few letters," of the New England states to the shouting of New York and the merely suggestive nature of signs in Ohio. He explores this early on in his journey and, by the time he got to the big western states, had moved onto other subjects. This leaves me utterly unprepared for Idaho.

Growing up in the Midwest, one doesn't get much experience driving through mountain passes or cattle drive routes. Our hills are imperceptible and our cattle docile and fenced in. Things I've never thought about until now, as I wheel down a 75-degree grade marked with a sign reading "CHAINS RECOMMENDED" and an 18-wheeler bearing down behind me. If that weren't sufficiently stressful, add complete confusion followed by wrenching fear upon seeing the next sign, which simply reads:

FROST HEAVES

Frost heaves? What the hell does that mean? And how do you adjust your driving for it? Frost *heaves!* Is "heaves" a verb or a noun in this case? Does frost actually heave? (And if so, what does that look and feel like?) Or are frost heaves a physical condition I might encounter? (And if so, what does *that* look and feel like?) Steep mountains rise on

249

either side of the road, uninhabitable land with no one around to whom I can pose these questions, if I could even turn off before being run over by the eighty-ton madman behind me. Knuckles white, I execute a hairpin turn smoothly, and see no indication of heaving frost. I'm just starting to relax when I pass another sign that reads:

OPEN RANGE—WATCH FOR STOCK

I'm pretty sure I know what "open range" means, having learned the song "Home on the Range" at a young age. "Stock" seems like all too local a term to use in case an easterner decides to drive through Idaho, though. A few miles later, as if some easterner *had* driven through and *had* had some trouble understanding what stock was in this part of the country, another sign defines it:

STOCK, it reads, beneath a black silhouette of a cow.

So, as some frost-based meteorological phenomenon could potentially heave me off the mountain, there's also a good chance that, because fences are expensive and time-consuming to erect, some rancher's two-thousand-pound cow might wander into the roadway. And as if that weren't enough, more animals—of so many varieties that they have to be lumped together on a sign that merely reads GAME to cover all of the possibilities—may leap in front of Mom's Honda around any blind curve. (This one doesn't worry me so much as it intrigues me, though. It would be exciting to see some wildlife up close, even if it would mean severe damage to the car.)

I stop for the night in Arco, or Atomic Arco, as it is known. Located just north of Craters of the Moon National Monument (the coolest sounding of all our national parks, if not the most remarkable), Arco earned its nickname by being the first community ever to be powered by nuclear energy. With a population of just over one thousand, it can't use much energy at all, no matter how it's being produced. As I pull into town, the lack of lights on in homes and businesses gives Arco an eerie feeling. The feeling is furthered by the fact that Arco is flanked by Craters of the Moon and other national forests and the massive Idaho National Laboratory, whose nuclear facilities are understandably protected by a good deal of dark land between them and the town.

As I rent a room at the first motel in Arco, the darkness spawns enough fear to give me a shiver. Or maybe it was the thumb-sized black insect I saw running from beneath the space heater in my room into the bath. Or maybe I'm just shivering because there's no way that space heater can warm this room. Though Lost River Bowl is closed when I arrive, I decide to spend as much time away from the room as possible.

After an Atomic Burger (it's just a regular burger, only it's made in Arco) at Pickle's Place, I head over to the Sawtooth Club, the only evidently open saloon in town, for a cold one and some local conversation.

Inside, a group of six sits side by side on one end of the rounded bar. Upon my entry, conversation seems to shift a bit. I'm not sure what they were discussing before, but somehow it's moved on to a contest to see who's got a bigger/better/stronger/easier-to-kill-a-man-with knife. Watching a man demonstrate (with knife in hand) how he uses his steel-handled six-inch knife to gut a being of some sort, I consider the penknife in my pocket that I'd once accidentally nipped my fingertip with, nearly causing me to require a Band-Aid. I'm doubtful it will be very useful in an Idaho knife fight. Suddenly the motel looks less foreboding. Time for bed.

Twenty-five miles north of Boise lies the mountain home of Ed and Peggy Wuelfing.

Ed was a longtime business associate of my father's, having started his own company just a few years after Leo had and became a sounding board for ideas as well as a customer and friend.

"We each made about every mistake someone could make," Ed says over elk Stroganoff one evening. (Elk, I learn, qualifies as "game," as opposed to "stock," in road sign lingo.) "We'd call each other up and share stories and ideas, give each other advice."

Some advice was better than other advice, as I learn when Ed relays a story about a semi-illegal scheme he'd suggested to help Leo recoup a large sum of money owed him by a dishonest contractor. I must have been too young to remember it, because I'm sure having a sheriff come to my house and question my dad would have been exciting to me as a child. I decide to weigh any of Ed's suggestions very carefully before acting.

Well-fed and rested after a few days with the Wuelfings, I come off the mountain to take the Boise media by storm. As I arrive at Emerald Bowl, the radio is covering Secretary of State Colin Powell's presentation to the United Nations chronicling Iraq's breeches of UN resolutions. This might be a tough news day for a fluff piece about bowling.

It is not. In spite of undoubtedly more pressing hard news to fill their broadcasts, all three local TV stations send crews to cover me. They all arrive within minutes of one another, which makes for some awkwardness among them as each sees the great exclusive scoop of the day slip from their grasp. But they get over it—everyone seems to know one another and one crew, ill equipped for the poorly lit bowling alley, even borrows a light from a competing crew to tape their segment.

Despite being out of practice after my low-profile jaunt through the mountain states, I manage to get out enough of Miller's talking points that some even make the final edit, to Russin's delight. I was starting to sense a lack of confidence on his part and that they might be questioning their investment, so this is a relief. I'm beginning to understand the pressures Tiger Woods feels to perform well so his sponsors don't drop him for underperformance. I make a note to mention that to Tiger if I see him, and leave Idaho for Utah.

Utah ★

IN Salt Lake City I again stay with friends of my father and my brother Peter through the heating and cooling distribution business. Karen Roberts, her sister, and a group of their friends treat me to a seafood dinner at an upscale restaurant and proceed to disprove my long-held belief that, due to the Mormon church's powerful influence on the state's laws, one can't get drunk in Utah. The next morning, while dealing with the repercussions of this revelation, I visit Mormon ground zero.

There's no better way to go visit a place like Temple Square, headquarters of the Mormon church, than hungover. The dehydration, vitamin deficiency, and mild nausea work together to produce a deadening haze not too different from the thick cloudiness through which a cult member might experience life. For the nonbeliever, a little booze-induced fog helps level the playing field.

The main feature of Temple Square, a ten-acre campus in downtown Salt Lake City, is a massive granite temple book-ended by three Gothic spires on either end. Awe-inspiring and captivating, it is not open to the public. The famed Salt Lake Tabernacle, home of the Mormon Tabernacle Choir, is also closed, which leaves me to wander the bright sidewalks between the two visitor centers and admire the building exteriors. The cold, fresh air helps the hangover, though I remain paranoid that in my weakened condition I may just get converted to Mormonism.

Famously evangelistic for their missionary visits to living rooms everywhere, the Mormons around the Square are suspiciously uninterested in me. At every turn I expect to be cornered for a "let me ask you about your walk with God" sales pitch that will end only when I agree to accept the tenets of the Church of Latter-day Saints, but it doesn't come. Am I not Mormon material? Can they tell just from looking? Or is this reverse psychology in practice, designed to trick me into begging for entry?

As I read a plaque outside the temple, a smartly dressed woman in a long skirt and heavy overcoat approaches. I brace myself for the hard sell and for a "you're healed, sinner!" smack to the forehead.

"May I help you find anything?" she asks.

"Nice try, but I'm not falling for it," I reply with uncalled-for defensiveness.

"Well, let me know if there's anything we can help you with," she says with the most genuine smile I have ever seen. "Enjoy your visit."

Seeking respite from the cold, dry air, I enter a visitor center. Inside I study a genealogy diagram that links the ancestry of a number of world leaders and historical figures to Joseph Smith, the church's founder. One branch of the family tree leads to Winston Churchill, another to Thomas Jefferson, and yet another to George W. Bush. Amazing. It is here, as I guffaw at what I'm reading, that a young woman in a long skirt and a blazer with a name badge on approaches me.

"Interesting, isn't it?"

"Yeah. Hard to believe," I reply, taking a mild shot at the display and preparing to be interrogated about my relationship with Jesus. Instead, we have a pleasant conversation about genealogy and family history. I ask her what the most common questions people ask her at the visitor center are.

" 'Where are the bathrooms?' is number one," she says, smiling. "And then we get a lot of questions about polygamy and the differences between ours and other religions." All very matter-of-fact and pleasant, with no trace of a sales pitch or defensiveness about her. Quite suspicious.

"Okay, so how'd the church start?"

She explains that Jesus spent some time after his resurrection talking to the inhabitants of North America, after which a following sprang up. This was around A.D. thirty-four, long before Columbus's trip and well before missionaries started trying to convert the natives some sixteen hundred years later. The believers were persecuted until only one remained, and he buried some God-written tablets in the woods. An angel led Joseph Smith to these in the 1830s, and he translated them to English.

I'd always had the impression that the Mormons had fabricated a new book of the Bible on their own, which was why no other branch of the Christian church acknowledged this one. But now that I learn there exists some archeological proof—proof even more tangible and recent than the Old Testament's Ten Commandment tablets—I find I'm intrigued.

"Where do you keep the tablets? I'd like to see them."

Still smiling and not thinking anything she's saying has the faintest stench to it, she replies, "After Joseph Smith translated the tablets, they were taken with the angel back to heaven and will return when Jesus returns."

"Bummer. That would have made a good exhibit here. What about the polygamy?"

"God commanded that men should have multiple wives for a time during the mid-1800s. Joseph Smith and the other church leaders were challenged by the command but obeyed it under close regulation. Then, after a period of time, God commanded that it stop. Some people, who are unaffiliated with the church, still practice it. But the church is officially against it and excommunicates any members practicing it."

Karen, my non-Mormon host, sheds more light on God's thinking on the matter.

"They just gave it up for statehood," she says disdainfully while giving me a tour of nearby Park City.

Apparently Utah's admission into the Union was running into opposition from some prudes in Washington who didn't think multiple wives worked well within the nation's morality and laws. So it would be more accurate to say that God wanted statehood for Utah and thus commanded a reverse in His polygamy policy.

My mind much clearer now, it is time to return to an activity less subject to God's apparently ever-changing will. I make a pilgrimage to Ritz Classic Lanes.

At the front desk is sixty-nine-year-old Vera May, a grandmotherly woman with brownish red hair and a small but sturdy frame. This is one of the few days in her life she is without friend and co-worker Arlene Johansen.

"Arlene and I have worked here together for forty-four years," Vera May tells me. "It's too bad she's not in today—you'd have enjoyed meeting her."

I've been to a lot of bowling alleys: forty-four years is a long time by industry standards. A really long time. Despite Ritz's recent transition from longtime family ownership to being owned by AMF, the staff has remained essentially the same.

"This is Bryant," Vera May introduces him to me. Bryant looks to be in his early thirties. His head is shaved, and a thin beard frames a warm smile. "He was coming in here every day and bowling, and one day I just said, 'Why don't you just work here? You're here anyway—you may as well get paid for it!'" After eleven years, Bryant is one-fourth the way to Vera and Arlene's employment duration.

Vera continues. "This is the Friday morning seniors' league. They're like my extended family. Everyone here is like family."

She smiles reflectively as she organizes some papers behind the counter.

"I lost my husband five years ago," she says. "These people saved my life."

"These people" includes Ken and Fred, fixtures at Ritz Classic who come here nearly every day with a small group of friends around the lunch hour to eat and talk. The conversation is almost exclusively about bowling, despite my trying to steer it elsewhere. The more I talk with them, the fewer words it seems to take them to get to bowling no matter what I ask.

"Where'd you grow up, Ken?"

"I was born on Okinawa, but when I was twelve we moved to Seattle. I joined my first bowling league in 1957."

"So what brought you to Salt Lake City?"

"After high school I got a job at a tooling company. Bowled with the foreman."

"Fred, tell me about your family."

"Well, my wife—she doesn't bowl. . . ."

Out of necessity I stick to questions about bowling. "How has Ritz changed since the ownership changed?"

"It hasn't changed much," Fred answers, "except for the food. It used to have a great diner with homemade soups and daily specials. It's still decent, though. And the coffee's still free after you buy your first cup."

In preparation for my upcoming six-hour drive through the desert from heaven-ordained Salt Lake City to devil's playground Las Vegas, I pay eighty-nine cents for a cup and gulp down a week's worth of coffee between frames in this, my forty-third state.

MY good friend Morgan again joins the road trip in Vegas and we do Vegas things, most of which I won't recount—not to protect the guilty but because Vegas stories are all the same: drinking, strippers, hookers, drugs, rare white tigers, ten-minute marriages, sleep deprivation, gambling, Elvis, arrests, limos, drinking.

It's a sharp contrast from the Mormon wonderland I just left, but Las Vegas doesn't feel any more sinister than the Mormon campus. Just more straightforward about it. We burn through more money than we'd planned and kill fewer brain cells than expected: the lights and scale of the place aid in our disorientation sufficiently to require less alcohol. After only twenty-four hours, we day-trip to Hoover Dam to regain our bearings—detoxification by sightseeing. The dam is large and disorienting as well.

Back to the Strip for more drinking and blackjack, more disorientation. Morgan is up, at least for this round, and I am remembering why I've left every casino I've ever entered vowing never to gamble again. I return from the ATM and join him, cursing my lack of discipline and confident that I'll quit once I get ahead.

Two beautiful college girls take the seats next to ours. They are dressed for Vegas—glittery halter tops, tight black pants, cleavage—and are friendly and outgoing, flirtatious but not hooker flirtatious. Better men than Morgan and I would have charmed them into dinner, dancing, and groping. Instead Morgan and I stumble over ourselves with good-byes as they grow bored, play their last hand, and go to another casino. Morgan finally loses to the house, and we're faced with a choice of sleeping for the first time in thirty-six hours or going bowling.

We bowl. It is close to midnight and the seventy lanes at the Orleans are nearly empty. More college girls a few lanes away from us, lingerie saleswomen at a local boutique, or so they tell us. Judging by the lacy triangles of thong underwear emerging from the tops of their low-cut jeans, I'm inclined to believe them. In another embarrassing display of our lack of mating ritual aptitude, Morgan and I manage to lose their interest and are left bowling alone but for a man and woman two lanes away.

"Tough luck with the ladies, eh?" Bob teases. Bob has tattoos. Bob rides a Harley; it is his only means of transportation. He is a chef at one of the expensive restaurants in one of the Strip hotels. His wife, Tina, looks like a stripper. Correction: Tina looks like a *former* stripper. It turns out Tina *is* a former stripper, or, more accurately, like the title of a movie I'm pretty sure can be found on Cinemax at 2:00 A.M., she was an "accidental stripper."

"I was working as a bartender and the bar owner decided to turn it into a strip club," she says. "I'd just turned forty and needed a self-esteem boost, so I got these and did some stripping. I don't anymore, though." ("These" are breast implants.)

Tina is blond, and her skin's smoothness belies her forty-four years, but her eyes reveal the mild weariness that comes with age. Shiny black half helmets, the kind that just cover the top and part of the back of the skull, rest on the table with their beers, the portable roof of the family car.

Morgan flies home to Cleveland the next morning, with no helmet. I depart for the Grand Canyon, grateful for his company and his help in binging and purging the Mormon from my system. I'm now hoping that what Clark W. Griswold, in one of the great road trip films of all time, called "the biggest God-damn hole in the world" will purge the Vegas from my system and I'll reclaim equilibrium.

★ Arizona

IN that movie, *National Lampoon's Vacation,* the Griswold family, short on money and running out of time to get to their destination, takes all of ten seconds to soak in the Grand Canyon, one of the largest and most spectacular sights in the world. Taking even a few minutes longer than they did, I decide, would be an affront to the spirit of my own trip. After all, aren't our real national treasures to be found in dive bars and bowling alleys, not in the world's largest crevasse and the mile-deep cross section of rock that makes up its walls? The sight of the Grand Canyon is truly unrivaled and impressive; the expanse is staggering and its colors change with the light before your eyes. It's impossible to not be awed at first sight, and likely possible to be awed continuously at it over long periods of time. But I think Chevy Chase's Clark W. Griswold, Jr., had it right: if you can't spend a week or a month exploring it, a quick glance before jumping back in the Family Truckster gives you the idea. For me this entails standing uncomfortably close to other tourists (why not invade people's space as they behold something so vast?) and saying disappointedly to myself, "I thought it would be bigger."

In Phoenix I take to the airwaves on the ample back of my former camp counselor, Brady Bogen, who plays sidekick to host John Holmberg on a show called *Holmberg's Morning Sickness* on a hard rock station. The outrageousness of quitting a job to drive around bowling lends itself so well to the shock-jock format—though I could as easily end up being mocked savagely as I could be elevated to folk hero status. Recent bits on their show have included a hot mom contest and a segment in which they paid a man $550 to eat peanut butter from an English bulldog's hindquarters (the Maricopa County sheriff threatened prosecution for this one). I'm fairly confident my interview won't take a turn like this, but I think back to Brady's influence on impressionable young people at a church camp in southern Ohio to gather material for my defense in case I walk into the studio to find a donkey and a jar of Vaseline.

There were six cabins for male campers at Camp Akita, each housing about ten campers for a week during the summer, and each was presided over by a college student whose duties ranged from babysitter, to drill sergeant, to comic relief, to spiritual guru. Campers fought to be in Brady's cabin, as his ability to balance these traits was legendary. Campers in Brady's cabin would run out of underwear midway through the week from wetting their pants in either fear or laughter—usually a combination of both. For example, there is story of a wrestling match between a 220-pound Brady and a 110-pound camper that ended with the camper gasping for breath after having the wind knocked out of him by a body slam onto a four-inch-thick Army surplus mattress. Brady, fairly certain the kid was okay, revived him by getting inches from his face and shouting, "Your dad's not a lawyer, is he?!"

In the *Morning Sickness* studio, Brady welcomes me warmly and Holmberg gives me free reign to exact a small amount of good-spirited revenge on behalf of campers everywhere.

"Everyone wanted to be in Brady's cabin," I tell Holmberg, "because at the end of the week they would give all his campers a rag doll and a felt-tipped pen so we could show the camp director where Brady had touched us."

By the end of the interview, listeners are e-mailing in obscene pictures they'd drawn of rag dolls marked where Brady had touched them, too.

Later that afternoon I meet a seventy-six-year-old man for lunch and three games of bowling at Kyrene Lanes in Chandler, Arizona.

In 1990 George Alces was on his way to a wedding in New Jersey from Arizona by way of Florida. Ten years retired, he had time for such a road trip.

"On a whim I threw in my bowling ball and shoes, thinking I might stop off and bowl in each of the twenty-some states I'd be driving through," he says. Upon completion of those, he decided he may as well finish all fifty, and proceeded to do so over the course of four years.

I had always assumed I wasn't the first to make this quest—surely professional bowlers hit every state over the course of their careers—but I hadn't expected to meet anyone else who had until George e-mailed me after reading Mark Brown's column in the *Chicago Sun-Times*.

Sitting next to me at the Kyrene Lanes snack counter, George is wearing the shirt given to him at Arctic Bowl in North Pole, Alaska. The back, in ironed-on black letters, reads: "ALASKA . . . MY 50TH!"

"I had a friend up there who arranged for the bowling center and the area bowling association to present me with this and to commemorate the accomplishment," he says. "My first ball there was a strike."

My first ball against George Alces on his home lanes is a strike.

"And the bowling went downhill after that."

As does mine. George beats me soundly three games in a row.

"People in bowling centers are about as friendly as you can find," he says. "Even when I didn't tell them I was trying to hit all fifty states they all treated me like family."

"Did you have a favorite place to bowl?"

"Lots stand out, but you know, Mike, the trip itself was the real destination."

"What did people think of your doing it?"

"Most understood it, though some thought it was pretty frivolous. Mostly nonbowlers in that camp. Overall, though, it was just good to have a goal, something to try to accomplish. It makes life more interesting."

Because I'm curious as to whether George's approach was more methodical than mine, I ask him the most common question I've been getting on this trip.

"How'd you decide where to bowl in a state?"

"Usually I'd just stop in a service station and ask where the nearest bowling center was," he says.

A great strategy, to be sure.

After losing three games in a row to a seventy-six-year-old, I opt for a confidence booster and go with my friends Ben and Bryan Smith to Frontier Lanes, just up the road from their couch. Which was convenient for me, as I'd been sleeping on their couch for the past few nights.

Bryan, it turns out, rolls some inspired frames, and I'm regretting his being there. Ben, for his part, bowls like a child: spirited but erratic. Soon, however, the bowling takes a backseat to the show.

It's a Thursday night. At 10:00 P.M. sharp the lights go dark, replaced by the familiar strobes and lasers of any rock-and-bowl program. But Frontier Lanes takes rock and bowl to a whole new level, courtesy of The Skullcrusher.

The Skullcrusher is a large man with wavy brown hair that hangs well past his shoulders. He wears a black cap with a skull on it with the words "Skull Crusher" surrounding it. His T-shirt is black and printed from neck, to sleeve, to waist with a gigantic green skull; it has its nose pierced. Bass thumps rhythmically over an impressive speaker system. The Skullcrusher is at the microphone.

"Ladies and gentlemen, welcome to Frontier Lanes Rock and Bowl!" he booms with the enthusiasm of a wrestling announcer. Then, to everyone's surprise, rather than wish everyone good bowling and ask for music requests, he goes on to introduce the entire staff in that same wrestling announcer's tone.

"Working the snack bar for you tonight and making sure those pizzas are piping and the nacho cheese is steaming, give it up for Ra-ooool!" People interrupt their bowling to cheer.

"Let's not forget the man making it all happen. Behind the counter . . . spraying your shoes and making sure the lanes are runnin' right . . . weighing in at one hundred and sixty-eight pounds . . . the one . . . the only . . . Ottooooooo!"

Once The Skullcrusher's done with intros and is just spinning tunes, I walk up to commend him on his work. The closer I get, the more menacing he looks. Then he smiles.

"Hey, man, how's it going?" he says. "I'm The Skullcrusher."

"Oh, really?"

In case I really did doubt him, The Skullcrusher gives me his card. It reads: "The Skullcrusher." Despite the name, he couldn't be friendlier or more upbeat. I decide to challenge the depth of his musical offerings by requesting Journey's "Any Way You Want It," figuring he was well stocked in current hits but limited when it came to bowling alley classics. Au contraire. My skull is soon crushed by a triple block of Journey, beginning with "Don't Stop Believin'," bridged by "Wheel in the Sky," and capped, grand finale style, with my request.

On my way out, across the bowling alley I send The Skullcrusher the "metal" sign, index finger and pinkie thrown in the air. He reciprocates.

Long live rock and bowl.

California ★

IT'S Valentine's Day. I'm spending the evening in a San Diego bowling alley with two men, one a friend from college and one a friend from the Oscar Mayer cult. None of us has a date. I consider calling Kalli to catch up and wish her well, but I opt not to for reasons I can't explain. The idea of trying to restart a relationship with her at the end of my trip has been coursing around my head, but I'm too chicken to admit that to her. The clearer the end of the trip comes into view—five more states until I have to decide what next to do with my life—the more I'm putting off any decisions. The prospect of completion, exciting on one hand, is terrifying on the other. This quest has so consumed the last year of my life between envisioning it, preparing for it, and now living it that I lack any plan for what is to follow. Perhaps it's because of the desert plateau landscape that unfolded on either side of me on the drive from Phoenix, but the image of the Looney Toons Coyote and Roadrunner series comes to mind. The Coyote's life is defined by the pursuit of the ever-present yet ever-elusive Roadrunner. Every waking hour is spent planning and executing elaborate plans to catch the bird, all to no avail. Yet the Coyote's pursuit continues; it gives his life purpose. What would he do if he caught the Roadrunner? What would he chase next? It may be more than a cartoon-born metaphor that's keeping me from calling Kalli, but I tell myself it's a question of venue: the crashing of bowling pins in the background would make it hard to talk. So I bowl.

Driving up the coast, I stop for a night in stunning Laguna Beach. Perfect weather amid news of a snowstorm all over the East Coast— Southern California has a certain appeal. From here I get the nerve to call Kalli. We have an amicable, if somewhat shallow, conversation in which she tells me of an impending ski trip with some friends and I shy away from initiating a "so, my trip's almost over and I'm thinking about moving back to Chicago" conversation.

I continue up the coast to Santa Barbara and a couch I'd been offered there. Its owner, Meghan, is my sister's boyfriend's brother-in-law's little sister. In other words, no one who should be letting a strange man spend the night in her home. I'm told she'll be a great host and really show me Santa Barbara.

"This will sound a little pathetic," she says when I inquire about the town's Thursday night doings, "but I've had a long week and I'm kind of looking forward to the finale of *Joe Millionaire* tonight . . . do you mind if we just order a pizza and watch it?"

Actually, I don't mind at all, but I mock her relentlessly for not showing me a better time anyway. In return for my lack of graciousness, she lets me stay for two more nights despite the fact that she'll be out of town on business. I imagine her sharing this with her family while she's on her trip:

"So, Meghan, how was Luke's wife's brother's girlfriend's brother's visit?"

"Actually, I'm letting him stay for as long as he wants. He's alone in my apartment right now."

Using Meghan's as a base, I drive up the road to Goleto and bowl at Zodo's. Recently renovated, Zodo's is open twenty-four hours to accommodate bowlers of any sleeping habit. Over an immense burger in the lounge, I discuss California bowling destinations with the bowling manager, bar manager, and chef.

"You've got to go to Jerry's Deli at the Sport Center on Ventura in Studio City," Steve, the bowling manager, says. "There is no better bowling center sandwich."

"And check out Hollywood Bowl on Sunset in Hollywood," adds Lawrence, the bar manager. "They filmed *The Big Lebowski* there."

On their advice, I drive south to Los Angeles, only to find that Jerry's is being renovated and not serving their trademark sandwiches. Following a map to the address where Hollywood Bowl should be, I fail to find it. Pulling over, I stop an elderly gentleman on the street and ask him where the bowling alley is.

"Most of it's in that pile of rubble right there," he says, pointing to a lot where a building has recently been demolished, cinder blocks and metal columns crushed and strewn about. "They knocked it down to build a school."

Cursing our educational system, I drive to meet yet another college friend and yet another Wienermobile friend at yet another bowling alley. Mar Vista Lanes is open, and I wait in one of the lounge's red vinyl booths for them to arrive.

A toothless man at the bar croons along with Louis Armstrong's "What a Wonderful World" in a perfect mimic of Satchmo's tremolo. People respond with applause and the bartender pours him a shot. He appears to be a regular and this performance a nightly occurrence.

A man in his forties wearing torn jeans and a faded black T-shirt encounters an old high school buddy at the bar. Their conversation turns quickly from the casual to the tragic.

"It's been a rough year, man," he says. "My kid died in a motorcycle crash in August. I got this tattoo to remember him."

A woman is telling her friend about a new diet she's on. "I've been eating nothing but oatmeal for a week," she says; her friend responds with a look of mortified disgust, as do I.

Two Mexican men are having an argument about Guadalajara, or at least that's what I decide I'll tell the cops if it escalates into a fist-fight and I'm called to be an eyewitness. "That guy said something about Guadalajara, and the other guy didn't agree with it," I'll say, proud that after four years of Spanish the only word I caught was the name of a Mexican city.

Wanton, who is not Asian, and Jon arrive and, predictably, we bowl. Afterward, Wanton puts me up in his guest room on a bed positioned just beneath a pastel painting of gunned-down rapper Tupac Shakur. There's nothing quite so restful as a night spent under the watchful likeness of a man whose life ended in a violent rain of gunfire.

My mother meets me at El Dorado Lanes near Westchester. She's been visiting her friends Barbara and Dale Boman, and will now join me for the drive to San Francisco. We have coffee and watch the bowling action.

Al Putziger bowls like he's in the Old West: dressed in a blue plaid shirt, navy blue pants, and suspenders, he moseys up to the line slowly, almost bowlegged, with the ball low on his right side like it's a six-shooter holstered just above his knee. When he releases the ball his hand snaps upward on his follow-through like it's responding to a gun's recoil.

John Laurcare is on the lane next to him, complaining about not being able to close a frame. "Nine! Nine! Nine! It's a German game all the time!" he says, likening his scores in each frame to the German word for "no."

"You're not from Germany, are you?" I ask him.

"No, I'm from Rhode Island," he says. We talk some more. He doesn't know my friend Spaghetti but has a childhood vocation in common with him. "I used to set duckpin lanes as a kid for ten cents a game. People would throw those balls down the lane like softballs—they'd almost miss the lane altogether. It was dangerous down there on the pin deck."

John and Al are bowling in a league where everyone puts a dollar in the pot for the bowler with the highest score. An eighty-five-year-old moving with all the athletic grace and speed of a chronic arthritic rolls a strike and uses the occasion to intimidate his competitors.

"You can pay me now or you can pay me later," he taunts loudly.

"Bitches," I add beneath my breath, finding great humor at the idea of him adding that word to underline his trash talking.

The Bowmans say good-bye to us and Mom joins me in Mom's Honda and we make our way up the Pacific Coast Highway's sharp curves and sharper drop-offs. The ocean out the left windows is dangerously beautiful, given that looking at it for too long may cause a driver to miss a turn and plummet into it. As she did on the drive to West Virginia, Mom keeps me well aware of every potential hazard. These are tense miles.

We stop for a tour of William Randolph Hearst's "ranch" at San Simeon. Including a castle and a number of guest houses with ceilings made of twenty-four-karat gold, it covers over ninety thousand square feet of living space, with fifty-six bedrooms, forty-one fireplaces, a 345,000-gallon pool ringed with Greek mythological statues, and another pool that is made of one-inch mosaic tiles in blue, orange, and clear-with-infused-gold. "Ranch" my ass. At Hearst's death in 1951 the complex was still being added to; one of the elements that was planned but never built: a bowling alley. An eleven-year-old boy reacts to that fact on the tour:

"It's so stupid. You don't have any money until you're old, and then you die before you can use it. This place could have had a bowling alley in it, but the guy died. That sucks."

Hearst probably had a bowling alley in one of his thirty other homes, but the kid has a point.

Having spent Valentine's Day in a bowling alley with two men, I'm now spending a night in wine country with my mother.

"Now, the room has two beds, right?" she asks the clerk at the hotel front desk. As if I hadn't made sure of that when I arranged the room, and personally called to double-check during the drive up.

There's something oddly uncomfortable about sharing a hotel room with my mother, and I sense she agrees. Our shame apparently stems from different sides of the same "grown man touring the country with his mommy" coin. Certain situations serve to compound this awkwardness.

Everything is in order in our wine country hotel room: two beds, a door on the bathroom, the works. And from the sound of it, everything is in order in the room above ours, where, just as we're dozing off, what must be either a newlywed or adulterous couple begins a rigorous marathon sex session that sounds like it might send their bed through the ceiling of our room. Mom is in denial.

"Why would they be doing repairs at this time of night?" she asks. "It's like they're hammering picture hangers into the wall or something. . . ."

Why'd she have to say "hammering"?

"Um, probably an emergency maintenance problem. I'll just turn the fan on a little louder to drown out the lovebirds—I mean maintenance man. Now just go to sleep, Mother."

Sexually active neighbors aside, it's a pleasure to have my mom along for a few days. We retrace steps in San Francisco from times she'd visited it with my dad and from the stopover she made on the way to join him in Taiwan just after they'd been married.

It's now been just over two years since he died, and she seems to be getting more comfortable with her new life, though it's also clear she resents it.

"I haven't heard from some of our friends since the funeral," she complains. "Just because Leo's not around does it mean I'm dead, too?"

★   ★   ★

After dropping Mom off at the airport, I set up camp at Kalli's best friend Erica's apartment. Erica and I catch up on my travels and she fills me in on the ski trip she's just returned from with Kalli.

"Who was there?" I ask, looking for news of our mutual friends. She lists them all, concluding with, "Oh, and John, this guy Kalli's been dating lately."

Apparently I don't do a very good job of masking my reaction; before Erica's even done speaking her voice takes on a "sorry to have to break this to you" tone. Nonetheless, I try my best not to seem too interested and even eke out an overtly insincere "good for her," my voice cracking as I do. Erica and I move on to other topics in our conversation, but I haven't in my head.

John? Who the hell is John? And why is Erica telling me about him now instead of Kalli doing it when we spoke about this ski trip a week ago? It's February. Weren't we having a "talk" by the Christmas tree just over two months ago? And she's already been dating someone long enough to spend a weekend away with him?!

I'm blind with confusion, self-righteous anger, and a need for answers. I'm sitting here with her best friend, who, though she may sympathize with my situation, is ultimately loyal to Kalli, and therefore my reaction to the news will surely get back to her. As I deny that there's any possibility I made our Christmas conversation out to be more than it was, it's all I can do not to lose my temper and scream, "When the hell was she going to tell *me* this?!" I open my mouth, not entirely certain that those words won't come out of it.

"Should we do some bowling?" I say cheerfully.

Erica and I meet a dozen or so friends at Presidio Bowling Center, a small facility on what was once part of an Army base and is now managed by the National Park Service. These are friends from college, former clients, the obligatory Hotdogger or two, a high school classmate's wife, and various others. The sweet release of hurling a heavy ball surrounded by friends and beer proves an effective coping mechanism.

The next morning, after breakfast with a freelance journalist who might write a piece on me for a free weekly—my only glimmer of media coverage for Miller in all of California—I hop in Mom's Honda en route for states forty-seven and forty-eight, the end of the contiguous portion of my trip now in sight.

Oregon ★

SAN Francisco is referred to as being in "Northern"
California. In relative terms, it is. The state stretches
south for over five hundred miles beneath it, and most of
California's population exists between the Bay Area and
the Mexican border. But make no mistake: Oregon isn't
just up the road. Between San Francisco and Oregon is a
350-mile swath of woodlands, national forests, and small
towns lining I-5 and Highway 101 going north and south,
and various smaller routes crisscrossing the woods. After
more than five hours of wondering when California was
going to finally end, I cross into Oregon ready to petition
for our geographic language to be changed so that San
Francisco is henceforth known as part of Central California rather than the North. Damn it, I'm sick of driving.

My Oregon destination is my good friend Michael
Bluhm's home in Corvallis. Bluhmer was a Hotdogger the
same year as I was, and the man knows his beer. Promptly
on my arrival he introduces me to the four taps of home-
brew that are the centerpiece of his garage.

The comfort of beer and familiar company is refreshingly grounding. Bluhmer and his fiancée, Kristin, listen
and struggle to find much merit in my side of the Kalli affair ("well, you *are* drifting around the country aimlessly
with no stated plan . . . and didn't you try to hook up
with some girl out east a few months ago?"). Nothing like
an old friend to set you right, ever so gently.

The three of us hit Highland Bowl, where we're greeted
by the most enthusiastic bowling center employee I've
seen in forty-seven states.

"Welcome to Highland Bowl," Santana says, smiling like he's been waiting just for us and all but leaping over the counter to shake our hands. "I'll set you up on lane five. How about some beers?"

On lane six a number of Oregon State students are bowling and practicing that drunken bowling alley tradition of making public displays of affection. Usually reserved for cosmic bowling when the lights are low and the music loud, the openmouthed kissing and hands casually in each other's back pockets are a little disconcerting in the bright light of open bowling—even for a seasoned veteran like myself.

Bluhmer slaps me on the back mid-sip of beer and I spill on the table and my shirt. Santana is there with a rag before the carbonation is gone from the puddle.

As we bowl, Kristin breaks a nail on a roll that slipped off her thumb earlier than she'd planned.

"Hey, guys! How about another round?" Santana is back, carrying four empty pitchers from other tables just as we're down to our last sips in ours. He returns with full ones as fast as they can be poured. Upon learning about Kristin's nail, he sprints for the first-aid kit and returns with a Band-Aid before we know it. It would not surprise me if he told us he noticed the tires on our car in the parking lot were a little soft so he took the liberty to fill them up. Before we leave for the night I dub Santana Most Valuable Bowling Center Employee in the Contiguous United States.

I leave Corvallis early the next morning smashingly hungover and dressed in a wrinkled High Life T-shirt, untucked because merely thinking about tucking it in hurts my head. My pants are wrinkled as well, and there are stains on them that I can trace back to Arkansas. I've done laundry somewhat regularly, but one can only get so much mileage out of three pairs of pants in five months without some permanent staining. Skeptical that anyone will show up here at Hollywood Bowl in Portland to videotape me for a news show, I decide my appearance matters little. I'll just spend a couple of hours there and get back to driving and brooding over my poorly played romantic hand.

Dan is working the counter at Hollywood Bowl and working the crowd of seniors bowling this Thursday morning, quick to respond to lane equipment malfunctions and facilitate their league's administration, lane assignments, and so forth. He is in his midthirties and his head is shaved to stubble.

"I got into bowling because my father wanted me to play baseball," Dan says, the first instance I've encountered of someone using this sport as an act of teenage rebellion. "He pushed me pretty hard in Little League and could criticize everything I did because he'd played baseball himself. Eventually I got so burned out working so hard during the Little League off-season that I wanted to find a sport my dad knew nothing about."

"Has that created a rift in your relationship?"

"Actually, I got him hooked on bowling and now we bowl together."

Dan no longer has to run laps after a bad game.

A man in a tweed jacket, blue shirt, and brown tie interrupts us. He has silver hair, perfectly combed, and a big smile, and I judge him to be the classic broadcaster. The smooth tenor of his voice confirms that judgment.

"Mike? Jim Hyde, FOX Twelve News," he says, offering his right hand. "This is a great story—I want to challenge you to a game."

Jim's energy is boundless and I immediately regret being hungover and looking it. It's just one affiliate in a fairly small market and Miller would certainly rather I be drawing bigger, *Tonight Show*–sized attention as the road trip nears its finish, but I wish I'd prepared better for this. Luckily, Jim is a pro and brings the best out in his subjects.

First he gets plenty of background footage of me bowling; then he asks me to elaborate on Miller's support for the trip.

"I just wanted to eat nachos and live the High Life for a couple of months," I say, looking just off camera. Jim then makes sure to get good shots of the yellow Miller High Life ball that Russin recently shipped me knocking over pins and coming out of the ball return.

"Gotta get the sponsor some credit, right?" Jim says, and I'm taken aback by his explicit recognition of the public relations game behind news stories like this. With most reporters it's a dance around the fact with the hope you can sneak in a sound bite or two they don't catch. "I can't guarantee it won't get edited out, but it's worth a shot."

He does a stand-up introducing the showdown we're about to have on the lanes, then laces up a pair of shoes from Dan. Jim and I roll a complete game and he beats me in one of my worst performances in forty-seven states and five months.

Jim interviews some of the seniors bowling and does some impromptu stand-ups.

"Wanna grab a beer in the bar?" he asks after the camera is being packed away. "Portland has some great local brews, you know."

Making sure the camera is really off, I accept on the condition that it's off-the-record and if anyone asks, I was drinking a High Life. We each have a pint glass full of dark, hoppy local beer as I share stories from the road and he shares stories from a life in journalism. I thank him and walk away with the feeling that his will be among the best pieces of video produced on this entire trip, even if it goes largely unseen for being on in a small market.

After a quick lunch in downtown Portland, I venture north to the last of the Lower 48 United States.

Washington ★

FACING the downside of being so near to completing the trip and the "what's next" decisions that will soon be upon me, I decide to call Kalli from the car as I enter Washington State. It's an awkward call to make from my position, that of being hurt because an unarticulated, inferred but not expressly implied relationship rekindling has been nixed before even starting.

Over an hour of awkwardness, the essential truths that Bluhmer and Kristin pointed out in Corvallis surface once again.

"It's not like I was seeking out a relationship, but you can't have expected me to wait around while you decide what you're going to do next. And I really like John. It's a really exciting thing for me."

"Fair enough."

"And what about Bowling Spice? And who's the girl in New Hampshire you mention on your Web site? And didn't you try to put the moves on some girl in Kansas on your way to my parents' house anyway?"

"Um . . ." Perhaps keeping a Web log, no matter how cryptically worded, wasn't such a good idea after all.

And so we leave it on friendly enough terms, implicitly agreeing that I couldn't have expected her to fight off the advances of men with jobs who treat her well and live in the same city for more than a day at a time—the same city in which she lives, no less—and that we could have communicated a little more openly with each other.

For about ten minutes I feel better; then on cue Seattle starts raining and I need to find a motel. I see one advertising thirty-nine-dollar rooms and enter the front office. Never mind my downbeat mood; this lobby would have deflated Richard Simmons.

The woman at the front desk delicately extinguishes her cigarette, careful not to crush the tip, and sets it on the counter's edge so she can finish it later. If the couch in the lobby is any indication, the furniture in the rooms will be brown, heavily soiled, missing cushions, and sprouting springs. The arms will be worn to the wood frame. I'm too tired and apathetic to get back into the car; the rain and dusk conspire to make me settle.

"Hi, I'd like one of the thirty-nine-dollar rooms for the night, please."

"Oh . . . we're . . . out of those," she says. "I mean, we only give the rooms in the back to the bad people."

My face reveals that I find this an odd way of getting me to upgrade.

"Not that there are any bad people here." She halfheartedly retreats before coughing a deep smoker's hack for what seems like five minutes. "It's just . . . the forty-four-dollar rooms are much nicer."

The faded photos beneath the glass countertop show rooms that match my mood. I'm pretty sure I've not seen worse in the past five months. The handwritten sign next to the photos doesn't do anything to dispel this: "No refunds after payment."

But what the hell. Maybe by some ironic twist spending the night in an awful room will cheer me in rainy Seattle.

I key into the door to a first-floor room and an ironic twist hits me over the head. It really is awful.

Two lamps hang from gold chains on either side of the head of the bed, their shades brown, with a thin coating of dust in the grooves of their accordion-shaped ridges. Casting their dim 40-watt glow on a powder blue, coral, and sea foam green bedspread, they flank a circular headboard that spans from floor to ceiling. Ringed by gold metal trim, it is filled with green carpet bisected by two swaths of light blue. The curtains, vertical stripes of brown, mauve, and cream, were meant for another room. What really completes the decor is two plantlike be-

ings that sprout six feet tall from round black cylinders—tall, narrow
trash-cans-made-vases. The "plants" (the word must be put in quotes
because they are not living and may or may not have ever been) themselves are leafy like ferns, but they are brown like a bear's fur. A
shaggy, ill-kempt bear. From the doorway it appears that there are two
Chewbacca figures guarding the bed.

The awfulness does amuse me at first, before nearly driving me to
tears. *This is how I'm spending the last night of the contiguous U.S. portion of my life's quest?* On cue, the people upstairs start at it.

Now, I've heard people having sex in some pretty disgusting motels, but this place takes it. I just can't imagine sharing such bare, exposed intimacy in *this* place, certainly not with a straight face. "Oh
yeah, right there. Hey, how about that carpeted wall, honey?" In this
case, perhaps indicative of a room-inflicted mood, the couple swings
several times from untamed arguing to untamed intercourse over the
course of the night. Plaster falls onto my bedspread during both types
of interaction.

Upon waking I spend thirty minutes in the shower trying to wash off
whatever I might have picked up from the bedsheets, which had
patches in places where the sheet had been worn through and re-
paired, like the knees of a child's jeans patched by his mother. I
shudder to think of what repetitive action might have worn through
the sheets such that they needed patching, and jump in the shower
for another half hour.

After scouring Seattle for a coffee shop and coming up empty, I
head for my final media event at Leilani Lanes.

While I await the adoring news crews I invited to cover my forty-
eighth state, Mark Bisbing, VP of tournament operations for the Professional Bowlers Association, joins me for a cup of coffee and a game.
He is a key part of the PBA's recent success.

The PBA had nearly folded in 2000, when three Microsoft

executives bought the organization with the dream of making the sport relevant again like it had been in the fifties. They began applying marketing lessons from their high-tech success experience. They structured the pro bowling tour like a golf tour, setting up multi-year sponsorships and regular ESPN tournament telecasts, finding ways to exploit the bowlers' personalities and the sport's underground popularity. Mark, who helped create the Nike Golf Tour during the time when a budding young golfer named Tiger Woods was getting his start, speaks of the undertaking with optimism.

"It's really not that different from a golf tour," Mark says, citing that before Nike got interested and Tiger became a household name, golf wasn't all that cool, either. Indeed, not a lot of twentysomethings were ever seen running around in Payne Stewart signature knickers. Still, Mark understands it's an uphill battle.

"When I talk to friends at Nike and tell them there is an extremely loyal market of three million people thirsting for them to come into a new sport and repeat the same success they had with golf, they perk up," he says. "Until I tell them it's bowling."

As we bowl, I watch the door for news crews or a columnist, but none arrives. This is puzzling given that the PBA headquarters are located here, and embarrassing since I'm wasting an executive's valuable time for naught. Mark's a good sport about it, and we're both a little relieved we weren't being filmed when we see our final scores. Rather low for the head of the PBA tour and a guy who's dedicated the last five months to bowling in every one of the Lower 48. I call Russin to let him know the event was a flop. He has news for me.

"Dude, Mike, you've been on in over a dozen markets this morning."

I'm confused. "I don't even remember leaving Seattle. . . ."

"We haven't seen the clip yet, but apparently the Portland spot got picked up on satellite and has played in Detroit, Columbus, Miami, D.C., on CNN Headline News, in Phoenix—all over. From the transcript it looks like they even played up the Miller angle." Later, when we look at the clips in succession it will seem like an extended Miller ad, with local anchors everywhere introducing and concluding Jim's story with phrases like, "A Chicago man is living the High Life. . . ."

Forty-eight states and some twenty-five thousand miles after I took her Honda and began this trip, I call my mother to share this bit of fortune. I'm not sure why, but somehow this is just the right capstone. We're both well beyond being impressed with me appearing on TV, but the fact that what Dad started is concluding as a minor national story seems something of a miracle.

I finish the media tour from atop the Seattle Space Needle with a phone-in to the Sterling show in Columbus, my hometown mouthpiece since I first called in from the other coast, in Brunswick, Maine. For some reason he throws me a curveball by asking, "Be honest with me here: This whole thing was just about getting laid in every state, wasn't it? How'd you do?"

This throws me off balance, not only because it's so out of the norm for Sterling's typical banter but also because my mom had told me when I called her that she would be listening with all the guests at a dinner party she was hosting. I picture her pushing her way through her guests and lunging for the radio's power button. I try to sound innocent without taking the wind out of Sterling's show.

"That's been one of the surprises on this trip, Sterling. It turns out that women really aren't that impressed with unemployed guys who spend a lot of time in bowling alleys."

"Well, regardless, congratulations, and thanks for calling in. You're my hero, man."

★ Alaska

A **LASKA** is one-fifth the size of the Lower 48, a fraction that doesn't seem very large until it's put into relative terms: California, Texas, and Montana—all quite large states—combined would not equal Alaska's size. Placed over a map of the Lower 48, the state's land (including the Alaska Peninsula and the Aleutian Islands) covers the entire width from Jacksonville, Florida, to the Pacific Ocean. Of the 586,412 square miles Alaska covers, less than 3 percent of it is privately owned. The federal government owns about 60 percent, the state about 25 percent, and native tribal corporations the rest. It was the forty-ninth state to enter the Union, but it could be its own country. To many who live here, it is. "The Last Frontier" is the state's motto, and the common name for the Lower 48 states is simply "outside." Many of those who live here like to tease Texans by noting that simply dividing Alaska in two would move Texas from being the second-largest state to being the third. Everything may be bigger in Texas, but nothing's bigger than Alaska.

My flight to Anchorage, Alaska's most populated city— about 350,000 people live here, compared with fewer than 300,000 across the rest of the state—arrives on the last day of the Iditarod Challenge dogsled race. To my disappointment, it's been an unseasonably warm spring and the snow I expected is nonexistent. In fact, for the race's ceremonial start in Anchorage the organizers actually trucked in eleven miles of snow from surrounding areas. This is easier than it sounds: about thirty-five miles in any direction from Anchorage puts you on a glacier.

Alaskans are rugged. In more remote areas this is the time of year when, as the snow melts, they find out who died over the winter.

"People get lost in a snowstorm," a man sitting with me in the bar at Jewel Lake Bowl says. "They get buried by snow and freeze to death."

"It must be a little unnerving walking around during the thaw wondering if you're going to come across a body."

"Yep. Or if you lost someone, wondering where they'll turn up. We call this funeral season."

Seeking a more upbeat conversation, I sit down with an aunt/niece duo who are beginning to bowl on lane nineteen.

"What's that tattoo on your wrist?" I ask the niece, who is twenty-seven.

"That's my ex-husband's name," she replies. "We just got divorced on Thursday."

"We're celebrating her freedom," her aunt adds.

"Well, congratulations." I wonder if the niece has anyone else she no longer sees whose name is permanently inked into her flesh.

Jack Anderson works at Center Bowl. He tells me of a bowling alley I'd have visited if time, money, loneliness, and fear of death were of no consequence. Some six hundred miles away from Anchorage (and yet still in Alaska), only accessible by plane, the town of Bethel has a six-lane house built on stilts. The tundra landscape requires that buildings be constructed this way to accommodate for shifts in the ground; every year or so people have to realign their houses, adjusting the height of the stilts to compensate for the way the earth has moved beneath their dwelling. This must play havoc when trying to pick up a difficult spare. Jack ended up in Bethel like all people must: by sheer random chance.

"I cut hair," he says. "A friend of mine needed someone to cover for him at his barbershop in Bethel while he was on a three-week vacation. I went up and liked it so much better than Washington that I never returned home." He just left his things in his apartment and let the lease expire so he could live in a place where it snows sideways because the wind only blows hard.

Chilkoot Charlie's is a legendary Anchorage bar, truly authentic and unique. I save a visit for my last night in town, using it as a time killer between dinner, a midnight bowl, and my 2:00 A.M. flight. Low ceilings, long bars, and sawdust on the floor would be a start at describing Chilkoot's, but only a start. Within the building there are no fewer than five bars, most operating and occupied, if not bustling, on this Tuesday night. One is oriented toward a stage; empty beer kegs with upholstered cushions on the top serve as chairs around squat tables of thick, rough-cut wood. The sawdust on the floor is more like hunks of trees, somewhere between logs and mulch. A Foosball table is wedged into a corner in the biggest room; down some stairs and around a corner is a room with pool tables. You could get lost here, if not for the immenseness of the building then certainly for its mazelike layout. Bumper stickers plastered here and there read: "My mom is in the 86 Club at Chilkoot Charlie's." The 86 Club is for people who have been "86ed" from the bar, banned for life for fighting or such behavior that would be considered inappropriate in a place with beer kegs for seats. And all of this is not to mention the Bird House.

The Bird House is an exact replica, except for the addition of a sprinkler system, of a bar that burned down in the midnineties. The replica is part of the Chilkoot Charlie's labyrinth.

The fire was a true tragedy for the original Bird House, a bar that earned a reputation for being a survivor when it remained standing after a 1964 earthquake that rocked Anchorage to the tune of 9.2 on the Richter scale. The quake caused the bar to slant to nearly a 45-degree angle, and the owners never bothered to fix it. This is a key detail of the replica at Chilkoot Charlie's: if you're not watching it, your beer will slide away from you and into a wall.

As at Marcy Skowronski's Holler House in Milwaukee, the Bird House is decorated with undergarments on the ceiling and walls, panties and bras everywhere. A bumper sticker behind the bar makes the invitation: "Welcome to the Bird House. Have a beer. Leave your undies."

Another sticker announces the four P's of the Bird House: Pickles, Poultry, Panties, and P-tarmigan. We've covered the Panties already, which, incidentally, is a phrase I've been trying to get into this book since Ohio. The Poultry is a bowl full of hard-boiled eggs sold as "boneless chicken" at rates of one for $.25, two for $.50, and three for $1.00. It takes me a minute to realize the joke—if "joke" is the right word for playing on people's expectations of a volume discount. The P-tarmigan is a horn-shaped instrument filled with flour that, when blown by an unsuspecting Bird House virgin, explodes all over the blower's own face. The Pickles are soaked in wasabi, and are as hot as they sound. Mine comes in a shot glass.

When you eat an entire wasabi pickle, you get to sign a guest book. The first pen they give you explodes when you remove the cap and startles you even if, like me, you'd just seen it demonstrated and should have known better. The second is a pencil with erasers on both ends. The third is shaped like a penis, and writes just fine.

Having endured enough abuse at the Bird House, I go back to Center Bowl, where the first half of my date with destiny takes place. Just after midnight on March 5, I bowl a 115 in the state of Alaska. Then I drive quickly to the airport to make a flight to Seattle. If all goes to plan I will successfully have bowled in both Alaska and Hawaii on the same date—a feat so dubious and unlikely that I will surely be the first to have accomplished it in the history of mankind.

My flight reaches Seattle at around 6:00 A.M. and I question the merits of red-eye flights. I'm some six hours away from bowling in my fiftieth state, feeling like and smelling like a guy who hasn't slept or bathed in far too long. A wasabi pickle funk rises invisibly from my pores, visibly bothering my in-flight neighbors. Onto the next plane I carry almost nothing, but it's just about everything I have: the note-books and laptop that contain all of my notes, all of the photos, and all of the e-mails of support that have emerged in the five months since I turned my life in a drastically different direction from the one in which it was speeding. I carry on my father's memory, my family's love, my friends' encouragement, more experiences than I deserve to have had in so short a time. And so on to the climax. On to state fifty.

The people where I'm going use it as both a greeting and a farewell. To me it symbolizes both an ending and a beginning, closure and pos-sibility.

Aloha.

Hawaii ★

As I am deplaning a United Airlines 767 in Honolulu for a short layover before catching an inter-island flight to Hawaii, also known as "the Big Island," my phone rings. It is Mark Brown from the *Chicago Sun-Times*. I had e-mailed him from Washington to update him and thank him for his column at the start of the trip, which had opened a lot of subsequent doors for me.

"I want to update my readers on your trip," he says. He's preparing a column to run in tomorrow's paper.

I give him the latest news, doing my best through sleep-deprived jet lag to give him an amusing anecdote or two for his column and to summarize what's happened since we last spoke. Doing so causes a moment of reflection that continues after we hang up and I'm boarding the plane for the last leg.

In 156 days I put 25,211 miles on Mom's Honda, not to mention the miles I put on planes across the Pacific, first north to Anchorage and then south and west to where I am now. I stayed with fifty-four different people, mostly old friends whom I was lucky to reconnect with for a few laughs and ten frames. I had never met eight of my hosts until I walked into their homes.

One of those eight, a man, sleepwalked into bed with me.

In all, I bowled 1,150 frames, or 115 games, in which I knocked down over 15,000 pins—which seems like a lot until you do the math and figure out that's an average of around 130.

I consumed, by estimate, some 450 bottles, cans, or

glasses of Miller High Life, and likely more. It's a harder stat to keep track of than bowling scores and mileage.

There can be no accurate measure of the number of cigarettes I smoked secondhand, and I would rather not know, lest it come up on an insurance questionnaire and drive my premiums higher.

In the forty-nine states leading to this I wore sixty-four different pairs of shoes—shoes that countless others with a size 11 foot wore before me, and have worn since. This makes me shudder when I recall the scare statistic I'd heard in high school health class that claimed when you sleep with one person you're actually being exposed to everyone they've slept with in the last ten years. How many people did I swap foot sweat with? Could my carrying of those germs to subsequent states possibly cause an epidemic?

The lower back pain I've acquired from spending my days driving and my nights lifting and rolling a heavy ball, then sleeping in a strange place, seems to be chronic.

And all this with a remarkable lack of planning and forethought. As I approach the rental car counter at the Hilo airport on Hawaii, I realize I don't even know how to get to Hilo Lanes, where I will be not only completing the fifty-state mission but also setting the Alaska-and-Hawaii-on-the-same-day feat. Hilo is a pretty small place, so the bowling alley should be easy enough to find, but it is 7:00 already, so I want to get in the car and start my search for it as soon as possible. All that stands between me and this great accomplishment is a five-foot-two woman named Li.

She proves to be a formidable barrier.

Having processed my credit card and driver's license, she needs one more piece of information from me before she can hand over the keys.

"And where will you be staying on the island?"

"Oh, I have no idea. I've just got to get to Hilo Lanes—do you happen to know how to get there?"

"You don't know where you're staying?"

"Nope." My tone is one of pride with a touch of nervousness caused by a suspicion the answer won't be enough for little Li.

"Do you remember if it was a big chain hotel? Or a resort? Or do you know the name of the street it's on?"

"Oh, I don't have reservations anywhere. I'll figure that out after I bowl."

She can't believe this. And there's a spot on the release form that requires this information for some reason. It's unclear why this is; it seems an odd requirement on an island, of all places, where it would be impossible for me to drive the car to another state, much less another country, and steal it.

"You came to Hawaii with no place to stay?"

"Well, I figured it's kind of a tourist's destination, so there are hotels everywhere. Aren't there?"

"Yes. There are many. Here, would you like a phone book so you can call and make a reservation somewhere?"

"No, I'd like a car so I can drive to the bowling alley. I can find a hotel by driving to one later."

This goes on for several more minutes, with Li insisting that I have to have local accommodations arranged in order to get a car and me insisting that I'm capable of finding them. Behind me in the growing line, a man leans forward and heckles, "Come on, just tell her where you're staying, buddy."

Whether persuaded by the pressure of a growing line or the tears welling up in my eyes as the hour of my date with destiny nears, Li relents.

"I will release this car to you, but please call this number once you determine where you'll be staying."

I grab the keys from her hand and jog to my barely acquired red Dodge Neon and make for Hilo Lanes.

At 8:00 sharp I roll my first ball in my fiftieth state. Hilo Lanes is about one-quarter full, and I am bowling alone there until a reporter from the *Hawaii News* arrives at 8:15. He interviews me over pupu (Hawaiian

for "appetizers") and we make arrangements for a photographer to meet me the next day to add a picture to the story that will run sometime later in the week. Such is the pace of an island daily newspaper.

The reporter leaves, and I stay and bowl a second game, reluctant to unlace my sixty-fifth pair of everyone else's shoes.

Outside, the lush fragrances from hundreds of tropical flowers combine sweetly in the air. Inside, the antiseptic scent of shoe spray mixes with the scents of worn leather, foot sweat, cigarette smoke, lane conditioner, fried food, and the hot electric motors in the hand-drying fans on the ball returns.

Outside, the view goes to the horizon on all sides, blue water, blue sky, a green flash at the moment of the sun's last setting, or so the locals say. Inside, the view goes to a beige wall, to beige wood floors, to fluorescent signs.

Outside, songbirds are bedding down for the night, singing briefly across the palm trees to one another; waves create a soothing white noise against the black volcanic sand beaches. Inside, a thud is followed by a rumble, which is followed by an explosion of pins in a strike, a hollow "pop" on a single pin spare, a disappointing lower-pitched rumble for a gutter ball. All are followed by a human reaction. A high five, a head shake, a fist pump. A drag on a cigarette, a swig of a beer, a team cheer.

I finish my second game, and consider bowling a third. Once I leave this bowling alley, the single purpose I've been living for these past few months is gone. I'll have caught my roadrunner and I'll just be a guy in his late twenties with no job, instead of a guy in his late twenties who's doing something admirable, if somewhat silly.

I unlace the shoes and return the ball I'd been using to its rack. Setting the shoes on the counter, I hesitate to take my hand off them. I think of my father, wondering how he'd have felt playing handball in his fiftieth state. In slaphappy fatigue I begin laughing, cackling like a lunatic at the front desk. A concerned look overcomes the clerk's face, so I leave, walking into the Hilo Lanes parking lot laughing myself to tears.

I celebrate with a massive steak dinner, and sleep well.

Epilogue ★

I do not call Li to tell her where I'm staying.

I spend the next few days doing as little as possible, though I do visit a bowling alley in Kona on the opposite side of the island from Hilo, for old time's sake. I hadn't gone two days without bowling in five months. A visit to Volcanoes National Park, where lava drools from the ground in molten ropes that cool to twisted black masses that you're welcome to walk on at your own risk; turn around if you feel a hot spot. A few days at a steam vent–fed spa where the shower is outside and the water is heated by the same lava. An accidental, eye-opening afternoon at a nude beach. A few days at my friend Joe Enos's home overlooking Kona, whales surfacing in the Pacific and the elusive green flash of the Hawaiian sunset's last moment.

On my return to Chicago I have lunch with Bowling Spice and trade bowling stories without either of us falling in love. I have lunch with Mark Brown at the Billy Goat Tavern, a legendary reporters' hangout just around the corner from the *Sun-Times* building, to thank him in person. Not long after that I have lunch with Kalli to see her new engagement ring and wish her well.

I return to my old job, this time on better terms and with a much-improved perspective. Not long after my return, though in no way related to it, the agency wins a major new client—a Milwaukee-based brewing company named Miller.

On a post-trip visit to Columbus, my brother Peter presents me with a gift, something he'd taken from the wall in our father's office. It is a rudimentary map of the

United States, measuring 20" × 30" and colored in blue, green, and varying shades of purple and pink, each state a single color. On it are small circular stickers, about a quarter inch in diameter in either green or yellow, each with a number on it. There is one on each of the fifty states.